OVERLA...
TOP...

A DOG'S LIFE

Ian Hall

Overland with Top Deck: A dog's Life.

Publisher. Dog Press. 2022.

ISBN: 978-0-473-65935-6
IBSN: 978-0-473-65935-3 Softcover (Print on Demand)
IBSN: 978-0-473-65935-0 Epub
IBSN: 978-0-65935-7 Kindle

Copyright © 2022 by Ian Hall.

All rights reserved. No part of this publication may be reproduced, stored in a retrieval system or transmitted in any way by any means, electronic, mechanical, photocopy, recording or otherwise without the prior permission of the author.

National Library of New Zealand/ Te Puna Matauranga o Aotearoa
Creator: Ian Hall, author.
Title: Overland with Top Deck: A dog's life.
IBSN. 978-0-473-65935-6
Subjects: Hall, Ian.
Travel.
Tour Guides
Biography.
Travellers.
Biography.
International Travel.
Dewey Number: 910.4

This book Is about...

- *The 'hippie trail'.* London to Kathmandu. Many did it. Walking. Hitching. Local buses. 'Magic' bus. VW Kombis. Cycling. Motorbikes. Trains. In a Mini. With cats and dogs.

- *The adventures of an everyday person.* First as a Capricorn P33H passenger in early 1979 and then as a double-decker tour leader three times from October 1979 to September 1980. I also squeezed in an eighteen-day Aussie overland there somewhere. Doing the very contrasting winter and summer/ monsoon overlands was an achievement. The situation was volatile in Iran, Iraq and Afghanistan. A Turkish coup d'état. Syrian rebellions.

- *People.* I refer to passengers as punters (gamblers) as "they pay their money and they take their chances." Normal everyday interactions. Travellers' experiences. Fun. Laughter. Squabbles. Niggles. Romance. Rejection. Jealousies. Living cheek-by-jowl with others. Cramped quarters. Limited privacy. Cooking for 20. Cooking whilst on the move. Making either 'barely edible' or 'delicious' meals or something in between out of dehydrated and tinned foods supplemented by local meat wherever possible—goat, buffalo, chicken. Shopping and haggling in local markets. Eating street food. Eating in local restaurants. Coping with 'Delhi belly' and 'starting-block' toilets.

- The *places* travellers came to see and *why* we came to see them: Varanasi, the Taj Mahal, Kashmir, Cappadocia. We followed in the footsteps of historical figures: Buddha, Alexander, Jesus, Anthony and Cleopatra, Marco Polo, Rudyard Kipling, Gandhi.

- Encounters with different cultures and religions. Interacting with local people—hotel managers and waiters. Rickshaw drivers. Diesel attendants. Bureaucratic officials. Police. Local guides. Thieves. Houseboat builders and houseboys. Local tradesmen with ingenious ways to fix things. Observing how the less fortunate earn a living. Receiving incredible hospitality and generosity. Meeting Bedouins.

- The overland crew 'brotherhood'. Particularly the Top Deck 'band of brothers'. Team work. Problem-solving. Improvisation. Keeping the tour moving and on schedule. Night drives. Initiative and resourcefulness. Driving the rough 'roads' of India and Pakistan. Accidents. Breakdowns. Ingenuity. 'Heath Robinson' repairs. The 'number 8 wire' mentality. Border crossings. Baksheesh. Corruption.

- The 'ordinary' incidents you could expect whilst travelling.

- The *extraordinary, the unexpected, and downright dangerous*. Revolutionary Iran when US hostages were seized in Tehran. Getting caught up in anti-western riots in Lahore. Being held up by machine-gun toting militia in Syria. A coup d'état in Turkey. A broken bottle-wielding taxi driver in Jerusalem.

- *Growing up. Maturing.* All who travelled and did overlands—punters and crew—grew up and learned about themselves. Many originally travelled "the hippie trail" for spiritual enlightenment. This can take many forms. Punter Ric told me that his *Befa* overland changed his life forever. Many overlanders could say that. Overlanders can look back on their experiences with pride.

Their challenge <u>now</u> is to convince their kids and grandkids that their adventures were true and not the figments of an overactive ageing imagination.

ACKNOWLEDGEMENTS

- Graham (Skroo) Turner for his ingenuity in starting Top Deck. And in supporting this book. Through his company, he has positively shaped the lives of many staff, crew and punters.

- Bill James for interviewing and appointing me and giving me opportunities to shine.

- Trevor Carroll for writing the first TD crew member's book, being the enterprising trailblazer and paving the way for others.

- Trevor encouraged me to post on the TD web site. I received much positive encouragement—'evocative writing', 'exciting prose', 'jogs the memory banks', 'love your detail'—which helped me complete this book.

- To the many Top Deckers I met in person and online.

- To *Lemming* and *Befa* punters for photos and anecdotes.

- To the many locals I met.

- Traveling and seeing the sights is much more enjoyable with someone close to you. To the young ladies who shared my adventures. For their affection, warmth and fun.

CONTENTS.

This book is about iii
Acknowledgments. v
Contents. vii
Prologue ix
1: London in Spring 1
1: Stunning Sydney 7
2: The Australian Overland: Sydney to Perth 13
3: Another job offer 39
4: A month In Kathmandu 41
5: All the world's a stage … 65
6: 'Mr. Cranky' 71
7: On the 'frog and toad' 77
8: Varanasi 85
9: Varanasi: Visiting the ghats 93
10: Gotta pick a pocket or two 97
11: Driving, accidents and breakdowns 99
12: Every cloud has a silver lining 105
13: Always look on the bright side of life 109
14: Smooth running 115
15: The Taj Mahal 125
16: Jaipur 133
17: Jaipur's Amber Fort 139
18: The Palace of the Winds 145
19: Bustling New Delhi 149
20: Jammu and Kashmir 157
21: Amritsar 173
22: Lahore 179
23: The North West Frontier 187

24: The Khyber Pass and Kabul	193
25: 'Off the beaten track'	201
26: The Bolan Pass	207
27: Quetta	213
28: The road less travelled	223
29: Crossing borders	233
30: Iran. November 5/6 1979	237
31: Iran. 1980. Summer	243
32: Iran. February 1980: Winter	253
33: Eastern Turkiye	259
34: A side trip to Ankara and Istanbul	275
35: Syria: Peace be upon you	279
36: Jordan	289
37: An Aussie jailbird	305
38: The Holy Lands and then … Mesopotamia	309
39: Turkiye: The Turquoise Coast	325
40: A coup d'état	329
41: Pammukkale	331
42: Ephesus	341
43: Kusadasi	345
44: Selcuk	349
45: Exhaustion	361
46: Troy and Gallipoli	363
47: Istanbul	371
48: Egypt	379
49: The last stretch to London: Europe	387
50: The end is nigh…	397
51: Reaching 'Old Blighty'	399
Epilogue	401

PROLOGUE.

I left Aotearoa NZ late January 1979 to embark on my OE.

And … to have a break from a tough four years.

I have no siblings. My father passed when I was four. Simultaneously my mother almost died from peritonitis. I ended up in an orphanage for the time it took for my mother to fully recover.

My mother was diagnosed with breast cancer in May 1975; events went downhill and she passed in June 1976. In November 1977, her mother, my beloved Glaswegian grandmother, passed, mortified that her only daughter would pass before her. My stepfather spent three years disputing my mother's will. I found it difficult to handle a multitude of pressures. I had married at 23 and was now 28. My wife and I separated. I am sure that if my mother and grandmother had continued living, they would have dissuaded me from a dissolution. I was close to breaking point. I had bitten off more than I could chew.

Three days after leaving Aotearoa NZ, I arrived in Kathmandu. My Contiki overland was cancelled: Civil war raged in Afghanistan and the Soviets were preparing to invade. Iran was in revolution. Transferring to *Capricorn P33H,* I arrived in London in early May. 'The winter of discontent' was easing. Margaret Thatcher was elected.

I came to Europe to travel, aiming to become a courier—tour leader in modern parlance. By May 30th, I was a tour leader for Tracks Travel. A training tour, a Russian/Scandinavian (3RS6) and a European tour (4CE10) followed. Changing to *Top Deck* in late September, I travelled to Kathmandu on *Casper* and returned on *Befa*.

This narrative begins with *Befa* arriving back in London after a tough winter tour. I fly to Sydney to get some sun and am talked into leading an Australian overland. Another Asian overland on *Lemming* soon follows.

Lemming is the main ongoing narrative.

I weave in anecdotes from other tours in appropriate locations. These stories are in italics to distinguish them from the lead story.

London in Spring

London. Tuesday, April 2nd 1980.

I was physically exhausted. Spent. And cold.

I watched the second hand of Victoria Station's clock methodically ticking off each second with a loud clunk. A cacophony of noise reverberated in the cavernous station. *Befa's* punters farewelled each other with cuddles, hugs, kisses and warm two-handed handshakes. Tears glistened in many eyes. Mine included.

Befa's punters: intelligent, articulate, fun-loving. Culture vultures as well as party lovers. Resilient. Hardy. Adaptable. Their 'winter tour' had been tough, *very* tough at times. Discomfort was a large feature of that adventure. They had achieved something which had not been easy. Leaving Kathmandu on January 15th, temperatures deteriorated until snow descended south of Isfahan. Within days it was minus thirty degrees. Even once the full snow drifts had gone, the temperatures, sharp biting winds and gloomy grey skies reminded you that … it was winter.

Stragglers struggled with their backpacks, eventually dispersing. Wandering outside to contemplate my next move, I encountered a drab, dismal world. Grey buildings, pavements and skies. Thick layers of dull stratus clouds moved listlessly overhead. Light 'pretend rain'—drizzle—was constant.

Flurries of cold wind rifled the news agent's green canvas awning and ruffled the magazine displays. Pavements were puddled, greasy and slippery. Umbrellas bobbed up and down as commuters scurried past. Raindrops trickled from brollies. Coat collars covered pink ears. Woollen scarves were swaddled around flushed sallow faces. Shoulders were hunched, hands either deep in pockets or enveloped in gloves. Eyes stared ahead, brains calculating destinations on autopilot.

I had been eagerly anticipating London. Reality was now sinking in. "What was the rush?" Robert Louis Stevenson had written, "Better to travel hopefully than to arrive." The journey, not the destination was to be savoured.

Six tours in fifteen months. As a tour leader I was available 24/7. No wonder I was fatigued.

Hefting my backpack over my shoulder and grasping my briefcase, I took the tube to NZ House in The Haymarket. Mail and NZ newspapers beckoned. What was happening 'down under' besides the Flight 901 Mt Erebus disaster last 28th November? What was PM Muldoon up to? Wage and price freezes every few months? Fuel shortages? Carless days? 'Think big' projects?

I wasn't expecting much mail. Capricorn P33H's Liz wrote to say she had a new boyfriend and wished me well. Jane from Tracks' 4CE10 had written from Palmerston North. We had chemistry but she was only in

Europe for six weeks. Murchison's mischievous Wendy, now working in Sydney, beckoned me. Tempting.

Giving Sydney genuine consideration, the green District line rattled me along to Kensington High Street. I could browse for hours in their well-stocked bookshops. I passed former employer Tracks Travel in salubrious 'Adam and Eve Mews', and ambled a kilometre south. Past Trailfinders' to downmarket Earl's Court (Kangaroo Valley) and Top Deck HQ. Into their 'dungeon', to collect my battered suitcase containing my spare clothes.

Handing in my accounts and punters' tour reports, I hoped curly-haired, easy-going Mick Carroll was payroll master. He was fast and efficient. One of three directors. The evaluation reports were hopefully positive. Punters had heaped praises on Iain and myself.

Making a spontaneous decision, I booked a Quantas flight to Sydney. My savings were dwindling. I'd have to find work in Australia. Returning to reception, an attractive 5' 8" brunette, long shapely legs sheathed in the latest Levis, was demurely waiting for me. I gasped. Susie was from *Casper*. Effervescent. Irrepressible. I told her I was bound for sunny Sydney. "OK, stay with me until then." Cheerful and upbeat, she was a rainbow compared to the greyness outside. We had a low-key catch-up, fondly recalling our tour and what we had been doing since.

Susie was one of two cockneys on *Casper*. The other was Mac. When I first heard their diction, they sounded brusque and abrasive. Trouble? Couldn't have been further from the truth.

My fascination with the accent had been triggered by Michael Caine and then by 1970s TV dramas like "The Sweeney". Born within earshot of Bow's Bells. London's East End. Dropped or substituted letters: Ts dropped in the middle of words. Scottish becomes sco'ish; h dropped from the beginning of words—hopefully becomes 'opefully; th became f so that think became fink and the g dropped off endings so that nothing became nothin'. This was before you got into their 'rhyming slang': 'have a butcher's/butcher's hook' = "look"; 'let's get on the frog and toad' = 'road' and 'use the apple and pears' = stairs.

At week's end, Susie drove me to Heathrow. The windscreen wipers aggressively batted drizzle away. Hugging her warmly, I then winged my way to Kingsford Smith Airport. I did intend to correspond but I only looked at her address whilst on the plane. It was scrawled on notepaper which had become soggy and wavy with damp. Sorry Susie. Indecipherable.

Stunning Sydney

Autumnal Sydney was balmy. The skies were blue. Mid-twenty degree temperatures. I located Wendy, who had travelled in tandem with *Casper* on *Rags*. I'd first noticed her in denim dungarees through the flicker of the campfire flames in Kavalla where she had joined her bus. Diminutive. Smart. Bright-eyed and bushy-tailed. An office receptionist.

Sydney 2017.

How could you not be impressed by Sydney's weather, the skyscrapers, the harbour, dazzling water and sandy beaches? 240 kilometres of shoreline. I took in the iconic harbour bridge and Opera House. Indigenous people have lived here for 30,000 years. Cook charted it in 1770 after six months spent mapping NZ. The first fleet of convicts landed in 1778. Sent from 'the motherland' to do hard time.

For the next two weeks, I job-hunted.

Approaching the local education authorities for relief teaching, the receptionist announced that Sydney had a glut of teachers. I was given short shrift. I commenced a hospitality course to train as a waiter and was hired for an afternoon washing dishes for a private party. Upmarket house. Extensive harbour vistas. Pocket money.

Ringing a George Street luncheon bar, the receptionist scoffed hearing my male voice. She doubted my speed to spread margarine and fill sandwiches at warp speed. Having run five week-long school camps in seven years during which, as chief cook and bottle-washer, I had prepared three meals a day for a horde of hungry kids, I felt underestimated.

After a week of job hunting, I rang Top Deck Director Bill James in his North Sydney office. We arranged to meet at a harbourside bar. Bill was tall and lean with the obligatory '70s gun-fighter moustache. His eyes were wise. Intelligent. Considered. Knew how to listen carefully and 'feed' off what you said. Didn't miss much. He spoke softly necessitating me to lean forward and turn an ear to listen over the hubbub of chatter, chuckles, giggles, raised voices, clinking of glasses, knives and forks on plates and the honk of boat ferries.

As we were chatting and drinking, I recalled when I had first met Bill. Late September '79. I'd only just completed the breakdown-plagued Tracks 4CE10 tour. Two of my three tours, all in J Registration Bedfords, had mechanical issues. The last had breakdowns every three days in the final two weeks. I wouldn't put up with that again. Tracks were unfazed by their coaches' mechanical incompetencies. They offered me the very tempting 4 week 'Oktoberfest and Greek Islands' tour. Many crew would have 'given their eye teeth' for that combo. I had misgivings.

Unbeknown to me, Tracks was the butt of jokes with other tour companies. I wished I'd heard these before I'd signed up. "How do you overtake a Tracks coach? Answer: Very easily. They have usually broken down." To paraphrase Meatloaf "Two out of three ain't good!" Peter Goodman admitted on the Top Deck website, "Tracks taught me a lot about non-professional tour companies."

I clashed with Tracks Director Bill over breakdowns and inadequate funding. An inordinate amount of time was spent chasing funds around European banks. More often than not, the funds weren't at the designated bank. After the fourth time, the novelty of this 'treasure hunt' wore off. The final straw? Management suggesting I borrow off punters.

I joined Tracks to do European tours and possibly a London-to-Johannesburg overland. The ultimate expedition. The prospects of that were now zero. I realised they needed mechanics. If their Bedfords weren't maintained enough to get around Europe, how well were their four wheeled drives prepared for Africa?

"G'day Dog, you old bastard! How's it going?" was how Ron Clark had affectionately greeted me in Florence's 'The Red Garter', two weeks before. I was polishing off my second 'Zombie', an addictive combination of cherry brandy, dark rum, light rum and pineapple juice with lime. Ron was knocking back an amber ale. He was on my Tracks training tour but they hadn't offered him a job. Instead he went off and talked himself into a superior deal with Sundowners.

Sundowners had just offered him an Asian Overland tour. He rejected it. Didn't fancy it.

I did! Challenging. Exciting. Adventurous. Dangerous. Off the beaten track.

It was nearing the end of the summer season. European winter tours hadn't begun in 1979. I would need a winter job. This could solve that problem. One tour there. A return tour in time for the summer season. Even if I led the Tracks Oktoberfest/Greek Island combo, I would still be back middle to late November needing a job.

In Earl's Court, I scooped up armfuls of free magazines like LAM, Trailfinders, the Australasian Express. Finding an Irish pub, and ordering Irish stew and dumplings to accompany a Guinness, I flicked through the classifieds.

Overland with Top Deck

My spirits plummeted. My favoured combined duo—Sundowners/ Capricorn—weren't advertising. They were initially separate camping companies then amalgamated. 'Top Deck' was advertising. Having scrutinised a bus in Aqaba they were not appealing. The tour leader looked young, bewildered and out of his depth. The driver looked like wild and unkempt like a Neanderthal man. Little did I know that would be me and my driver in four weeks' time.

I pondered. Overland in double-decker buses? No need to erect tents or a separate cooking-trailer as with Tracks. Hmmm. It certainly had novelty value. Maybe this idea did have 'legs'.

I legged it around to the Top Deck offices at 64 Kenway Road and picked up their latest Asian Overland brochure.

I imagined future conversations—

"Ian, how did you get to Kathmandu? Car? Motorbike? Rail? Local bus? Four wheeled-drive truck?"

"No. A double-decker bus!"

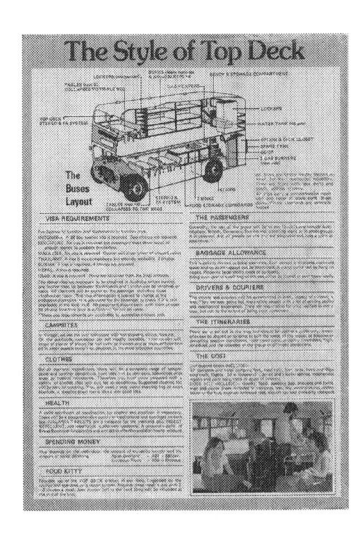

I have had that conversation... numer-ous times. At the mention of double-deckers, reactions cover a gamut from surprise to worry. Responses include eyebrow raising, widen-ing of the eyes, wry disbelieving smiles and the shaking of the head to the furrowing of the forehead as frowns settle in. Say what? Back up ... double-decker buses?"

In the 1979 edition of 'Across Asia on the Cheap', including the 'Bad News Supplement on Iran and Afghanistan', Tony Wheeler gives a précis of overland companies

— 10 —

like Capricorn/ Sundowners and four-wheel-drive trucks like Exodus Expeditions and Encounter Overland. Top Deck does get a mention … *"Top Deck travel overland in, believe it or not, (sic) double/decker buses—accommodation is on board, upstairs! Their ten week trip costs £360.00 or A$520, food not included." (P10. 1979).*

I had reservations. Top Deck's European itineraries were infamous, legendary, indeed fabled, for their partying. Did their overlands attract a more serious 'culture vulture' clientele to the European tours? Hopefully.

Against my gut instinct, I took a punt and applied. I had no 'Plan B' apart from a last Tracks tour.

I was interviewed in a Spartan back office at 64 Kenway Road by Bill James one afternoon. What a contrast between the two 'Bills'. Tracks' Bill Stephens dressed in grey three-piece, pin-striped 'power' suits. He was smart and savvy but rule-bound and formal. He could switch his pale blue eyes from friendly and collaborative to chillingly cold and impersonal in an instant.

Aussie Bill, dressed in quality jeans and an open-necked shirt, was intuitive and astute. But informal, amiable and laid-back in the archetypal 'down-under' way. Bill had 'street' credentials. Familiar with 'the frog and toad'. He was on the first 1973 tour (which in 1975 became Top Deck) with Graham 'Skroo' Turner and Geoff 'Spy' Lomas in 1973 and was tour leader on Grunt in 1975 for their first London to Kathmandu and Kathmandu to London in 1976.

Having completed a successful summer season as tour leader as well as an overland as a passenger where Greg Marks, the Capricorn courier had mentored me—the route, Visa procurement, border crossing procedures, keeping to itineraries and schedules, etc—were all familiar.

Stressing my professionalism, organisational and communication abilities as a teacher, I added my BA in History included papers on 'Medieval History' and 'Byzantium', the latter covering much of present day Turkey, Iran and the Middle East.

"Useful." He suggested that I could compile a set of overland notes for crew to use.

Bill abruptly surprised me by suddenly saying he disliked poaching couriers. Gulping, my counter was a little like the Liam Neeson quote from the 2008 film 'Taken'. I said he wasn't poaching. "Bill, you advertised a position. I have a specific set of skills that I have earned over two short but effective careers. Skills that should make me a delight for managers like you. I'm a perfect fit."

We were eyeball to eyeball. I waited. Tacitly. Smiled buoyantly. Bill was a thinker, a calculator, well aware of 'the big picture'. He was also a master of 'the pregnant pause', the blank unreadable gaze. By not revealing his hand immediately he left the other person squirming.

Ultimately he grinned. He had been teasing me. "Hired".

I thought I had all the credentials for Top Deck except ... the macho attitude, colourful vocabulary and DIY skills. My ego was telling me Top Deck would have been foolish not to hire me.

Within four weeks I was doubting the wisdom of my decision.

No written contract like Tracks' 9 point 'Contract Operator Agreement'. No rigorous training as prescribed by Contiki's John Anderson for his staff in "Only two seats left". No job description. Just a firm handshake. I was elated. The rest is history. Two successful overland tours with Top Deck.

The Australian Overland: Sydney to Perth

The next evening, the flat's landline trilled three times after dinner.

"Bill speaking. Ian ... I've been thinking ... Interested in being tour leader on an Aussie Overland leaving May 8th?"

The Aussie Overland had started in March 1977 to make a mammoth three-part, twenty-week tour. "Yes." I was flattered. I chuckled, "But I've only been in Australia two weeks."

"Ian, you are more than capable. A map and a guide book and you'll be away laughing!" He didn't say who would be buying those.

The flattery was questionable. He'd read my first set of reports in Kathmandu last Christmas. They weren't too good. That tour had been a 'baptism of fire' and hell for me with driver Mr. Cranky. Bill told me to collect more than thirteen reports next time. But there were extenuating circumstances: we were travelling east and more than half were felled by diarrhoea. Most didn't attend the tour farewell. Filling out reform forms was well beyond their energy levels. Plus there were four Germans who couldn't speak or write English.

My *Befa* reports were excellent but they were in London. Did Bill phone Mick Carroll to get an opinion? I doubt it.

Bill saw opportunities quickly and was an opportunist.

So was I.
A 'win-win' situation.

He needed a tour leader. I needed a job. Snap.

I would accept the flattery and adapt my skills to Australia. I'm an avid reader of guide books. Have a decent memory for facts. In the right place at the right time.

This was unexpected. I instantly forgave him for 'shafting' me the previous Christmas. Swings and roundabouts. You win some, you lose some. Trevor Carroll, a Top Deck senior crew member in Kathmandu directed me, in late December 1979, to lead a 28-day 'Around India' tour. UK £149.00 plus £8.00 a week food kitty. I prepared a bus with driver Steve Pyatt, bought provisions, collected and briefed punters and travelled 200+ kilometres to the first night's stop in Pokhara. A long and winding road.

Bill intervened from London, abruptly replacing me with his nephew Peter. Nepotism. I was around the campfire after dinner, beginning to get to know the passengers and remember names and backgrounds, when I received the news. I was NOT impressed. As a teacher I had reached middle management level, organising people, events, week-long camps. Wouldn't think of asking someone to prepare a student camp and then replace them after they had started.

I was prepared to attempt to reason with the boss but … no-one else was. Trevor was acquiescent. "Do as you are told!" was his wordless frown which followed a shoulder shrug. "What can you do?" He knew Top Deck's culture. I was quiet after my first tour. Hadn't yet regained my confidence. In teaching, I was used to 'robust debate' with colleagues. Steve kept his head down. I was the Lone Ranger. Tonto was nowhere to be seen.

Talking to Peter before handing over, Peter said he was exhausted. HE didn't want to do back-to-back tours. Bill was trying to do his nephew a favour. Give him extra experience. Understandable. He should have known via communications that Peter's tour was late. They often are. I collected my backpack and returned to Kathmandu on *Slug* with Iain McKinnon with whom I did my next tour. That turned out to be an inadvertent but compatible, very successful pairing.

A dog's life

In 'the Lucky Country', I would be travelling in my father's homeland. Arthur George Hall hailed from Auburn, north of Adelaide. It would be interesting to glimpse the area he was raised in.

Bill invited me home to lunch with his charming and attractive wife Liz. Ham, salami, cheese, tomatoes, fresh bread rolls and salad. They were a very down-to-earth and hospitable couple. I couldn't imagine a similar lunch with South African Bill from Tracks. Liz and Bill had met on a Spain, Portugal, Morocco tour. The small talk turned to the route to Perth, the bus I would be using and the advertisement we would write to attract a driver.

Root, the double-decker, was outside Bill's parents' home in Willoughby. It no doubt lowered house prices a tad. "It isn't as good as the ones you've driven through Asia Ian." Bill warned sheepishly.

"In fact it's a bit of a mess!"

Man, was *THAT* an understatement.

Bill said its name was '*Root*'. It was *rooted*. A kiwism meaning stuffed. On its last legs! 'Not long for this mortal coil' in Monty Python idiom.

Root was a 1947 AEC Regent III Australian-made model that originally did Sydney suburban routes. Route 69 was on display above the cab. It looked ancient and had a pushed-in black snout like a 'pug' dog. Pugs are cute. This 'dog' of a bus' wasn't.

The decrepit double-decker, Registration ISN 334, brought tears to my eyes. Not only was it long overdue for a visit from a window cleaner, net curtain washer and all round dynamic handyman, it should have been in a museum. How was I going to scrub up this relic and make it roadworthy? It had spare parts strewn under the seats and in the aisles, thick layers of dust everywhere, cobwebs, spiders, ants, dirty dishes and cutlery in the sink, an inch of dirt and grease veneer on the lino, filthy curtains and windows you couldn't even see out of, smeared greasy benches and fat and food encrusted burners!

It had *not* been cleaned … at all.

A trip to the nearest hardware store selling detergents, brushes, sponges, scourers and cleaning products was top of my 'to-do' list. A solid week of early mornings followed, taking me to late April. Paid work. Extra pocket money. Hard work and elbow grease combined with hot water and detergent. At last the interiors were hygienic, liveable and presentable. I mentally listed the following: Curtains washed, ironed, refitted. Tick. Mattresses inspected. Clean covers. Tick. Cupboards scoured. Tick. Crockery and cutlery checked and/or replaced. Tick. Lino scrubbed and mopped. Tick. Oven and burners scrubbed with a wire brush. Checked to make sure they worked. Tick. Camping gas topped up. Tick.

Not bad even if I do say so myself. But you can't make a silk purse out of a sow's ear. Its deficiencies were obvious. I drove *Root* around the block to get the hang of the four speed, pre-select gearbox. Not initially easy to grasp. There was a knack.

April 30 turned to May 1. Departure day was May 8. The advertisement Bill and I penned for a licenced, capable driver-mechanic elicited fifteen replies. Former drivers from Sundowners and Autotours took one look at *Root* and laughed maniacally.

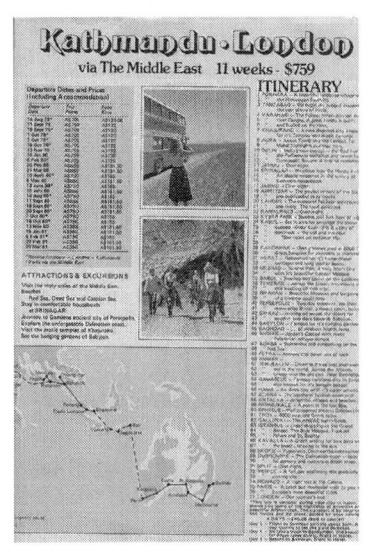

"*Mate*, you *cannot* be serious. You *must* be kidding."

Two days until departure. Out of the blue, who should turn up but a quietly spoken Pom? Jon Chadwick. He'd joined Top Deck in October '79, and, like me had flown to Australia to see a girlfriend. Whilst here, he rang Bill to arrange a beer. He had Boris Becker-type looks. Amiable. His timing was immaculate. For HIM. All the 'heavy lifting' was done.

A dog's life

The 1979 Top Deck brochure had the August '79 to March '81 twenty-week departures.

Sydney to Perth was the first section. Eighteen days. 3,200 kilometres. For thirteen of the seventeen passengers, this was the beginning of their marathon adventure. Cost = A$2583.00. Food kitty = A$198.50.

They would leave me in Perth. For the second section, another tour leader in Bali would escort them through Indonesia, Singapore, Malaysia and Thailand to Burma. I have been to Bali, Singapore and Bangkok but hadn't done that section overland in depth.

From Rangoon, a flight to Kathmandu to pick up a ten weeker.

On departure day, ominous clouds assembled overhead, gradually evolving from several shades of grey to jet black. The bus resided in the St Leonard's railway station carpark. After 8:00 am, punters arrived. Fresh-faced. Many first-time travellers. Excited. Twenty-somethings, snatching overseas travel before settling down. Most had Aussie or Kiwi accents. A married couple came over to chat—Kiwis Morris and Trish. Morris was reserved, an electrician by trade with a droll, dry sense of humour. He was beanpole lean with a tight beard which complemented his shaggy locks. His attractive wife was natural and unpretentious. Trish was vivacious with an exuberant playful quality in her eyes. They got along well but appeared opposites. Morris must have had some pretty cool chat-up lines. And successful too. I had to learn from him.

The apparition in front of the punters left them all gobsmacked! This was NOT the image they had seen in the brochure.

"That can't be OUR bus … SURELY!" That won't get us out of this carpark, let alone out of Sydney."

Dog's reaction to *Root*. More about Dog in a few pages.

Chad and I had scrubbed up well. Jeans, T-shirts and track shoes. Hair combed. Fixed smiles in place. Like the Queen and Prince Philip. I was aiming for the 'crew not looking as decrepit as the bus' look. We welcomed them with positive cheerful smiles and firm handshakes to hide our embarrassment about the bus' condition. Chad nudged me lightly in the ribs with his left elbow and, his palm covering his mouth, confided "If I was a punter, I would go back to Top Deck and demand a refund. RIGHT NOW!"

Well-wishers were difficult to distinguish from punters. Parents were farewelling their youngsters on their big OE. Champagne was in plentiful supply. Corks were popping and bubbles were rising in tall plastic champagne flutes. Kathy was one such bundle of excitement. Her friends and family were there in numbers, clinking each other's plastic glasses and proceeding to down the bubbly. Annoying younger brother Paul stuck his movie camera, with extendable boom microphone into our faces with the banal hackneyed commentary "And this is the tour leader … over here we have the driver." Kathy's father, besuited, grey-haired, middle-aged, stern, obviously aware of his standing in society, introduced himself as a magistrate. He quizzed me adroitly on Afghanistan, Iran and Iraq. I was on solid ground. My answers brought forth nods and mutters of approval.

Someone somewhere remarked, "Aren't they so young?"

The overall impression of the bus wasn't aided by the ruminating, rumbling and flashing of the erupting electric thunderstorm and the consequent trickle … then cascade … of water down the stairwell as the rain found its way through the roof seams. I was relieved punters hadn't unpacked or their gear in their lockers would have been soaked. Smart-arse Paul quipped "Hey, there are shower facilities after all!" It was a scene from a horror movie. All we needed was a hunchbacked, gecko-eyed Igor played by '70s comedian Marty Feldman to round off the farce.

Downstairs, I hushed everyone, and, with clipboard in hand, called out each name. Julia Ralston. Tick. Kay Russell. Tick. Cress and Angie looked cheeky. I was aiming for the poised, self-assured look to impress parents and relatives. "He looks as though he knows what he's doing. Our kids are in good hands!" I was used to addressing school assemblies with parents watching. Parents, relatives and friends looked on solemnly. A few eyes glistened with tears. The names matched up with punters. They embraced their loved ones and choked goodbyes. It could be months, even years, before they would see each other again. Chad clicked *Root* into gear, and without scrunching the gears, swept out of the carpark and onto the highway.

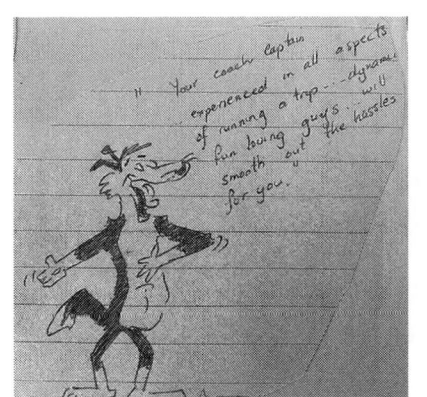

He and I had practised our departure route. I switched on the PA system announcing that we were both new to Australia but would ensure they had a good time. Several passengers' faces paled and they gulped! I added (tongue-in-cheek) "Anyone know how to get out of Sydney?"

This subterfuge caused *considerable* consternation. We had a plethora of volunteers scrambling to direct us.

Our naturalistic 'method acting' was of such high quality that the punters really *did* think we didn't know our way out of Sydney!

We reached the Hume Highway heading south and inland. Shortly after a Mittagong lunch stop, we diverted to Birema to have a cold ale at reputedly the oldest continually-licenced pub in Australia. Since 1834. As I did on European tours, I brought out wine, cheese and crackers mid-afternoon. That broke the ice, the passengers soon engaging in animated discussion. I smiled listening to some of the conversations. They knew more about Australia than Chad and I.

As we drove, I reactivated the sound system and warbled off facts about the route and Canberra. I had gleaned those from my trusty paperback 'The Encyclopaedia of Places' that morning. For some strange but fortuitous reason I had brought it from London. We reached Lake George and the outskirts of Canberra by seven o'clock. Before pointing out the campsite's facilities, I spent a few minutes summarising the daily chores and routines. A few drinks in a local dimly-lit bar followed grilled pork chops and sausages and potatoes in tin foil on the barbie. A successful first day drew to a close.

As I was dozing off, a perfumed feminine form tried to sidle into my sleeping bag. She was vivacious and charming. Wanting to be loyal to Wendy in Sydney, I turned her down.

Canberra is a 'manufactured', city, planned in 1911 by Chicago architect Walter Burley Griffin. After visiting the Australian Coin Mint and Parliament House, the day's highlight was the War Memorial Museum. Huge paintings, dioramas, tanks and aircraft from all the wars Australians have fought in were exhibited. The Gallipoli section meant a lot. Gallipoli links Aussies and Kiwis in a common bond.

Away the double-decker chugged by 6:45 a.m. on the 300 kilometre trip to the Victorian border. The punters were already learning the routine—the engine idles while I make a brew, scan a map and memorise facts from 'The Encyclopaedia of Places'. I had mentioned at last night's briefing that that was the cue for an imminent departure.

Punters scrambled for the nearest toilet block. Conditioning. Akin to Pavlov's dogs.

Duty rosters were underway. So was the Trip or Day Book, often seen on tours of 'my era'—usually a hard-covered exercise book in which the tour leader put the route for the day, the kilometres to travel, the touristy highlights, where we would be camping and maybe a postcard. Punters were invited to write observations on the tour. If successful, the book was auctioned off at the end of the tour. I used a Trip Book on all of my tours. The rare one wasn't successful.

'**Dog**' made an appearance. Dog was NZer Murray Balls' creation. I had first read the 'Footrot Flats comic strips a week before departing NZ, long after the characters had become national icons. On the second day of Capricorn P33H, flames burst from the engine canopy as the coach was climbing the steep hills outside Pokhara. The hot engine has ignited some wiring.

Waiting to be rescued, I appropriated the Trip Book and, sitting by myself, attempted to compose a cartoon. I love dogs and anthropomorphism—giving the dog human traits, emotions, thoughts and feelings. I created the dog to represent a person on the tour. Drawing with a ballpoint pen, they were pretty rough. They deserved more time. I should have edited with pencil and rubber. I tried to modify dog to make him mine but I hadn't owned a dog for fifteen years and couldn't think of a distinctive look.

I wasn't intending to draw each day. In reality, I wasn't expecting to sketch at all. But the humour found an audience and there was a lot happening to draw inspiration from. By week's end I saw Rob climbing onto the coach, picking up the Trip Book and asking, "What's 'Dog' got to say today?" Like a syndicated newspaper cartoon. By day five, Tineke remarked, "Can hardly wait to see the complete manuscript of Ian's (S)TRIP BOOK". That Trip Book was auctioned off at the end of that tour.

A group of P33H friends met regularly over the years and in the new millennium, Tineke, who had publishing connections, sent me a copy of the Trip Book replica—"For DOG, who has given us so much pleasure during the Overland and whose comments livened up the original P33H Trip Book … Liz, Jules, Jude, J-9, Barry, Charlie, Barb and Tineke."

I cherish that replica to this day.

I instigated a 'King' and 'Queen' for each day. They could 'fine' people as well as give out the 'dummy' award for misdemeanours and blunders.

Drizzle drifted down as we drove through yellow, parched rolling hills. The grass needed precipitation. The colour of the paddocks had morphed from Sydney's green to brown to orange and yellow to bleached white the further south we went. Tall white gum trees, their bark unravelling in long thin curled strips were everywhere. We smelt the distinctive fragrance of the bush and native flowers. Native birds and insects made a din in the trees and scrub. I had been away from NZ sixteen months. The 'down under' sights, sounds and smells were a tonic. Revitalising. Invigorating.

I was discovering stories which make up Australia's history and folklore. "Well there's a track winding back to an old fashioned shack, along the road to Gungadai. Where the gum trees are growing and the Murrumbidgee's flowing, Beneath the sunny sky"—an Australian folk song. Five kilometres from Gungadai, we stopped at the 'Dog on the tuckerbox' monument—the camping area for the bullock-driven teams, settlers and sheep herders who were westward bound in the 1850s. One version of the story tells of a driver who got bogged down in a swamp. To lighten the load and extract himself, he left behind some cargo and his dog to guard it. By the time he returned the dog had died.

Awww …. A Dog = Unconditional love. Loyalty.

One of the beauties of travelling via Top Deck, even in one as dilapidated as *Root*, was the ability to move around, go upstairs, read, sit at the table to play cards, chess or backgammon, make yourself a coffee or have a nap on a bunk.

A dog's life

The group was gelling. Showing a sense of fun. Morris was doing a 'Stephen Spielberg' with his Super 8mm movie camera. Its pistol shape would later get us into trouble in Syria. Trish asked "What do you hope to get from the tour?" Jeff, a mechanic, expected to "have a good time, some excitement, see the world and enjoy life." He didn't realise the excitement he would experience in Syria. Chris looked more naïve than most and would learn a lot in the next twenty weeks. He summed up the intentions of many a Top Decker, "To see as much as possible on as little money as possible!"

Prankish Scotty often thrust the camcorder into your face at unexpected and inconvenient times. One morning, after having driven during the night before, I was attempting to catch up on some much-needed sleep. A shoulder shake shook me awake. I turned over to find Scotty with Morris' camcorder inches from my face with Scotty asking some inane question. Considering the circumstances, I forced a smile and was *very* restrained in my reply.

A highlight any day was *if* we passed another vehicle. Punters would let out a joyous *whoop* to encourage the driver to go faster. Top speed was 35 kph. We averaged 25 kph on the downward slope of rolling hills, once reaching 45+ kilometres an hour on a downhill gradient with a tail wind and in the slipstream of the truck in front. If anyone complained at *Root's* slow pace, Chris' quip was "This is on *purpose*. You see much more at this speed."

I had secured the kitchen fixtures tightly but they vibrated and rattled, creating an almighty din. Together with the engine noise, the cacophony ensured that passengers had to lean into each other and shout to make conversation. They didn't seem to mind. The smarter ones went upstairs where they could hear themselves think.

The next day, as the birds were limbering up for their raucous dawn chorus, we chugged off towards Melbourne, quickly reaching the New South Wales-Victoria border. Usually there is a search for fruit and vegetables which are prohibited from one state to another. 6.30 am was apparently too early for the Customs officials to be up.

Victoria is the second smallest state and was part of New South Wales from 1836 to 1851. Gold was discovered in the 1850s near Ballarat and Bendigo, prompting an influx of immigrants. Glenrowan was our breakfast stop. On the top deck, some 'scrooges' saved the sixty cent entrance fee to the Ned Kelly exhibition by peering over the six foot fence.

The Irish got a bad deal from the British in their homeland in the mid-nineteenth century. The potato famine killed a million while another million fled the country. I felt for them. My great-grandparents were from Donegal and County Armagh. They married in 1875 in Derry and immigrated to Scotland in the 1890s and their children immigrated to NZ in 1907. All for a better life.

STEVE HART   NED KELLY   DAN KELLY
THE KELLY GANG — From an original Photograph

'The Wild Colonial Boy' was a popular tune with an Irish lilt when I was a boy. Many Irish came out as convicts. Ned Kelly was the infamous bushranger who lived circa 1854-1880, played by Mick Jagger in the 1970 film—a 20th Century rebel playing a 19th Century rebel. Ironic. I presume Director Tony Richardson did that on purpose.

Born in Victoria, Ned Kelly was one of eight children to an Irish convict from County Tipperary. Without a strong law-abiding father figure, he got into horse stealing, was convicted and fled into the

Australian bush. With mates, he indulged in numerous illegal activities. Eventually, dressed in innovative suits of home-made armour, he got into a gunfight with police at Glenrowan in 1880, was wounded in his unprotected legs and captured. He was tried, convicted and hanged in Melbourne. Regarded as Australia's version of Robin Hood he was a later version of the bushranger Ben Hall who lived from 1837 to 1865 in New South Wales. Hall? Any relation?

Root rattled and juddered, making steady progress to the outskirts of **Melbourne** by three o'clock. Punters disembarked for a fun three hours at Luna Park before retiring for a quiet night at the West City Caravan Park. I departed for Melbourne in a tram to collect Angie, our last passenger, accompanied by a perky curly-headed pom, with a distractingly lazy left eye which had a mind of its own. One eye would be looking at me while the other, slightly askew, was looking over my shoulder.

The penetrating gaze of either one of those eyes would make anyone nervous. 'Curly' had a razor-sharp wit being ultra-quick with the snappy putdowns. The poster girl for sarcasm. And a flirt. With me. That, combined with her glares, the kind pythons make before they crush and devour you, made me aware of her capriciousness. Alarm bells sounded.

Angie's broad face matched her hips and was to prove hilarious, compassionate and pragmatic in the coming days. Angie and Curly proved a fitting pairing for duties and the chemistry between them, always roguish and prankish, was immediately obvious. Cress matched Angie in the loud and bubbly mould and between them, they were 'the three musketeers'. One for all and all for one.

In the evening, with Chad catching up with an old flame, I escorted punters to the 'Astana' Indonesian restaurant. All looked stunning. Jan and Trish reached the glass entrance door together. They laughed at their reflections and broke into paparazzi poses. Once they had vogued to their satisfaction, they entered the restaurant. As they walked towards our table I saw a few male heads jerking upwards from their entrees, necks twisting around to follow them and jaws dropping. Trish was natural and understated. The girl next door. Jan was the pin-up girl for refined elegance. She was my height, with a generous portion of that lithe leg. During the meal, she leaned across the table, rested her chin on her palm, and quizzed me comprehensively about the Kathmandu to London route. If she was attempting to look pixyish, a la Audrey Hepburn on the poster for 1961's "Breakfast at Tiffany's", she was successful.

I 'worked the room'. The meal included tender lamb kebabs in a peanut sauce, similar to 'The Showboat' in Amsterdam. Questions about the decker's route across Asia made me a little maudlin. I said the tour would change their attitudes, values and ways of viewing the world. Travelling that route was like turning the pages of a history text.

By Day Three, the battery was grumbling that it didn't like waking up each morning. If Bill knew of the battery issues, he didn't tell me. He *did* have the wisdom to take out an AAA membership though. The Regent III's gearbox didn't allow push starts. The AAA rep fiddled and fumbled. Our departure time changed from seven o'clock to ten. A battery salesman rescued us and got us going. But he didn't get a sale.

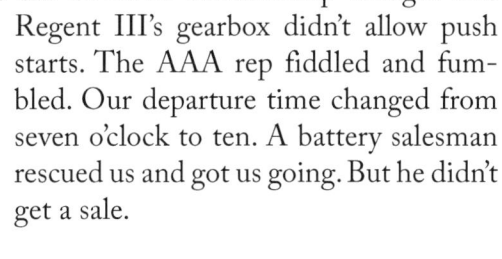

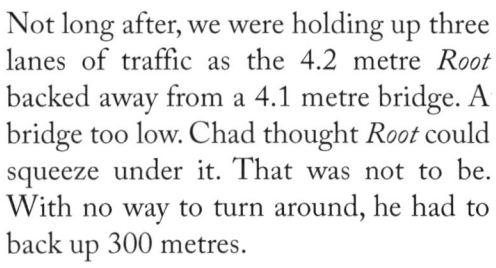

Not long after, we were holding up three lanes of traffic as the 4.2 metre *Root* backed away from a 4.1 metre bridge. A bridge too low. Chad thought *Root* could squeeze under it. That was not to be. With no way to turn around, he had to back up 300 metres.

Local rush-hour commuters who also had to back away, were *not* amused judging by the frowns and the horn tooting. We eventually found an alternative route and continued on, Chad earning the 'dummy award'.

It was time well spent at Sovereign Hill, a replica 1860s goldrush town. Through 'Bath's Hotel Stables' you could see the town below. The west coast of the South Island went through a similar experience at a similar time. Some of our punters sluiced and panned for gold. The small quaint schoolhouse had wooden desks with bench seats all as one unit.

Not far from Sovereign Hill is the Eureka Stockage Memorial. In 1854, miners rebelled against the government. They erected the 'Southern Cross' flag. Some were jailed. Others shot.

The left-hand head-light of *Root* was determined to shine directly into the bushes beside us. Not straight ahead. To correct this, Chad and I pulled over in a small country town. Chad pulled out tools for a tinker. I sat in the cab determining if his tinkering and tampering were resulting in the two lights being aligned. No. With a frustrated sigh, he eventually secured the headlight in place with a piece of string.

Fortunately the 'local' was opposite. We were soon hailed to come in for a drink by four nurses who had called in an hour earlier and stayed to work the bar. They were noisier and more 'under the weather' than the patrons. After several ales we left. Chad and I alternated driving until midnight.

Early morning starts are delightful—my initial 'cloudy head' soon clears. I check the oil and water, start the bus to let her idle and have my first caffeine of the day. The early morning chill is bracing. Helps me wake up. A thin strip of light appears horizontally above the horizon and gradually expands upwards. Stars shine brightly in contrast against the dark blue. Pale smudges of clouds can be seen. Birds get their vocal cords ready to cheerfully welcome the new day. The gradual lightening of the sky over the silhouetted gum trees, leaves a vivid impression. The landscape is vast and seemingly stretches on forever giving a feeling of space. Infinite freedom.

The journey to **Adelaide** was faster than expected, despite crawling slothly around Mt Lofty. Adelaide is beautifully laid-out, founded in 1836 as a planned colony for free immigrants. It's renowned for its gardens and colonial churches and winding Torrens River. Punters went shopping along the main thoroughfares. Later we located the West Beach Caravan Park in Glenelgs. A few beverages were consumed at the St. Leonard's Inn before retiring.

Chad and I spent ninety minutes of the next morning cleaning the four six-volt batteries with bi-carbonate of soda. After our combined elbow grease they gleamed like new. It would have made a humorous movie shot—start with several seconds of Chad and I admiring the clean battery terminals, tilt the camera slowly down to beneath the engine where the sidewalk was newly stained and the worse for wear around our feet.

Farewelling Adelaide in our wing mirrors, *Root* headed to the Barossa Valley, a renowned wine-producing region. Named after Spain's Sherry district, Prussians and Silesians settled here in 1842. A few kilometres north of here, my father, grew up. Unfortunately I didn't have time to explore. After dinner and showers, the group settled into the local for a few after-dinner drinks and night-caps and games of pool and table tennis.

Day Nine. Again *Root* refused to start! Bill had hinted strongly that this *could* be *Root's* last Overland. Don't spend excess money, Ian. Nurse the fossil to Perth.

A dog's life

Photo: Chad trying to be a blur so he is not associated with *Root*.

Hindsight is a wonderful thing. I *should* have purchased new batteries, enhanced the firm's reputation by having a reliable bus, pleased the punters and saved Chad and myself a lot of stress. Instead we were doing a tour of Australia's Automobile Associations. If I came this way again, I should be able to call the AAA representatives by first name.

At the Kaiser Stuhl distillery, punters completed the forty-minute tour. This was the era of wine casks. Few were purchased but the accompanying crackers, dip and cheese vanished within minutes. A brief excursion into 'Hardy and Penfolds' had the same dearth of purchases. Watching the punters climb on board *Root*, I wondered why their pockets were clinking. They were now armed with an abundance of tasting glasses. We continued to Port Augusta at the northern end of Spencer Gulf. Behind the township are the Flinders Ranges, the last hills we will probably see for 2500 kilometres. We were now on the 1600 kilometre Eyre highway. We were following in the footsteps of pioneer Edward John Eyre who crossed the continent from east to west in 1841.

Kimba to Ceduna was smooth travelling. The Trip Book had a raft of humorous comments. Dog made cameos, usually on his knees praying for *Root* to start or else pushing the bus. Chad was a candidate for the 'dummy award'. He accidentally smashed a pane in the cab's door when he almost tumbled out of it. He was perched precariously beside me on a night drive.

However at a pub one evening, not to be outdone by Chad, I left my leather pouch with passport and tour funds on the table beside Curly. I realised as soon as I exited the pub and immediately returned. It wasn't on the table where I'd left it. I gulped. When asked, nobody had seen it. Heather, Kay, Kathy, Cress and Angie were trying very hard to keep straight faces, bite their lower lips and stifle smirks. Tears glistened in their eyes. If they held the laughter in any longer they would burst.

They reluctantly returned it, declaring that the 'dummy' award was mine … For the rest of the tour!

Early next morning, we pulled into a service station to top up with fuel and use the hot showers. Bliss. Thereafter it was 300+ kilometres through low-lying scrub and bush to Ceduna. The Nullarbor is unlike the deserts of Pakistan. Although trees are non-existent or rare, there is continual scrub and tussock and the highway is tar-seal, a far cry from the pot holes and corrugations of the 'Pakistani Highway' between Quetta and Zahedan. *Root* kept a constant speed. The townships we passed through were so small they look like a single service station rather than a village.

The Yalata mission displayed skilfully crafted indigenous artefacts. From there to the town of Nullarbor it was a straight run through monotonous desert. Occasionally there was twist in the highway. High-pitched female squeals behind the driver usually meant kangaroos and the occasional wombat had been spotted. From Eyre onwards for one-hundred and fifty kilometres, the road cliff hugged its way along the coastline. Jagged promontories and bluffs jutted out. Surf pounded onto black glistening rocks. The timeless battle between the relentless waves of the Southern Ocean and the cliffs and shore have resulted in beautiful wind-swept surf beaches.

Punters were revealing their quirks. Subby was a diminutive, attractive kiwi who was traveling with friend Jenny. Unlike Subby, Jenny had killed off a few brain cells through inhaling her fair share of weed. Subby steadfastly refused to squat in the bushes at bush-side toilet stops, crossed her legs and arms and defiantly argued, "I'll wait until the next service station!" She also pranced around in very brief, almost transparent pyjama tops in the mornings or cotton dresses split to the thigh to reveal a vast expanse of short but toned leg—a look I have a weakness for. In Asia she'd be in trouble. She thought I was 'taking the Mickey' when I suggested more modest clothes.

Despite the battery charger being on overnight, dirty terminals caused an hour's delay. Nothing was said to me directly but there had been grumbles from punters who expected a trouble-free tour. In a 1947 Regent? One or two were mumbling about doing a 'Fletcher Christian'. Fortunately *Root* was no 'Bounty' and I no William Bligh. The mutiny idea dissipated.

The day from Mundrabella to Norseman passed quickly.

The plain is so flat, the road so straight and devoid of oncoming or passing traffic that Chad and I allowed a couple of passengers to drive the bus for a while. Chad or I squeezed into the cab beside them. Their grins were enormous. Jeff Spann was a mechanic. He fancied a driving job after his brief driving bout. After chatting with Chad about his skills, I decided I would recommend him to London HQ. At a roadside restaurant, we spoke to a young couple cycling from coast to coast. Just when you think you are being intrepid, you encounter someone else-hitching, or cycling or on a motorbike usually—who are *really* adventurous.

On another clear blue day, broken only by an occasional jet trail kilometres high, we drove to Kambalda and Lake Lefroy, a salt lake. Once a gold-producing centre between 1897 and 1906, it was closed down until 1966 when it had a rebirth when nickel was discovered. The district then produced one fifth of the world's nickel.

Boulder was a one-horse town about five kilometres from Kalgoorlie, connected to part of the 'golden mile', the richest square mile of gold-bearing earth in the world. Gold was discovered in Kalgoorlie in 1893. Mount Charlotte, the last gold mine, was closed down in 1976. The town has long spacious streets flanked either side by early twentieth-century wooden hotels replete with balconies.

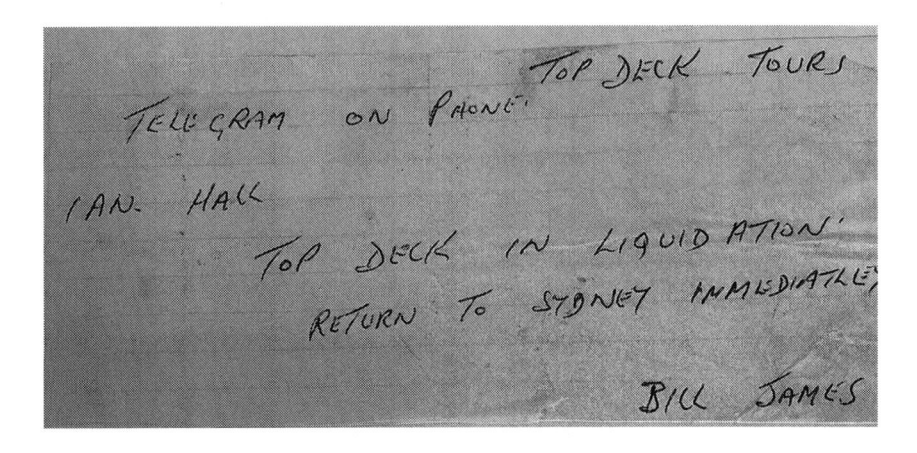

> TELEGRAM ON PHONE:
>
> TOP DECK TOURS
>
> IAN. HALL
>
> TOP DECK IN LIQUIDATION!
> RETURN TO SYDNEY IMMEDIATLEY
>
> BILL JAMES

Once we were settled in at Westnova Camping, a receptionist hunted me down and handed over a 'telegrammed' message. There was a hint of a smile as she walked away. Top Deck had gone into liquidation! I shared this with Chad. Our initial consternation turned into sceptical guffaws once our finely-honed detective skills kicked in. We speculated as to which of the passengers had cooked this up? Trish? Roguish? Maybe. Julia? Kay? Not practical jokers. Cress? Angie? Curly? Possibly! Who can't spell 'immediately'?

Chad and I kept mum while trying to spot furtive looks and stifled giggles. We let the schemers wonder whether we had received it, although later I thought, if we had pretended to fall for it, the perpetrators would have owned up quickly as they wouldn't have wanted to return to Sydney.

Mutiny was contemplated when the bus failed to be coaxed into life the next morning.

A dog's life

When it did start—the bus—not the mutiny, we drove to the Hainault mine. Opened to the public in 1973, it goes down one thousand feet with cross cuts every two hundred feet. A guide explained the dry and wet drills, the ventilation shafts, railway haulage carts, the health problems incurred and the long hours worked. This was a fascinating new world for me but probably not for Aussies and West Coast South Islanders.

Not daring to turn off the engine for fear it wouldn't start again, we drove from Coolgardie through the night to Perth. Five hundred kilometres. At one stage a plague of mice crossed the road. Thousands moved towards and around us in unison. A moving chattering carpet. Perfect breeding weather? Bumper grain harvest? You couldn't see tarmac beneath them.

Trish, Morris, Jan, Jeff and Subby, lean and agile enough to squeeze into the cab beside me, took turns chatting to keep me alert. Others of bigger girth knelt on the seat behind and shouted over our shoulders. Around two o'clock, Chad took over. No sooner had I wormed myself into my sleeping bag in the 'bed' directly behind the driver's cab, than the police waved the bus over to check faulty rear lights. They discovered the string holding the headlamp in place. With his broad English accent, Chad was feigning innocence of all regulations. Stifling a chuckle at the brilliant timing and grinning broadly, I tugged the sleeping bag further over my head in an effort to doze off.

Thirty minutes later, Chad reached under his driver's seat for something ... only to touch a warm, soft and very much alive body! The hair on the back of his head stood up in fright and his bowels loosened! "Bloody hell!" he roared as he abruptly swerved to a stop to bolt from the cab. I had to grab the seat I was lying on to stop myself from landing on the floor in my sleeping bag. Grabbing his torch, he discovered the offender was a fruit-bat, just as frightened as he. And *much* smaller. It was hard to feign sleep amidst all these shenanigans so I assisted him. We covered 'Bruce the bat' gently with a tea towel, removed it, released it in the bush and were soon off again.

After dawn rain, the day turned sunny. Welcome to Perth. The Bali-bound punters trooped into the London Court Top Deck office, where I introduced them to Greg Ettridge, nicknamed Wombat, a colourful veteran of the London to Kathmandu route. While Chad and I chatted to Wombat, *Root's* passengers unfortunately weren't too impressed by his office staff's answers to their queries.

"When do we fly out?"
"Dunno."
"Where are our passports? Do we have all our visas?"
"Dunno."
"Are we flying straight to Singapore or Bali first?"
"Dunno?"
"Who's our tour leader in South East Asia?"
"Dunno."
"Who's our courier from Kathmandu to London?"
"Dunno."
"Typical Top Deck!" they muttered. "SNAFU." (Situation normal all f**ked up).

The punters' unfavourable view of Top Deck was disappointing. The first three questions could have been answered. The tour leader questions were different. I explained why. With many tours on the road at any one time, breakdowns, late arrivals, weather and local politics can stall tours.

In Fremantle we stocked up on fresh fish, scallops, oysters, mussels, meat and vegetables from the quayside markets. Steak and fish sizzled away on the barbecue that evening to celebrate the tour's end. Unfortunately the hijinks, fuelled by over indulgence in alcohol, went too far. Jenny hid Chad's clothes and despite me cajoling her for their return, for some unfathomable reason she refused. Chad hauled Jenny from her bunk, her friends loudly objected and Chad fell from 'hero to zero' in the blink of an eye.

The tense atmosphere continued the next morning. Just what we needed on the last day! I turned firefighter trying to smother the flare ups. I called a 'round table' conference to clear the air. Having had a discreet chat with him beforehand, Chad begrudgingly muttered an apology. It was a good Marlon Brando imitation for he could have been mumbling anything. A handful of punters had grumbled to me about him. Few said anything. Typical! Some make bullets for others to fire. Jan was close to tears and was talking about going home. Toughen up girl! She could/would encounter much rougher crew in Asia.

We drove south to Brunswick Junction to a lush, green dairy farming area where we met Alan Rose, aka Camel. He was so nicknamed because, just as a dromedary can hold its water, he could hold his beer. Wombat had hinted he was a strong possibility for the group's tour leader in Kathmandu.

"Tour leader?" Some queried me incredulously." He's never been that way before!" That never deterred Top Deck. They would probably pair him with an experienced driver and he'd learn on the job.

Camel guided us over shingle roads and along fire breaks through lush native bush to see 'tall trees' unique to that area. By the end of the day, I noticed his radar had pinged on Jan. She was easy to look at. Camel's challenge was not to be caught looking. Jan either hadn't noticed him or was playing coy. Chalk and cheese. Earthy no-nonsense 'salt of the earth' pragmatism versus elegance and a fondness for quality things in life. Perhaps high maintenance? Opposites attract.

On Sunday, our Catholics went to mass. Two nuns were invited back to look around the bus. Upstairs, Angie, of the Dawn French build and associated wicked sense of humour, tried to keep talking while at the same time spreading her arms wide to conceal male and female seminude pinups taped to the walls. As one nun descended the stairs she remarked, "You all sleep up there? Males and females? Oh dear. Three

Hail Marys and Mother of God!" Cress grinned like the proverbial Cheshire Cat.

At the Swan Gardens Motor Camp, passengers cleaned out lockers, washed clothes and packed. They cleaned the bus outside and inside. Cathy climbed on Chris's broad shoulders to clean the bus' top windows. We were going to leave the bus better than we found it. Punters dined on chicken, prawns, ham, luncheon and salads and money from 'fines' went towards alcohol. I had the most fines! Huh!

Around 9.00 pm, Chad and I stood and solemnly bought proceedings together. Chad would read—"The first award for this evening is the Cordon Bleu Award ..."

A dog's life

I would read "… and the nominees are …"

Chad would announce in his best Oscar voice, "And the winner is …" An envelope was opened, the winner came up for hugs and kisses and their gift. There was a surfeit of attractive girls to embrace …

Ahhh, Dogs always like cuddles.

Cress received a curtain as an apron and a cook book for the Cordon Bleu Award. Appropriate. She intended to get into the English hospitality industry. Chad received a cushion for 'the best bum', Trish and I were handed a bottle of wine each as Miss and Mr. Top Deck. Beanpole-lean Jenny received 'The Drunk Award' and a bottle opener and aspirins, 'Curly' earned 'The Quote of the Trip' award as well as a wooden spoon for 'Constant Stirring'. Jeff won 'The Worst Joke' award.

The party raged until the small hours. The Caravan Park made a note to refuse Top Deckers in the future. I thought we were very civilised. I hadn't consumed much. There were heavy heads the next morning but the bus had to be thoroughly cleaned. More drinks were consumed in the Airport Bar. Morris, usually droll and deadpan, surprised Chad and I by being close to tears.

Both Chad and I were gifted photographic books. A card had these well composed words for their 'coach captains'. "We the unwilling, led by the unqualified, have been doing the unbelievable, for so long, with so little, we now attempt the impossible with nothing!"

> May, 1980.
>
> To
> Our Illustrious Courier,
>
> Ian Hall
>
> In Gratitude For Services Rendered
> We Would Like To Present You With
> The
> "Where Is It?"
> Award.

Barbara, Anne, Kelvin and Steve were remaining in Australia. I said "Goodbye" to the thirteen flying to Bali, not realising I should have been saying "*Auf Wiedersehen.*"

Chad and I had another drink and reflected on the tour. Both amateur photographers, we had shot some spectacular images. We had worked well together. Complemented each other. We shook hands and wished each other well on our next ventures.

Whatever they were. We were both now unemployed. At loose ends.

Another job offer

Aboard a modern coach, Sydney-bound, I was dispatched overnight across the Nullarbor. With plush reclining seats, targeted lighting for night-time reading, air conditioning and piped music, this was light years away from *Casper, Befa* and *Root*. I managed to slumber fitfully. Looking at the inky black night with lights twinkling intermittently in the distance, my serious reflection stared back at me in the glass. I pointed at the reflection. It pointed back touching my finger tip. I told my reflection that he was a lucky man. Or dog. My smile and words ricocheted back at me. In eighteen months, 'Dog' had driven across the European and Asian continents, the Indian Subcontinent and now the Australian sub-continent.

I thought of John Clarke's '70s alter-ego Fred Dagg who said, "You don't know how lucky you are."

Within a day of returning, Bill rang. His usual time—after dinner, thoughtfully interrupting me doing the dishes. "Hi Ian. Bill speaking. I have read the evaluations and punters were glowing ... of your leadership and your ... knowledge (chuckle, chuckle) of Australia ... Sorry, I never did give you a guide book or map, did I?"

I could hear the smile in his voice. He paused briefly, "Will you do a four-week 'flier' from Kathmandu to London? We need an extra bus in Europe for the summer season. I can book you a flight via Bangkok." Boy, he sure was making up for scrubbing me from that 'Around India' tour. Another bone for the dog! Two job offers/bones in a month! They can't have enough crew in Kathmandu if they have to fly me from Sydney. Tours were obviously approaching Kathmandu but wouldn't be there in the required time scale.

After an animated discussion with Wendy, I rang back to confirm. Australia, though *very* enjoyable, felt far away from 'the action' in

Europe. For both of us. Once Wendy had saved more, she too wanted to return to London.

Perhaps, as Vera Lynn predicted "We'll meet again, don't know where, don't know when …"

I had a week before departing. I soaked up Sydney's atmosphere. Ate Morton Bay bugs. Visited harbour-side cafes and bars. Knocked back a few Fosters. Went on a harbour ferry cruise taking in the iconic harbour bridge, the Opera House, Manly beach and Toranga Park Zoo. Loved the world-renown Bondi Beach. Sun. Pounding, rolling surf. Surf. Cafes. Bookshops.

Down under. The antipodes. The colonies.

Wonderful. *Auf Wiedersehen*.

A month In Kathmandu

Saturday June 14th, 1980.

Bangkok. Tasty food on the plane. A one-night stopover. Decent five-star hotel. Smorgasbord breakfast included. Onto Kalkotta. Three hours on and 'Royal Thai Airlines' was circling Kathmandu. Leaning forward to peer through the window, I glimpsed the city I had departed just six months before. Nepal's 140,000 square kilometres was rugged, hilly, bush-covered terrain. Parts appear like NZ Aotearoa from this height. Population 12 million. A Buddhism/Hinduism mix, its monarchy dates from the 1760s when one King conquered other kings in the Kathmandu valley and brought the country together. In 1951, Nepal opened to tourists. On May 29th, 1953, Everest (I prefer the local name Sagarmatha) was conquered. A coronation present from NZ Aotearoa to the new Queen Elizabeth II.

Spiralling slowly towards Kathmandu, the sprawling mass of dishevelled shanty buildings that constituted much of the Nepalese capital stretched out below. 300,000 people in 1980. The plane banked, tilted and settled into a glide path. Buildings then grass and tarmac blurred past. The plane touched down with a jolt and taxied slowly towards the terminal buildings. The engines whined on a few seconds then diminished. Within minutes the aircraft steps were wheeled up. As soon as we walked outside the plane, the mid-year heat and humidity smothered me. Had someone thrown a blanket over me?

The caustic pungent smell of jet-engine fuel, a kerosene-petroleum mix, hung heavy in the air. I liked that smell. You only get it at airports therefore to me it meant going somewhere, adventure-bound. Passing through customs, I scooped up my backpack from a squeaking juddering carousel. The first time I'd arrived in Kathmandu, February of the previous year, a wiry elderly Nepalese elbowed me aside, grabbed my suitcase with one hand, handed it to me and with the other, asked for a tip.

Steve 'Hulk' Prosser greeted me with a bone-crunching handshake. Solid and strong as his nickname implied, with dark hair, piercing inquisitive eyes and a full tight beard, Hulk was dressed in black shorts, black T-shirt and jandals. In 1983 when Top Deck restructured into ten divisions, Hulk was in charge of 'Asia'.

Climbing aboard *Boogie*, Hulk introduced me to Nick Duce who drove us to the Hotel Blue Star. We navigated a maze of corridors. We eventually found Room 107 of 'driver's alley', my 'man cave' for the next month. The room, an annex off the main block, had thick curtains, a queen-sized bed, clean sheets and bedding, a roll-top wooden desk, a deep weathered armchair and decent carpets. Last time I'd been here, for a month, I had slept on *Casper*. Other crew had rigged up a makeshift outside shower in a corrugated-iron lean for the crew's use, as hot water in 'The Withies' was doubtful at the end of the day. I now had an en-suite. This doghouse was doggie heaven compared to *Casper*.

Hulk said the buses were at 'The Withies'. Crew were at the Blue Star, a three-star hotel already used by Sundowners/ Capricorn, a more upmarket venue for tour leaders to greet punters. Whilst there, I became confidantes with 5'4" Manik Shestra, the Blue Star's diminutive Nepalese manager. He was always immaculately groomed, a smooth, natty dresser. Dapper. His trousers were always sharply pressed. My reflection smiled up at me from his polished shoes. He ran 'a tight ship', was astute, appeared respected by staff, professional and helpful. We were to share experiences via a mutual love of a tumbler or two of whisky or rum in the hotel bar most evenings, the only way to round off a busy day.

A dog's life

Within an hour, I returned to 'The Withies'. Double-deckers were jammed in side-by-side and nose-to-tail beside two beige coaches with German signing. Surrounded by a brick and stone fence with lockable iron gates, 'The Withies' was reasonably secure. What was once lush green grass was now dry and patchy and strewn with extensive oil splotches, tools, paint tins, brakes, tyres, clutches, differentials and other assorted engine parts.

I received a warm hug from 'Aunty' and a firm handshake from 'Uncle' Arnu. They ran a basic backpackers hotel.

I had first met them in mid-December 1979. Within days they had arranged a meal for the recently arrived crews of *Casper*, *Rags* and *Boogie*. After a gruelling tour, that was a friendly welcome to Kathmandu.

They provided invaluable assistance over the next months before *Befa* departed 15th January. Both knew where to direct you when you needed mattresses, mattress covers, towels, utensils, cutlery, crockery, spare parts and where to go for an assortment of items that needed fixing. Usually for a pittance. Aunty had a reliable contact for fresh, tasty inexpensive honey.

On very hot days when we were working on the bus, their son could be relied upon to come up with a well-made 'cuppa' in the morning and a chilled longneck in the afternoon.

Photo: Iain McKinnon. Repairing the roof he dented en route. January, 1980.

There were more crew working on buses in the Withies Yard in January 1980 than July 1980.

A band of brothers. During the Christmas/New year period there were crew coming and going continuously. Most brought in tours then departed 'down under' for Christmas. Doug Foskett arrived on Boxing Day and stayed to work on buses and take a later tour back. Like me, he had a degree and had trained as a teacher. Unlike me, he had never taught. He was literate and erudite, was a 'have-a-chat' with the gift of the gab to keep other people entertained.

When I was with Tracks, I rarely saw other Tracks coaches on the road. In contrast, Top Deck was like a brotherhood, a fraternity. Like a family, you got along with some and not with others. A varied lot. Most had nicknames. I rubbed shoulders with: Have-a-chat, Tricky, Dillon, Hulk, Diesel, Festus, Studley, Coxsley and Dirty Pierre. Macho. Rough diamonds. Some 'polished' rough diamonds with a smidgen of finesse and subtlety when it was called for. 'Characters' all. A few were quiet and considered. The commonality was that they were professional, knowledgeable about their jobs and committed to getting their bus to its destination, sometimes via routes that weren't in the brochures.

'Hands-on' stuff was not a strength of mine. This was an opportunity to learn new skills. Skills I might have had if my 'blue collar' grandfather and father had graced this planet a little longer. I relished learning from fellow crew and mixing with people who knew things I didn't.

I was introduced to Trevor Carroll in London by Skroo Turner. Rags was travelling in convoy with Casper. Trevor, the tour leader, was a lean, good-looking, personable maverick from Broken Hill with a drooping handlebar moustache and a mischievous grin. His eyes had 'rascal' in them. At times those eyes were dead and blank like a shark's—usually when he had a few. Which ... apparently wasn't rare.

Trevor could talk. Like Doug, a real "have-a-chat." As we did the shopping for Rags and Casper at the Alliance Store in Action before the tour, there was a steady flow of nonstop information, advice and chatter coming from him. The constant chin wagging was annoying. I tried to avoid him.

The next day I realised there was much more to him. A classic case of 'Don't judge a book by its cover' Ian. Trevor strolled to the Victoria Station meeting *point, under the clock, thirty minutes after his designated time. Mr Cool. Mr Unhurried. That dyed-in-the-wool' Ocker macho persona emanated from him in spades.*

However Mr. Congenial Conversationalist was efficient and effective. He was a seasoned raconteur knowing how to tell stories. As the train rattled its way to the white cliffs on the coast, I quietly observed him. Punters had tears welling in their eyes at his droll anecdotes. So did I. He loved being the centre of attention. Punters hung off his every word.

Also called 'Tricky Trev' or 'Trick', I briefly wondered how he obtained that sobriquet. It soon became obvious. On our train journey to the coast he asked if I would 'trade' Pam on my bus for a female punter on his. Gordon on his bus fancied Pam on seeing her at the station. That was quick. Trevor assisted in the matchmaking, making sure Gordon owed him one.

Casper caught up with Rags at the Oktoberfest. After my first stein, nature called. I was at a urinal when Trevor materialised beside me. "G'day, mate." We chatted. He chuckled. To convince his punters to go to the Beerfest instead of Paris, he said that he had "vital spare parts" to collect in Munich. I believe in transparency so simply said. "The brochure says Paris. The Oktoberfest is a once a year event and this is its last week. Munich or Paris?"

Bruce Hyslop summed up the pulling power of the Beerfest on the website. "I know buses from most companies changed itinerary to do the Beerfest... a Top Deck bus doing a 'UK Ireland' trip also made it to the beerfest once." I chuckled. Diverting from somewhere in Central Europe, sure. But from Ireland? Ingenious.

Trevor departed Kathmandu in late December '79 for SE Asia. Mike McWha and Brian 'Dillon' O'Sullivan were two remaining senior crew members. Dillon, pictured above working on Befa, was my height at 5'8" and of lean build, with thick dark hair framing his face and a moustache that drooped over the corners of his mouth.

Dillon had confidence, self-assurance and panache to complement his alpha-male strut. He hailed from Hawkes Bay on NZ's North Island and reminded me of the 1970's kiwi middle distance athlete, Rod Dixon, who was just as cocky.

There were two contrasting aspects to Dillon's personality. On the one hand, was that macho swagger. Contrastingly, he gave helpful advice without being impatient or condescending. Dillon was patient and encouraging with my initial attempts at being practical. I felt I was making progress with my DIY skills.

Hulk introduced me to PDL 518—on which I was to do the flier. *Lemming* was so named because a driver had parked without securing the handbrake. She had rolled forward, her momentum only being stopped by an inert building.

It was an absolute mess. Another *Root*. There was a common theme arising—me getting buses road-worthy. I felt like Steve McQueen in 1965's 'The Sand Pebbles' when he is introduced to the engine room of his Yangtze River gunboat—"Hello engine, I'm Jake Holman."

Instead—"Hello *Lemming*. I'm "Dog". Can't promise I'll have you looking like new but you'll certainly look and run better than you do now." I began work knowing what was required and within my skill set. I intended to call on Hulk and Nick when it came to mechanics. Nick was tall with flowing, brown untamed hair and a full luxuriant beard. An energetic live-wire, always helpful, great sense of humour and fun to have around. I asked Hulk and Nick to come for a drive with me. Listen to the engine. Anything amiss?

In the heat of summer, the sweat just poured off us and Uncle's young son did a roaring trade in chilled soft drinks and bottled water.

Free Time. Late afternoon, after *Lemming* had been worked on, I downed tools to scrub hands and nails, shower and freshen up. I wore the Top Deck baggy orange cotton 'shorts' with cream pockets, a 'Dog' T shirt from a past tour and jandals. When I'd first seen those shorts last Christmas, I'd thought "Ridiculous! There's no way you're getting me into those!" Now in the summer heat they caught the breeze and were a god-send. The pockets were deep enough to hold a cold beer and that chill, when the rest of you was covered in a light layer of sweat, was most welcome.

After downing a chilled longneck, I was off to explore Kathmandu, loving its energy, hustle and bustle. Its winding, narrow alleys have a medieval feel where the ancient wooden and buildings lean inward towards the top. Durbar (Palace) Square is its heart with its ornate wooden palace, temples, monuments and statues.

The steps up to the pagodas are laden with vegetable produce. Numerous rickshaws, pedal and automated, were alert for custom. Women dressed in colourful saris. Shoeshine boys do a busy trade. Emaciated stray dogs roam about, their rib cases prominent, ever optimistic that they may find a morsel somewhere. Being a dog lover, I found that hard to

A dog's life

handle. Men were curled up sleeping whilst passers-by weaved around them. Kids curled up with dogs to keep warm. Well-fed cows sprawled about wherever they pleased. Postcard sellers thrust them in your face, eyes wide, loud sales pitch, spittle flying. "Good price. Best price!"

There are other squares with statues and pagodas with intricate carvings and designs.

Plumbing is primitive. On more than one occasion, women tossed dirty water out into the streets from their homes. Communal wells and washing facilities were well-frequented where men and women would draw water to take home in metal or clay pots, where women washed their hair or scrubbed away at their clothes, often kneading them like dough.

Down nondescript lanes, there was a host of pie shops like the 'Chi and Pie'. Apple, chocolate, lemon meringue ... I haven't got a 'sweet tooth' but these were tempting.

Cafes and restaurants like KC's, Aunty Jane's and the Anan, were popular. Ideal for the budget-conscious. Many had ambitious menus that didn't match the quality of their cooking facilities.

I tried to extend my list of favourite restaurants but wasn't always successful. At a bistro near the Blue Star one evening I encountered this experience.

"May I have a seafood cocktail?"
"I am sorry sir. We are out."
"Okay. Let's see... Could I have the grilled cheese?"
"I'm sorry, sir. Cheese is out."
"Roast chicken?"
"Yes, sir."

Ten minutes later. "Sorry, sir. No roast chicken!"

A young lady at the next table had secured the last portion and silently mouthed "Sorry." I gave her a wan smile … and stifled the urge to walk out, settling instead for the pan-fried chicken. My reward was a very generous portion.

The Anan was more reliable—renowned for its buffalo steaks, sweet and sour dishes, garlic chicken and prawn dishes. One evening over Christmas, Wendy and I had a couple of Kukhri rums with the meal and more in the dimly-lit bar. We got into an animated discussion with a local journalist.

It turned heated as he was critical of Edmund Hillary. Being patriotic kiwis, we defended him to the hilt, disputing the journalist's claim that Everest's conquest in 1953 had done a lot for Hillary but very little for Nepal. We countered with his work on bridges, schools and hospitals for the Himalayan Trust—this despite his wife Louise and daughter Sarah dying in an aircraft crash whilst visiting him. I thought I was conducting a pretty coherent argument until I walked outside into the fresh air, immediately stumbled and fell flat on my back. Wendy had to help me 'home'. More inebriated than I thought.

Near the Withies, the 'Gangri' Restaurant (nicknamed 'Gangrene' by crew) was a regular lunch destination usually for grilled cheese and chicken jaffles. Sonan the proprietor, knew my favourites and often anticipated my order. "The usual?" His 'tomato and egg-drop' soup was scrumptious.

There were numerous narrow alleyways branching off Durbar Square. A boy with a homemade charcoal burner was intently grilling his sweet corn turning the cobs over. For the family or for sale?

A dog's life

Along some thoroughfares, wizened beggars held out small wicker baskets pleading for coins. One afternoon, one thrust his shallow wicker bowl plaintively towards me. I picked out a coin and said "For me? Thank you very much!" His face dropped. Minutes later another street person, nursing a covered flaxen bowl, asked for baksheesh. I pushed back the lid to extract a coin and disturbed a curled comatose cobra. I gulped, feeling the hair stand up on the back of my head. No more Mr. Smart-A*se with beggars!

Having a chai at a café and watching the world go by, I noticed scams. A Nepalese was keeping an eye on tourists. When he spotted a likely suspect, he would bolt over their way, suddenly develop rickets and break into a spiel to elicit money, the diatribe involved his many kids dependent on him. If successful, his thank you's would be many and dramatically delivered. If unsuccessful, he would retreat and repeat the act elsewhere. It left me wondering how you distinguish those who are genuine from the scammers.

Many 'shops' were narrow and shallow, their wares spilling out onto the pavements. I located a dingy, well-stocked shop which became a regular. It imported 'Time' and sold second-hand books discarded by travellers heading home—the latest Robert Ludlum and Frederick Forsyth. I purchased 'Freedom at Midnight', 'Lords of the Golden Horn' and Lonely Planet's 'Across Asia on the cheap: With a 'bad news supplement on Iran and Afghanistan'. 50 rupees each.

Kathmandu is dirty and rubbish-strewn. Rats in gutters are commonplace. One alley near the Withies was nicknamed 'Sh*t Alley'. Locals dropped their trousers and 'dumped'.

Along the Bagmati River, vultures scavenge through rubbish heaps. Walking along a narrow track near the river, a scrawny girl suffering from diarrhoea, relieved herself loudly. The results must have been like pellets fired from a scattergun. I grimaced! Many Nepalese have the habit of clearing their throats and spitting into the streets, a practice not likely to promote good hygiene.

Carpet shops were abundant. Cottage industries. I explored many. Weavers worked in basic conditions but always sported broad smiles. These people seemed eternally optimistic. Nepalese carpets are made of wool, silk and cotton and are double-knotted in distinctive designs. I bought two of them from a small family operation where those that did the hard graft would hopefully get a bigger cut of the price.

Exploring. Bicycles were available for hire to explore Kathmandu's environs. As well, I boarded local buses, a unique experience in itself with its eclectic clientele. I wanted to rub shoulders with and observe the locals. I travelled to Baktapur, sixteen kilometres away—Nepal's third major city and my favourite. It was like passing through a time-warp. In a time capsule. A medieval village over a narrow muddy river perched on a hillside; no electricity, cow dung drying on the sides of houses to be used as fuel or in wall construction, women spinning long yarns of wool and weaving carpets, old men and boys making pottery bowls and plates in the twisting winding alleys.

Like other cities, its centre is a Durbar Square. It has a golden gate made of brass and a pagoda. I was more interested in people watching. How people go about their everyday tasks. Medieval cities must have been like this.

Another day I hired a bicycle to cycle to Baktapur and then on another ten kilometres to Nagarkot. Two boys offered to take me to where I could view Everest/Sagarmatha. I wasn't going to get any closer but I had to glimpse the tallest mountain in the world. I tipped my guides. Oh to have time to explore Chitwan National Park, to spot tigers.

On my first cycling expedition to see water fountains in Kathmandu, two youths said they would look after my hired bike for a few rupees. I declined as I had a chain and lock. When I returned to the bike, the tyres had been deflated. Older locals were embarrassed and assisted me. Protection money. What's a couple of rupees worth? I don't like succumbing to threats or encouraging crime but… These people are very poor. Make it a "win-win".

Preparing the flier. Following days of toil, *Lemming's* interior was approaching readiness. Floors, ceilings, windows both inside and out, cupboards, benches and all surfaces had been cleaned. Lights, stereo, intercom and electrics checked. Brakes checked. New tyres. Check. Spare diesel, oil, grease and camping gas. Washed curtains, bed coverings and linen. The support fittings for the burner were replaced and windows upstairs needed fixing or replacing. When it rained, the interior of the bus was inspected for leaks and seepages. I clambered up on the roof to inspect the seams. Unlike *Root's* they seemed weather proof.

I could see the 'big picture' clearly. I'm a 'list' person. By jotting items down I could sequence the work. Initially the 'to do' items *far* exceeded the ticks beside them. Little by little, in piecemeal fashion, that was reversed.

Anything mechanical? That was Nick and Hulk's area of expertise.

Once fit for viewing and with the appropriate bus carnet and insurance, Bill and I composed an advertisement, reproduced photocopies on Manik's photocopier and plastered them on the windows.

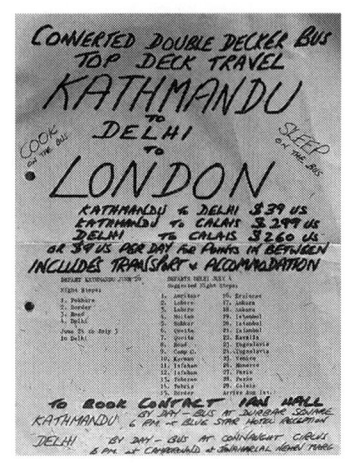

With the Lodekka parked in Durbar Square, it soon elicited interest. Getting to London in a month could be a challenge. I was concerned about drug takers causing border crossing hassles as I would be held responsible for onboard drugs. A young American aiming to work for Cosmos tours was attracted as were two guys bound for Calais. Two Melburnians' destination was Delhi. The bus' layout impressed many.

Deposits were paid. I recorded interested punters' names and their Kathmandu addresses, their intended destination, contact details in Kathmandu, fares paid and receipts given.

'Time' magazine updated me about international events especially Iran. In April, President Carter sent 90 commandoes into Iran to snatch the 52 hostages—Operation Eagle Claw. In a night sandstorm, one helicopter collided with a transport plane. The Iranians released photos of an Ayatollah grimly surveying the wreckage and charred corpses. One grotesque, carbonised arm reached skywards, the fingers grasping for help like a claw.

As well as getting to know Manik well, I also got to know Seru, at the opposite end of the Blue Star's pay scale. Diminutive waiter Seru adopted a brotherly attitude towards me and brought me breakfast every morning. He doubled as my alarm clock. Punctual. Reliable. Every wake-up was like Groundhog Day, a repeat of the day before. "Breakfast Sir? Pineapple juice? Eggs?" He served mango fruit juice and poured my tea. No milk or sugar. Every now and again he'd vary the

A dog's life

routine—"Thought you'd like porridge today Sir. That'll fill you up!" That was *in addition* to my usual masala omelette.

Ahh … This is the life … a dog's life.

Seru had been at the Blue Star for three years, earning 300 rupees a month to support five daughters and three sons. He looked barely old enough to shave let alone sire EIGHT kids! Obviously he was busy in his spare time. He had never been out of Kathmandu but hoped to go to Pokhara one day via Sundowners.

Woftam's Woes. On Thursday, June 19, just a few days before the express' departure, a watershed moment occurred. The bus with the best name in the fleet—*Woftam* ('Waste of f**king time and money')— *limped* in with Ian McDonald and Peter Brown (aka 'Filthy Pierre'). They had had a hellish tour, were utterly fed up and weren't ready for another ten weeker. They booked flights home within a few days and poured out a catalogue of woes to me that evening over a few beers in the Blue Star's bar.

Woftam was in *no* condition to return to London as scheduled with 'my' Aussie Overland punters, now travelling up through S.E. Asia with Rusty Stewart. *Lemming* was better prepared but still needed work. *Woftam* needed several spare parts and much mechanical attention.

Over a meal at the Anan, Hulk, Nick and I discussed the options. *Lemming* would be ready to leave in three weeks' time on the July 10 departure. Possibly with me. Hulk and Nick would work on *Woftam* for a delayed flier.

In Sydney, Bill agreed with my logic of taking 'my' former punters on to London. Continuity. I was a popular entity with the punters. He repeated that they had 'raved' about me in their evaluations of the tour. "Ian. Wise thinking. Use *Lemming* for the ten weeker. Put the express on hold. Contact those who have booked and inform them that the 'flier' will proceed when *Woftam* is roadworthy."

After that initial telex to Bill, I corresponded with London. Telexes tell the story.

17/06/1980
"Hulk on *Boogie*. One tool kit between two buses. *Lemming* no spare tyre, only part of rim. Large battery needs rebuilding. Four back tyres almost bald. Need replacing, unavoidable. One back tyre has ripples under surface. Shot. Have spent $300 in 3 days. Will buy new tyres in Isfahan. Need at least $1,500. Get Camel to get Iran visa. *Lemming* has Iran carnet".

```
8955339TOPD G
244 ATTOUR NP
REF:  85/6

KTM 19/6/1980.
TELEX TO TOPDECK TRAVEL LONDON 8955339.

ATTN: DILLON.

LEMMING HAS VERY LOUD PISTON SLAP.
DOES LAST DRIVER KNOW WHETHER IT'S SERIOUS OR NOT?
I AM NO MECHANIC. IT'S A LONG WAY FROM HERE TO DELHI.

CHEERS AND BEERS
DOG.
244 ATTOUR NP.

IS THERE ANY MSG PL?

DOG LA  LAST DRIVER HAR GONE HOME  WHERE IS CAMEL?
    IS DOG HALL THERE ?????TKT
NO  HE IS not HERE   WE WILL CONVEY THIS MSG TKS
```

"Is Dog Hall there?"

24/06/1980
"Peter flies out today. Ian booked also. I will get as much done on *Woftam* as possible. Camel arriving July 4. Needs big end bearing and piston. *Lemming* needs 4 new tyres. Cheers, Dog."

24/04/1980
"Try to get to Iran for tyres. Who needs pistons, etc.? Dillon."

Five o'clock next day I received a telex. The July 10 departure was mine! Thanks Bill.

My small four-week overland 'bone' had been swapped for a bigger more juicy one. A ten weeker. Well done Dog! Thirteen out of twenty-one punters inbound for *Lemming* were doing the twenty weeker. Sydney to London.

Peter gave me a set of medical stamps so that I could stamp punters' vaccination certificates. 'Liberating' stamps and forging signatures must be in the fine print of Top Deck crew job descriptions. I had prior 'form' in forging Indian diesel permits. In Durbar Square, Peter and I shared experiences and had a few laughs while he tried to sell off his extensive tool kit before flying to Bangkok. I smiled when he told me about being waved over by the Polizei in Munich last year. Peter showed his Queensland truck licence and tried to talk his way out of trouble. The officer let him ramble on a bit then abruptly stopped him in his tracks by declaring that *he* had worked for the Queensland police for ten years. He *knew* Peter's licence was not valid. Peter got a 240 DM fine on the spot, the passengers all got off and Peter took the empty bus back to the campsite. He was told to find a driver with a valid licence. The *irony* was that tour leader Doug Foskett did the rest of the driving in Munich and he only had a car licence. That made *me* reflect. All I had was an international car and motorbike licence which I renewed each year. Fortunately I was *never* pulled over and asked for my licence whilst working for Top Deck.

Ian McDonald was an ex-probation officer from Christchurch and knew my Outward Bound instructor, Terry Easthope. It's a small world. Ian asked me for a reference, as leaving Top Deck so suddenly, he wondered if he'd get one from them. From conversing, he seemed like me—quiet, more reserved than some crew and therefore able to provide a balance to those who were more tempestuous. After a decent rest, Ian was keen to do another overland.

Ian's girlfriend Gail developed gall bladder problems and ended up in the local hospital. 660 rupees for two nights. Ouch! As there were beds for relatives, Ian stayed the night. The bed sheets were freshly laundered but Gail considered the blood stains from a former patient off-putting!

On July 1st, I drove Ian and Gail to the airport in *Lemming*. He identified the clatter in the engine as piston slap and suggested I do something about it if I wanted to reach London. Ian wished me well. Gail hugged me and confided in her broad Yorkshire accent, "Ian, You're quiet and reserved but I think you're a *sly* one. You definitely haven't led a sheltered life as you keep telling us. You're *quite* fun really."

Was that a compliment?

Lemming was now fine-tuned and ready for inmates. I checked *Lemming's* share of the staples bought at the cavernous Alliance Store in Action—rice, pasta, cooking oil, tinned meat, spam, sugar, flour, salt, tin foil, matches, tea bags, coffee, Milo, cordial, corn flakes, porridge, baked beans, spices, jam, ketch-up, Marmite, Vegemite, peanut butter, washing up liquid, tea towels, cleaning agents, Dettol, tins of Westler hamburgers and hot dogs, Erin dried peas and mixed vegetables and Batchelor's dried steak and kidney, chicken oriental, beef stroganoff, beef goulash, chicken and beef curry. I enjoy cooking. I had ten recipes for twenty people in my briefcase, should punters need them.

Concluding *Lemming's* makeover, the back porch area was painted green, the mud flaps, engine cowling and radiator black and the hubs and wheel-trim white in contrast. I painted the cab black but Hulk had other ideas.

Beginning to grow bigger and turn green with annoyance, the Hulk demanded "It looks like a f*cking U-boat Dog. It's summer. Black will be too hot. Repaint it!"

Supports were made for the burners and stove, a cassette rack for downstairs, a toolbox, map box, and coffee cup holders for the cab.

A reunion

On Thursday July 3rd, the RNAC flight arrived.

'My' former punters descended. Hiding behind a thick concrete observation pillar, I intended to surprise them. I failed. Miserably. Cress, Angie, Kathy and Kay almost immediately squealed and pointed me out. Cathy Ogilvie waved and in doing so, reminded me she was a nurse. Nicknamed 'Flo' for Florence (Nightingale) to distinguish her from the other Kathy. Always positive and willing to help and use her nursing skills. They might be useful.

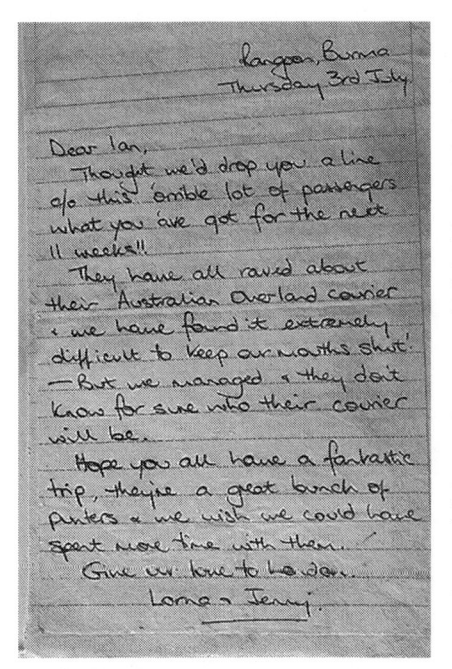

Everyone came over beaming wide smiles. I received handshakes, claps on the back and hugs and kisses all round. The latter two thankfully *not* from the guys. A few punters seemed even *more* pleased to see *Lemming*, a far cry from *Root'*.

Cress passed me a letter from two of *Woftam's* punters they had met in Rangoon. I had been spotted pretty quickly as though they were searching for me, the giveaway line in the letter being "… they don't know for sure who their courier will be."

I handed out mail from the post office. Letters and aerograms were devoured voraciously. News from home! Usually a delight. That evening we caught up in the comfort of the Blue Star's bar.

Parking *Lemming* at the foot of Swayambhunath, we climbed the steep steps to get up to the stupa. The Monkey Temple is 2,000 years old and has eyes on every side, forever on the lookout for righteous behaviour. Kathy and Jan stepped over the sleeping homeless, spun the prayer wheels wishing for a magnificent tour and took in the extensive views of the Kathmandu valley.

After more than ten weeks together, cliques had developed. It was now a veritable witches' cauldron. The innocence of *Root* had vanished. My alarm system warned me not to be enticed into anything 'political'. Beware of fluttering eyelashes. The less I said, the healthier I'd remain. The tousled-haired, lazy-eyed one continued the stirring and flirting that she had started in Australia. Barbed ad-lib lines. Mercurial. Machiavellian.

Irritation was about to bubble over between Kathy and Trish. Each had plausible stories. In tears, Kathy sought my 'advice'. I was being played like a violin. Others saw me taking sides. I felt like a teacher breaking up playground fights.

Tread carefully Dog or forever remain … in the doghouse.

Alan Rose, aka Camel, arrived four days before departure. What's with these drivers? Arriving when *all* the heavy lifting has been done. And they often complain we don't get our hands dirty. Camel had been changed from the regular departure to the flier … then back to the regular departure.

Thinking he was doing a flier, Camel sold a passage to a neighbour. 'Pop' had a tight basketball-sized stomach that strained rebelliously at the buttons of his white, short-sleeved monogrammed shirt. You could see the basketball coming around the corner before you could see who was carrying it. Pop had a tanned face, an amiable smile and blue eyes that didn't miss much. Although thinning on top, his fine white hair was long and slicked back behind his ears. Camel was caught out by the changes but was loyal to Pop who at 65 was somewhat outside Top Deck's 18-35-year-old demographic.

I wasn't the only crew member to have a punter that was not in the age demographic. I suspected some senior crew went through pax lists when travelling in tandem with others and 'cherry picked'. I would imagine they'd win some and lose some with that system. I was dubious about Pop's ability to cope with the style of the tour and the heat. It was a source of tension between Camel and I initially, and occasionally, during the tour. As far as Camel and Pop were concerned, it was a fait accompli. But the tour leader is the one who has to 'sell' any irregularities to the passengers, field complaints and soothe ruffled feathers.

The driver gets to work with objects that are mute and don't answer back. I was discrete and Camel and Pop did not hear many complaints.

Pop was a grandfather-like figure. Sometimes he took a hotel room. He seemed to be a gentleman towards the ladies, making efforts to respect their privacy. I heard a few complaints but I usually slept downstairs directly behind the cab. One disgruntled Yorkshire native referred to Pop as "sweating, smoking and a right pain in the bum."

But ... what an adventure for a Dutchman in his sixties!

I purchased two distinctively-patterned Nepalese carpets for 1000 rupees each (NZ $84.00) storing them in the U turn under the stairs, together with the two cases of Indian whisky which I intended to sell to Akram in Lahore. The contraband pens that an enterprising, glib-talking

Indian entrepreneur tried to convince me would make me a fortune in Delhi failed to show. They sounded suspect anyway. Anything could be in boxes labelled 'Ball point pens'.

I reserved a table at the Anan. When the buzz of multiple conversations diminished, I toasted the newbies as well as the veterans. Twelve courses. A room to ourselves, white starched tablecloths and silver service by attentive obsequious waiters. The experienced tour leader living up to his reputation!

Enjoy the kudos while you can, I thought. I will certainly make mistakes in the next ten weeks and whenever I do, the naysayers will drag me down 'from hero to zero' in the bat of an eyelid.

Over the meal, I encouraged punters to hire bicycles or use local buses to get out to Baktapur and Nagakot and even further to see Everest. Don't spend money on taxis when pedal and auto rickshaws get you closer to the locals. And they are more fun.

I announced that Top Deck had approved Jeff, with his driving and mechanical skills, as a trainee driver. He would be taught to drive the Lodekka, work with Camel and gain a job with Top Deck once in London. Jeff blushed and beamed sheepishly, unsure where to look. Jenny whispered, "Jeff's so chuffed, I thought he was going to kiss you".

I'm glad he resisted that urge.

Five of the seven remaining passengers had arrived. The others drifted in. I checked them off against my master list and wrote official letters for those needing visa extensions. Angie and Curly were the first cooking-duty pair. The fun-loving combination were competent bargainers for fresh fruit and vegetables in the markets. I bought pillowslips, a food-kitty purse and padlocks. Paying for the many telexes I had sent—1750 rupees ($147.00)—I was told "Only Mr. Trevor has had more than that."

All the world's a stage...

Camel, Seru, 'Dog' and *Lemming*

A few minutes before I was to brief punters, I sat at my desk and jotted down briefing points. One point would have a natural link which prompts the next. The bullet points on paper in my pocket were in case of brain fade.

As a teacher I had learned to 'project' my voice. At Outward Bound in Anakiwa we always had an assembly after breakfast. The students stood in a circle around the instructor. We started with notices and what was happening that day and ended with an inspiring quote. Today's became a favourite quote of mine, especially in hard times. It was President Teddy Roosevelt's "In the arena"—"It is not the critic who counts, not the man who points out ... how the doer could have done better. The credit belongs to the man in the arena ... who strives valiantly, who errs and falls short again and again: there is no effort without error..."

The instructor caught my eye and held out the book, "Ian, would you read this for us?" I was caught by surprise but walked into a position where I could see everyone. I skimmed the passage rapidly to catch its rhythm and began. I looked up several times to catch the eyes of the listeners. After the assembly and as we prepared for kayaking, several of my 'Cook Watch' asked me "Where did you learn public speaking?" I didn't see it as public speaking. That to me is speaking without preparation or notes, "off the cuff". That would *really* scare me. This was just communicating what was on the page in front of me.

Shakespeare was correct when he wrote, "All the world's a stage and all the men and women merely players. One man in his time will play many parts".

Twenty-one strangers, different nationalities and personalities, ages, sizes and shapes, confined to a small confined space for ten weeks in tryingly hot conditions: long drives, limited sleep, little privacy, humidity, clashes over duties and bunks. That would be a suitable topic for a doctoral thesis. A social anthropologist or sociology major would have a field-day.

Having been a teacher for seven years, I had learned a little about personality types from interactions with students, staff and parents. This knowledge was transferable to Top Deck. Most groups gel well. Or at least parts of the whole do. With twenty punters there are at least two or three sub-groups that you get along with.

Having travelled through Australia with thirteen of the group, I already sensed some of those personalities. Most punters were one personality type with touches from at least one other category. Occasionally two. Within a week, the new punters would be 'showing their colours'.

There are those who like to be close to the crew, in a few cases, *really* close. Intimately close. It's a two-way street. Crew like a 'friend with benefits' on a ten-week tour. Female punters are often assertive, even bold, in pursuing crew. And if they are rejected … don't expect a glowing end of tour report. This category wants to bond with the driver and tour leader and by doing so, are in touch with the 'command' centre. 'The patricians'.

Where the decision-making is made. Some like to know what's happening before the rest of 'the plebs' on the bus. Consciously or subconsciously.

A second group see things in black and white terms. There is a 'right' way to do things. If something is in the brochure, you *have* to show it to us! If we are meant to be at a destination three nights, then three nights it is.

A dog's life

"Ian? What time do you think we'll get to our campsite tonight?"
"Aww… let's see. 5.30? 6.00?"
"Hey everybody. Ian says we'll be there by 5.36!"

A third group are gregarious and extroverted, the 'life of the party'. Indeed they *are* the party-goers. Lively. Fun. Charged with 'ever-ready, long-life batteries'. If they miss a monument because they are a little hung over, that's fine. They are *not* culture vultures. They are here for a short time *and* a good time.

Finally are those who are easy-going and laid back. Some are introverted and shy. Some are quiet to the point of appearing aloof and stand-offish. Many are helpful and considerate. They make the driver a coffee on long drives and climb up in the cab with him. They will do more than their fair share of jobs.

This category includes those who are 'dreamers', who are on their own planet, blissfully floating along, 'away with the fairies'.

Some are lazy because they have paid for this tour and paying money means they don't *have* to work. *Won't* work. Some don't realise that work needs doing. An Irishman on *Casper* developed 'avoiding work' into an art form. An embarrassment to his countrymen. He wrote (anonymously) in the Trip Book "This tour is a heap of sh*t" yet at the end of the tour asked for the Trip Book as a souvenir. Probably to be derogatory about it back home. Yeah? Nah!

In the comfort of the Blue Star bar, lounging back in deep sofas and sipping a chilled tipple of choice, the punters were a captive audience. I gave them a reality check. The seven newbies were novices to Asia and the summer heat and monsoons. As well as being new to the confines of a Top Deck bus.

Glossy Top Deck brochures put an attractive spin on the adventure. I wanted punters to know what Top Deck had left out: the long drives, the intense heat, the monsoons, mosquitoes, bugs, enticing street food cooked in unhygienic conditions, starting block toilets, the poor quality of some hotels and campsites, the challenges of living in close quarters, being in a gold-fish bowl when the locals surrounded us.

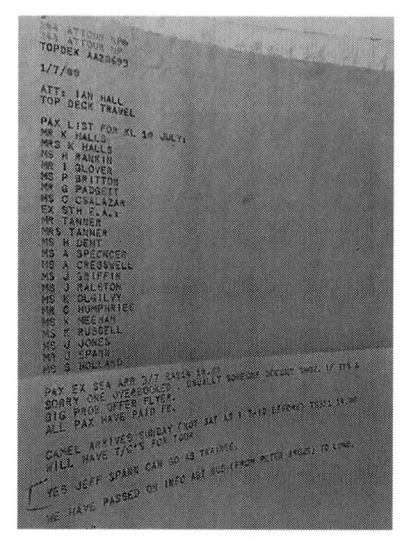

That kind of truth wouldn't sell tours.

I added. "You can smoke weed away from the bus. *Absolutely* NO drugs are allowed on the bus. Keep the bus tidy, upstairs and down. Take pride in it. Make your bunks up in the morning. Keep *Lemming* tidy. Be punctual with getting back to the bus. Don't keep friends sweltering in the bus while you *amble* back".

Lemming's July 10, 1980, pax list.

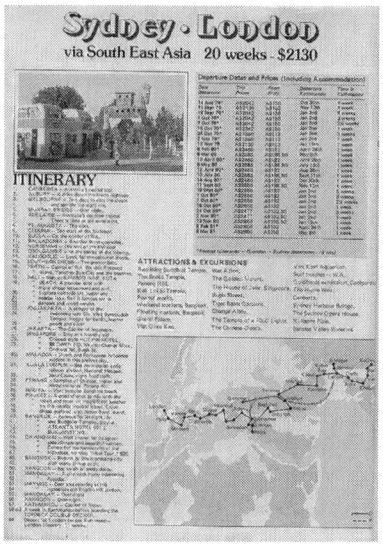

They would get 'Delhi belly' at some stage. Inevitable. One way to reduce weight. Wash your hands in disinfected water before boarding. I warned them how grubby a handful of rupees could be after going through thousands of hands. Wash your hands before cooking. Use pills to sterilise the water.

The 1979 Top Deck Brochure.

Casper's departure = Oct 1, 1979.
Befa's departure = 15 Jan, 1980.
Lemming's departure = 10 July, 1980.
No one told me these departures were eleven weeks. I thought they were ten!

A dog's life

One newcomer was Bolivian Cescelia Csalazar. 5'6". Short-cropped dark hair. Cherubic face. Smart. Stylish clothes. Quiet. How good was her English? I made a mental note to talk to the girls to make sure she bonded with buddies.

I must have laid the reality check on too thick for kiwi Sabrina, with the luminescent smile, who lightly touched my elbow, nodded towards an unoccupied corner of the bar and steered my elbow, with me attached, towards it. She reminded me of someone's sassy but annoying little sister. Aren't little sisters meant to teach you patience? She fluttered her eyelashes coquettishly. Sipping a cocktail delicately with slender pinky finger extended, she asked, her voice slightly husky and lips only a few inches from my ear "Ian, aren't we going to have any fun at all?" She finished with a well-practised hair toss.

Turning away, the last grin over her shoulder was not a wink ... but it was close.

I didn't think she was flirting with me. I wasn't her type. Or she mine. We didn't have enough common interests. Despite being attractive. She was early twenties. I was late twenties. That would be cradle-snatching. She was just making a point. She was to come out with similar gems later in the tour.

I polished off my double rum and coke and found a deep leather chair on the periphery to people watch. Always worthwhile and informative. In my mind, I opened my notebook of 'Personality Types' and besides "Easy going/Vacant" wrote Sabrina's name. It joined Nadine from a previous tour.

There was a clink on the table beside me. Camel sat down and carefully slid another cold rum and coke over to me.

"Good spiel, Ian. You could use this. Cheers."

'Mr. Cranky'

Camel appeared easy-going, calm and patient. A knowledgeable and capable mechanic and handyman. Like Chad and Iain before him, I trusted we would co-operate and complement each other.

But that wasn't always guaranteed. Not a 'given'...

In September 1979, just days after Bill James had appointed me, Graham 'Skroo' Turner drove me to the workshop to meet my bus and driver. Like Bill James and Liz, Skroo had met wife Jude on a tour. Her SPM tour in 1976 started off with one courier but he was abruptly replaced by Skroo. He hadn't done anything wrong. Skroo knew Jude previously in Australia and wanted to get to know her better.

Skroo was quietly spoken, considered and easy-going. He was a couple of inches taller than my 5'8", broad shouldered, lean and muscular beneath his shirt, a mop of fair hair which threatened to be unruly falling over his brow and a bushy beard that often opened to reveal a broad toothy grin. He had a degree in veterinary science hence the original name of Top Deck Travel— Argas Persicus Travel. (Turkey penis). Obviously had a sense of humour too.

I could tell his grey cells were working overtime as he made small talk. He asked what my Capricorn P33H tour was like, their route and accommodation. Were they doing anything different to Top Deck? I mentioned Egypt. That could be a destination too far from Top Deck's overland route. I recommended Jaipur, Khetri House, the Palace of the Winds and the Amber palace which didn't appear to be in the Top Deck 1979 overland brochure or on its map. Jaipur was a more direct route to Agra then Delhi. Khajakaho was 600km south. Skroo grunted noncommittally. He had a reputation for being inventive and innovative. He was chewing that over.

He forewarned me. "I'm afraid your driver has a reputation for being difficult to work with!"

I suppose I was thankful for the warning but it wasn't the wisest thing to say to a new recruit. And not the most judicious pairing. Mr. Cranky and a newbie? Tricky Trev and Cranky would have been a better fit. As a senior teacher, I was responsible for selections, placements and pairings within my teaching team. I chose them carefully with regard to personalities and experience.

Skroo introduced me to said driver who was tucking into his ploughman's lunch at a nearby pub and said farewell, wishing me a good tour. I soon found out that the driver had a reputation for being cranky and having a permanent scowl on his face. He was intelligent, savvy, lean, good-looking with a full thick beard, penetrating eyes and even white teeth. Through a mouthful of salad, he scrutinised me. He seemed satisfied that I had done an Overland before and had one season as a tour leader. Albeit with another company.

Baloney! He didn't hear me at all.

Casper. 1st October to 12th December 1979. Cranky was grumpy and abrupt. Right from the start. With everyone. I had completed two European tours in 1977 as a punter and four tours in 1979 and had never seen punters treated this way. Was this the Top Deck culture? Was it an intended niche market? To be abused by staff? Like restaurants who have Fawlty Towers nights with Basil Fawlty abusing guests. I had heard that Skroo was innovative but ... surely not! Cranky snapped at punters. Grunted and mumbled replies. Wasn't co-operative. No—"Sure we can do that". Refused impromptu toilet requests whilst on the road. "Tell them to piss in a bucket". I refused to pass that on and persuaded him to stop. He grumbled at some meals "I'm not eating this crap" and went off to a restaurant. He called female punters 'maggots'. Punters, both male and female, were intimidated and I received a barrage of "I'm scared of him" complaints in the first week. From everybody. Males and females. Logic wasn't his strong point. He was out-of-touch with reality. These were fare-paying passengers. Without them he wouldn't have a job.

Day One: In the late afternoon he asked me to drive the double decker. Surprise! Surprise! I don't recall Bill asking about my driving skills at the

A dog's life

interview. I had driven a delivery van around Auckland as a part time job for two years whilst at Teachers' College. But ... nothing like a Lodekka.

For the first few days, I didn't find it easy driving the Lodekka's 'crash' gearbox. You depress the clutch, move the gear stick into neutral, pause for a couple of seconds, de-clutch again to move the gear stick from neutral to the new gear. All the while keeping the revs up, being mindful of your speed and the incline/decline of the road.

Or as a veteran told me, "You depress the clutch, move into neutral, go off and make yourself a coffee, come back and complete the process."

I was conscious of my responsibility for the punters' safety. And ultra-conscious of grinding the gears. Thought the gear lever would never slip into place without resisting. Embarrassing. I had a lot to learn including remembering there was a 'second storey' of punters above me.

By the time we got to Venice, I was changing gears without scrunching and I half expected a sustained round of much-deserved applause from those behind me. Nope. Nothing to mark my achievement. These punters are hard to please! Once I mastered the gear change I lapped up driving. At the same time I revelled in the double-decker lifestyle. Like an enlarged VW Kombi van with friends. No tents.

Day Three. Cranky gave me a 'crash course' in handling the 'crash gearbox' for an hour whilst the punters were exploring Neuschwanstein Castle. Competent advice. Impatient delivery. Tips from the HGV licence. The recommended order of checking your mirrors before pulling out. Using the steering wheel from the bottom to turn.

Day Four. I was driving in the Brenner Pass. Well inside a tunnel something dented the roof. Cranky swore loudly. Punters stared at him aghast. Felt empathy for me. Couldn't believe that one crew member was abusing the other. We exited the tunnel OK.

Mr. Cranky had pointed out the route on the map. I assumed it was a Top Deck route and one he had travelled before. Any tunnel we encountered, we *could fit under. No. As '70s comedian Benny Hill joked, "If you assume, you make an ass out of u and me".*

Being new, I didn't treat him as he treated me. BIG mistake. I didn't scold him when he stuffed up. And he did. In the first four days he ran out of diesel and with a plastic container, sheepishly had to hitch a ride to buy some. I let it go. In doing so, a one-sided relationship developed. When I stuffed up, I heard about it. When he stuffed up, I was tolerant. I had to assert myself.

In Florence, Mr. Cranky dropped two female cooks off at the downtown markets to purchase fruit and vegetables. It's a steep climb to Campeggio Michelangelo, a great campsite with fantastic Florentine views and in walking distance from Franco's Red Garter. Even if inebriated. Which punters were … more often than not.

Mr. Cranky was knocking back a cold one when the cooks struggled in, arms laden. He didn't cop an earful. They zeroed in on the tour leader. ME. Canadian Theresa gave me a spirited bollocking in front of everyone. It was unreasonable to expect the cooks to lug heavy fruit and vegetables for twenty-two people uphill. She was 100% correct. Cranky kept his head down during the reprimand although a sly grin broke through his beard. Rather you than me, Ian. No support there. No—"That was my idea to drop you off there, Theresa."

By the time a month had passed, I had reached the end of my tether. We were opposites. Mr. Cranky was loud where I was quiet, rude obnoxious and offensive where I was patient, subtle and diplomatic, unsupportive when I was loyal and stoned when I was sober. At the Dead Sea, before entering Israel, I sought advice from Trevor who advised me, "He probably doesn't even realise he's being an a*sehole. Retaliate, Dog. Grow some balls. Bite back. Give as good as you get!"

I didn't think that would work. To paraphrase Hamlet, "To be here on this bus or not to be here? That is the question. Whether tis wiser and simpler to suffer the slurs and abuse of an out-of-touch grump or to take arms against a storm of abuse, and by opposing, end it."

A dog's life

I confronted Mr. Cranky. Out of punters' earshot. I talked, he listened. Trevor was correct. Cranky was surprised. Maybe he didn't realise how obnoxious he was to others. There was sensitivity in that persona somewhere. But deeply hidden. He was taken aback.

Our relationship improved for a while. He did make an effort. I snapped back if he was being grumpy or unreasonable. When he flew out of Kathmandu Airport at Christmas he said "Thanks Ian. A good tour. I'd work with you again". I bit my lip and didn't express my true feelings. Sure I was being passive/aggressive and should have been honest. What was the point now? He was leaving. I would probably never seen him again.

I had to adapt. Own the problem. It was part his and part mine. Independence is deep in my Scottish 'roots'. I am quiet but certainly don't like being bossed about.

Secondly, I was trained to be collaborative and collegial. If you have a beef with anyone, it's done in private. You don't 'go off' at a colleague in front of others. That's anathema. Absolutely ignorant. Unprofessional. You don't show fare-paying punters the crew aren't getting along.

Thirdly, teaching is predominantly a women's profession. I was now in a macho world. Testosterone was in the air as thick as a London fog. Adapt and toughen up, Ian ... pronto. Keep your values, ethics and professionalism but adapt to a new working environment. The hardest time to hold to your values is when you are challenged.

Most punters gave Mr. Cranky a wide berth in the first four to six weeks.

By the time we completed the Mirjaveh to Quetta 'highway', (photo), altitudes changed. He nursed Casper along in <u>very</u> difficult circumstances. All credit to him.

That's life. I could live with it.

He gained respect and received more glowing reports at tour's end than I did. I was seen as quieter and weaker. I wasn't too worried. Whatever you do, there are people who won't understand why you do things, won't like what you do and won't like you.

It was a growth experience. Adversity brings out character. Growing as a person comes from interacting with others. Giving and taking. Confronting. Arguing. Asserting yourself. Extending your comfort zone. What's the famous African proverb? "It takes a village to raise a child". It was a lonely few days in Kathmandu after I arrived. I sat upstairs in Casper and reflected. Dug deep.

Did I like the overland route? Yes. I loved it.
Did I like the Top Deck way of life? Yes.
Did I want to do more Top Deck tours? Yes.
Did I have the goods as a Tour Leader? Yes.

Most importantly. Did I want another Mr. Cranky as a driver? No. What could I do about that? Be assertive. Speak up. Express my opinion. Start quoting job descriptions. This was my job. One notoriously cranky driver wasn't going to make me leave.

I toughened up and ran future tours the way ol' blue eyes, Frank Sinatra, the Chairman of the Board, recommended —

"Yes there were times, I'm sure you knew
When I bit off
More than I could chew
But through it all when there was doubt,
I ate it up and spat it out
I faced it all and I stood tall

… and did it my way."

On the 'frog and toad'

July 10, 1980

Camel and I roused ourselves as dawn was breaking. We stowed the remaining gear on board with Morris, Jeff, Gary and George assisting. Opening my briefcase, I inserted my maps and trusty, dog-eared copies of the 'Encyclopaedia of Places' and 'Across Asia on the cheap', wedged my briefcase behind the driver's seat and my collection of music tapes and camera beside it. Passengers unpacked and claimed bunks.

From the left: Nick Duce, 'Dog' and Manik. Steps on the Blue Star Hotel.

Lemming trundled off by 8:30 a.m.

Nostalgia hit me as we climbed out of the Kathmandu valley above the low-lying morning mist into sunlight. A month in Kathmandu over Christmas. A month mid-year. Such a geographic and historical leap from Aotearoa NZ. I was blessed. I had lived and worked there, made friends, met locals, been on a first name basis with several restauranteurs, bar and shop owners and had glimpsed a different culture. I was grateful. A milestone in my life's journey.

We reached the crown and started to descend, the only ones on the road. The commanding views were of precipitous rolling hills covered in lush bush. Not unlike Aotearoa NZ but in places the bush had been cleared for round thatched-roof housing and the hillside terraced to grow rice. Water in the terraces shimmered, twinkled and glistened with the breeze and early morning light.

The tar-seal snaked away disappearing around tight bends to reappear fainter, further on. A thin, blue river weaved its way between hills.

On the far horizon, were the snow-capped Himalayas, at times hidden in parts by fluffy clouds.

At Trisuli Beach, the cooks prepared lunch. The 'Chi and Pi' savoury pies I had purchased that morning would complement the fresh salad. Camel and I plunged into the invigorating waters, soon followed by others. Pop created a tsunami beside us, still with a cigarette hanging out the side of his mouth. His pale, tight pot-bellied figure was in sharp contrast to others who revealed tanned, taut, figures. Many were undoubtedly slimmer than when they started out in Sydney.

At Pokhara's Green Lake Motel, the snow-capped craggy Annapurnas make a sensational backdrop. Macchapuchhare's twin peaks resembling a fish's tail are striking. I caught up with Nehru, the motel's 'go to guy' with whom I'd made friends while on *Casper*. Each tour I would give him a few T-shirts. He was beginning to acquire a reasonable collection and was always appreciative. I asked him to arrange Sabrina's birthday cake.

Casper. December '79. Annapurna, Fish Tail, in the background.

Over that evening's chicken curry, I recommended one-to two-hour mini-treks and photographic locations. We then headed to Lake Phewa Dal to try out the skiffs. They looked easy to row but there was a knack to steering them. I had learned kayaking skills at Anikiwa's Outward Bound and anything I commandeered usually headed in my intended direction.

Several punters paddled to the bush-covered island in the middle. Always looking for opportunities to have fun, I hatched an idea.

The following day, punters gathered at the bus for afternoon tea. Kathy spoilt us with fresh raisin scones. Down to the lakeside foreshore at 3:00 p.m. for boat races. Unbeknown to the 'plebs', Camel and I had eggs and flour bombs.

Punters got into teams of four. One team of two had to row around a distant buoy then paddle back to shore to hand over to the next two. First full team back = the winner. Camel was the 'buoy' around which the teams had to turn but, sporting a smirk, he kept back-paddling further away. Julia and I teamed up. She was athletic and strong. I chose well. We approached from the opposite direction to everyone else. Camel didn't do me any favours as he tried to move himself as the 'buoy' further away but eventually we rounded Camel to be first back for the changeover, done in waist-high water and out of reach of the opposition.

Gary and George took a while to get the hang of paddling. Kathy tipped sideways out of her skiff letting out an unfeminine oath. So did Pip but with her strong Yorkshire broque, it was hard to tell exactly what she said. Chris took it all a little too seriously, lost his cool and spat the proverbial dummy. Everyone claimed a victory! "Great day, Ian. Great fun!" Morris and Jeff laughed as they headed back to the motel for a shower and a cold one. Dessert was a chocolate mud birthday cake for Sabrina, conjured up by Nehru. The elfin was delighted.

Together with punters Kathy, Flo and Cescelia, I went shopping in Pokhara for plastic buckets and disinfectant. I always left a water bucket laced with Dettol beside the back door so that punters could rinse their hands. We found what we needed, and more, at the fibrolite and corrugated iron lean-to, quaintly labelled 'Provision Shop: Cheese, brown bread, white bread and other things.'

Along Pokhara's lake frontage are several restaurants. Most have ambitious menus that bear no resemblance to the kitchen's facilities. Often invited into a kitchen if I showed even a passing interest in the menu, most were Spartan, lit only by a single bulb handing forlornly from the ceiling and with a small fire burner. Heaps of vegetables and provisions were stacked on shelves. Waits of over an hour were not uncommon. The chefs knew their stuff though and the Chinese meals were of generous portions and invariably tasty.

On very rare occasions, I didn't select the restaurant well. On the <u>Befa</u> tour, as it was winter, my 'regular' was closed so, having few options, we went next door.

"*Night it came and time to eat
Little did I know what was facing me.
Ian he said, "The Luxman's the spot"
And so off we went then, at a trot.*

*Well his nickname is 'Dog'
And surely its true
To take us to Luxman's
What a terrible blue*

*Soup like kero,
Mutton like lead,
Chop suey so hot,
It turns the eyes red.
So our warning to Dog,
Surely must be!
If it happens again,
NO DOG THERE WILL BE!"*

You said it well Estelle. You win some and lose some!

Ten minutes after starting off at dawn, *Lemming* started to climb twisting roads. It was along this stretch that Capricorn P33H broke down eighteen months before. At the helm I frequently saw monkeys scampering along the roadside. Spiders' webs, draped between the prickly points of large cacti, glistened with shimmering droplets of morning dew. The higher in altitude, the more I could see behind us. The fog clouded the valleys. Small villages and single houses embraced and clung to the hillsides, which sloped away in steep, stepped terraces where rice and other crops were grown. There were orchards amongst the terraced hillsides. The odd black and white goat or two stood by themselves in lush green pastures.

The next day, *Lemming* reached the Nepalese/Indian border by five o'clock. As we closed on the border, we could hear roaring in the dense jungle. A tiger? I had been brought up on Jim Corbett's 'Maneaters of Kumaon' as a boy. Hunting man-eating tigers. One had killed four hundred people.

I noticed three things the first time I arrived at the Nautanwa border.

Firstly, bureaucracy in action. Three hours at least. For centuries India has had religions, traditions, rituals and ways of doing things.

Bureaucracy was extended by the East India Company. Three copies of everything is needed. My copies of passenger lists weren't accepted. A local was directed to laboriously write the list out by hand. I watched him closely and tried to assist him. 'The lights were on but nobody was home'. There wasn't much sign of intelligent life behind his brown eyes but he could at least cautiously craft English letters and words even if he didn't understand them. Probably very lucky to have such a job. An official higher up the pay scale saw me hovering and frowning, shooed me away like an annoying fly.

Indian officials are sticklers for detail. On Casper, in the melee of the customs building, I observed others being processed before us. I had a lightbulb moment realising that our duplicate copy of the bus authorisation did not have Skroo Turner's signature on it. Rags had been directed back to Lahore from the Pakistani/Indian border, just two weeks before for the same reason.

A dog's life

Nudging Loxley on the elbow, I nodded at Turner's name, my finger circling where the signature should have been. I knew there was another copy with Skroo's signature on it in my briefcase. Loxley twitched his eyebrows north in assent and rapidly back-pedalled to the cab to find the real McCoy. Returning, he surreptitiously added it to our paperwork.

Sometimes punters contributed to a long crossing. Some wandered away from the bus just as they were needed. To have a pee. To take a photograph. To purchase Indian street food. An official wanted to see the camera stated in the passport to ensure it hadn't been sold. Others filled out their forms incorrectly. Some didn't have the correct signature or stamp on their medical forms.

The second thing I noticed was the Indian head wobble. You'd be talking to a local and their head would be bobbing to show understanding. It's in between up and down and a sideways head shaking. A head roll combined with a head shake.

Thirdly—the distinctive Indian accent. I had heard Spike Milligan from 'The Goons' and the characters in the English TV sitcom 'It ain't half hot Mum' but thought that was a take-off.

Duh. No! They do speak like that.

On the Casper tour, after I had been ejected from the building for trying to be helpful, I chatted to a soldier. I was wearing shorts, T-shirt and jandals and was bathed in a light layer of perspiration. The soldier was wearing his uniform with the addition of a sleeveless sweater over a long-sleeved uniform shirt. To him it was late autumn and getting cold. Everything is relative!

Varanasi

I stirred at dawn, let *Lemming* idle whilst I made myself a black coffee. My 'time clock'/circadian rhythm must have been a blessing to my drivers, all of whom liked to sleep in. I was a lark (as with 'up with the larks'), not an owl. With mind still on 'autopilot', I absent-mindedly watched several colourful birds flit, flick and flutter in the trees. All manner of shapes, colours, stripes and spots were evident. The trees were buzzing with birdsong: chirps, chirrups, warbles, squeaks and twitters. I smiled. The uplifting innocence of nature.

I studied my Roger Lascelles' map, circled a couple of places in pencil then flicked through my resources. After flicking through Tony Wheeler, I also scanned 'The Encyclopaedia of Places'. That was a paperback I had stumbled across in Kensington High Street's W.H. Smith one wet Sunday afternoon before my first Top Deck overland. I was killing time. What a treasure! I thought of a number of places on the overland route that I'd seen as a passenger. They were all there. Top Deck did not provide me with any overland notes so I had to look after myself.

I was gifted with a good memory and three hours after linking 3-4 items together, I could switch on the sound system and rattle them off. In four tours, no-one ever saw me doing my 'homework'. All 'dead to the world'. Not that I would have minded if they had seen me.

The clean air had a faint whiff of a wood fire. Through a stand of trees I could see a mud and wattle hut and a stooped white-haired woman brewing water in a black kettle over an open driftwood fire. Goats were bleating in the fenced courtyard.

Music from Supertramp soothed me as I drove, the dawn mist above the farmland slowly lifted, dissipating and evaporating. The large fertile Indo-Gangetic Plain stretches across a huge area of northern and eastern India. People farmed here 5,000 years BC, paralleling what was happening between the Tigris and Euphrates. The melting snow and glaciers, combined with streams from the Himalayas, feed the rivers in the plain including the Indus and Ganges. This deposits rich sediment and alluvium making the soils ideal for farming. Reservoirs of underground water also feed irrigation canals. Fields of crops could be seen on both sides of the road.

Arriving at the 'Hotel de Paris' by 2:00 p.m., punters settled in quickly. I booked two rooms with the manager, Dav Banajee, so that punters could use the facilities. They immediately refreshed by having showers.

It was here that I first took an interest in how India's multitudes made a living. Many masseuses, manicurists, pedicurists and haircutters miraculously appeared to offer their services. Plus fortune tellers and tea-leaf readers. These artisans were savvy.

We were foreigners. White people = money. They traded their skills for our money.

Camping companies were lucrative targets. Arriving every few days. A Top Deck bus contained twenty-two potential customers over a two day period. A Capricorn/Sundowners coach had thirty-odd potential customers.

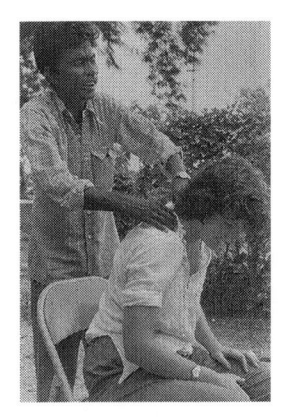

Most artisans were not on an hourly, daily or weekly wage as hotel workers were. Their livelihoods depended upon hustling and 'selling' their skills. Each day was different. Each artisan knew what a good day's return looked like and aimed for it.

I like a cut-throat razor shave so after he gave Julia an invigorating massage, I asked a lean swarthy 'jack of several trades' to tidy me up. He had skills ranging from haircutting and shaving, to massaging, manicures and pedicures. The more skills you have the better chance of making a 'sale'. I had used him before. Gentle with the blade. Inexpensive. Trustworthy.

Capricorn P33H had stayed at the 'Hotel de Paris'. I returned there on Top Deck, the only Varanasi venue I knew. I hadn't been given guidelines from Top Deck on campsites. It was where individual crew had camped before. Word of mouth. I did price comparisons. Favourable.

Despite being past its best, in the spacious rooms with high ceiling fans, the wicker and rattan sofas and chairs, the faded fittings and the indulgent attention afforded by the waiters, punters would glimpse what life was like under the British Raj. I imagined the ghosts of the 'stiff-upper-lip brigade' scowling down on me.

Staying there killed two birds with one stone. Firstly decent accommodation, hot showers, clean facilities, morning and afternoon tea facilities provided by ever-vigilant waiters. Secondly a history lesson. My strong suite. At the one venue.

The best insult ever directed at me was by my stepfather, "That boy's an overeducated upstart". He was disputing my mother's will at the time. Another favourite is Top Decker Doug Foskett calling me (tongue in cheek) "an upper class toff" because I went to the Hotel de Paris instead of the Dak Bungalow site he frequented. He favoured and often needed its garage and mechanical facilities.

Thinking of Doug's comment, I could swear my room trembled as my blue-collar, railway-trimmer/upholsterer father and Glaswegian boilermaker grandfather turned over in their graves. My father died when I was four and my grandfather when I was seven. Hence … no modelling of DIY skills. Leaving school I had to use the grey matter instead.

As I was listing receipts and aligning them with my records, the ceiling fan was circling languidly above me. A large speckled gecko with prominent protruding eyes, each looking in a different direction, was stealthily traversing the ceiling. Obviously has suction cups on its feet. Geckos

Overland with Top Deck

cannot close their eyes so their tongues clear them of dust. That gecko reminded me of '70s English comedian Marty Feldman who suffered from a condition causing his eyes to become mis-aligned and to bulge. He used his unusual appearance to his advantage in his career.

No sooner had I dropped into a cushioned wicker chair when there was a 'rat-tat-tat' on the frame of the door. In came a tall, humourless Indian with a thick mane of tangled, tousled, shoulder-length black hair, parted in the middle. His luxurious full beard showing the first strands of grey blended in seamlessly with his long hair. He was a striking image in his flowing red shirt, yellow silk sash tied diagonally and baggy purple/blue trousers.

Having seen him before, a virtual permanent fixture at these grounds, I predicted his 'sales pitch'. "Did 'Sahib' (me) want my punters to see his 'snake and mongoose' show?" No charge. They would 'pass the turban

A dog's life

around' for tips. How did he know we had arrived? The 'jungle drums' must have been beating.

Thirty minutes later, by which time I had rounded up the punters, he returned with several swarthy, turbaned accomplices. The captive passengers watched spellbound as a row of cobras were lured from their coils to sit upright as he played a bulbous looking flute-like instrument, made from a gourd. The cobras had been 'milked' of their venom or had their venom glands removed. Or they weren't the species that could spit their venom a distance of four metres. They were noble imposing creatures up close with their black and cream markings, shiny overlapping scales, distinctive flared 'hood' and their black penetrating eyes which dare you to move faster than them. Cobras are deaf and are responding to the vibrations in the air when the pungi is blown. Punters later watched a staged cobra-mongoose fight. The more adventurous of the punters had a python wrapped around their shoulders.

The snake charmers, rickshaw drivers, artisans, barbers, masseuses, waiters, and room cleaners I encountered were from the sudra/labourer caste. Occupation is an indicator of caste, your standing in society. Hindu sacred scriptures divide people up into four: Brahman/priest, Kshatriya/warrior, Vausya/ trader and Sudra/labourer.

Originally a person's caste was not fixed permanently by birth but that changed.

A person's caste was determined by parents and that reflected how well or how poorly one had lived up to their caste duties in past lives.

In 1980, about 6% of India's population were Brahman, priests and government employees. 14% were upper castes, typically landholders, merchants and shopkeepers. 52%, were lower castes, represented by cow-herders, labourers, artisans and carpenters.

18% were 'Dalits', the Sanskrit term for 'oppressed', their status so low they are without caste. Their jobs are often demeaning including human waste disposal and burning the dead. I caught up with the 'mature' waiter named Bachlal that I had met whilst on *Befa*. Usually standing ramrod straight, shoulders squared back military fashion, he dressed in a white uniform which contrasted with his sun-scorched, brown skin. As dark as worn leather and as wrinkled as parchment. Bachlal had a long lean face with silver hair and a grey luxurious, Hercule Poirot moustache. He spoke excellent English and took pride in his profession—serving people.

I was sitting on the steps outside my room one morning basking in the mid-morning sun. Bachlal served me chai latte—white teapot, cup and milk—on a silver tray. As he chatted, he squatted easily on his haunches. I added that to my lexicon. Doing 'a Bachlal'. Squatting.

Bachlal followed a strict code of conduct. He had been at the hotel for nine years. Previously he had spent fifteen years in an Indian air force mess where, he said puffing himself up with some pride, he knew 'important' people and received generous tips, often 100 rupees (NZ$13.00) a time. That would have added considerably to his lifestyle.

He, like others working at the Hotel de Paris, had guaranteed employment. A step above those who had to harass and hassle each day. He worked from six a.m. until six p.m. His wage = 200 rupees, NZ $26.31 a month. His tips doubled that some months. Of his family of seven, the youngest was six years old. Six! I looked at him and chuckled. He might be getting long in the tooth with snow on the roof but there's plenty of fire still in the furnace! Uncle at 'The Withies' in Kathmandu had the same active libido.

Varanasi: Visiting the ghats

India is a spiritual country. That spiritualism, that search for enlightenment, attracted many westerners to journey 'the hippie trail' in the '60s and '70s. Indians are driven, guided and protected by their faiths. Hinduism is the main religion but there are followers of Buddhism, Sikhism, Christianity, Jainism, Zoroastrianism and others. Hinduism dates back to 1,000 BC and has a pantheon of gods led by Brahma the creator, Vishnu the preserver and Shiva the destroyer, as well as secondary gods such as Hanumam the Monkey God and Ganesh with its elephant head.

There were millions of people in India in 1980. Most appeared on or below the poverty line. They are so poor they had to have something spiritual to hang onto, to give them hope, to help them cope with life.

In India, western ideas of materialism, competition and promotion seemed artificial. Life in India is life at its most basic. Living from day to day. Hand to mouth. People seemed happy and optimistic, able to cope on much less than the average westerner.

Varanasi is India's supreme holy city. Many come each year to bathe in the Ganges and cleanse their bodies and their souls. Despite being dirty, smelly, noisy and chaotic, assaulting the senses like most Indian cities do, Varanasi is unique.

Early the next morning a bus took us to the Ganges. The taxis had recently increased their prices from thirteen rupees to twenty rupees a head.

My most memorable visit was in February when, before dawn, I had marshalled barely-awake punters onto tricycle rickshaws. We were pedalled to the ghats, an eerie sight through the still, morning mist. The seats were initially wet with dew and had to be wiped down. The handlebars glistened with moisture. I was at the front and the others snaked in a long crocodile line behind me, 2-3 passengers, depending on their girth, to each rickshaw. A comment in the Trip book later was "Dog, this is Brett speaking. I think we have a convoy!"—in reference to the 1978 Burt Reynolds' movie 'Convoy'. It summed up the procession. Our rickshaw convoy had a surreal quality.

We weaved our way through narrow alleyways to reach the ghats. Varanasi is a rabbits' warren of bumpy potholed, uneven, smelly streets and alleyways with buildings leaning in on themselves. A myriad of dangling electrical cables try to ensnare an unobservant person. Standing respectfully aside to allow a funeral cortège pass, punters eyes grew wide in alarm when they realised a body wrapped in cloth lying on stretcher, was being carried aloft by the mourners just feet away.

At the Manikarnika Ghat, dead male bodies are swathed in white and women's bodies wrapped in pink. They are carried to the waters on bamboo stretchers by outcastes. Bodies are submerged in the Ganges before being cremated. Lower castes are cremated in a different area to Brahmins. Children and lepers are dropped in the middle of the Ganges. Funeral piles were lit, crackling and snapping before bursting into a roar. Colourful pink flower pedals were scattered around. The smell of incense and burning wood linger in the air. Bony-framed dogs sniffed for morsels ever wary of being shooed away. Baskets of ashes were emptied onto the steps where dogs and black ravens picked over juicy morsels.

We had boarded a wooden skiff and gently rowed past a few of the eighty ghats. At a respectable distance. The oars dipped rhythmically in the waters, barely making a splash. Our guide kept his voice low and punters whispered, playing down their voyeurism. You could see and sense the pilgrims' spiritualism, their genuine and sincere belief and devotion. As westerners we may not understand their pantheon of gods. But *they* do. It works for *them*. So be it.

More pilgrims arrived to be cleansed and purified as the sun leisurely rose higher in the sky. Bare patches of concrete or wood on the gnats were filled. The area teemed with life.

Sadhus (priests) sat and meditated. Their faces were weather-worn. Deeply-lined. What life stories could those faces tell? Some had long white hair. The tips of their wispy pointed beards caught the breeze. Lean muscular yogis twisted themselves into impossible distortions. Dark brown, sinewy, strong and focused. Legs drawn up behind their heads.

Devotees washed themselves, scrubbed their clothes and vigorously cleaned their teeth in the waters. Some scrubbed away a lifetime of sins. Fascinating. I felt guilty, an intruder observing someone's private religious observances.

Gotta pick a pocket or two...

As the sun sank lower and the day's shadows lengthened, most punters signed up to see that evening's sitar and dance performance. I was 'burned' on a past tour when eighteen said they wanted to see a show but only ten turned up. That show's organiser was distraught as his group had travelled some distance. He avoided me thereafter. A reliable contact lost. Since then I asked punters to record names on a clipboard 'Tonight's Show". Time: 7.30 p.m. Venue: The Lounge: Cost for the 60 minute show = 20 rupees. I hinted that I might charge them if they reneged.

Ravi Shankar's sitar inspired the George Harrison compositions "My Sweet Lord" and "Across the Universe". The Beatles travelled to Rishikesh in 1968 to attend Transcendental Meditation sessions with the Maharishi Mahesh Yoga.

In the evening, a power blackout interrupted the show. Blackouts are common in India. I had been updating the accounts at the antique teak, roll-top desk, the surface of which shone from years of buffing and burnishing. Camel was curled in a foetal position. Breathing deeply. As there was no light to work by, I exited the room intending to check on the punters. Everyone was engrossed. In the candle-lit gloom I couldn't tell whether their eyes were glazing over. Sometimes these events, although the production values were high, are best in shorter doses.

As I retreated down the walkway, five metres from my room, I heard a briefcase click in the still air. I was alerted. Camel had been catatonic when I left him.

He still was… almost in a coma… but a tall, lean teenager was moving furtively away from my briefcase, his hands deep in his pockets. I seized an arm and pulled a fist out. It was wrapped firmly around a wad of crisp new Australian banknotes. Pop had paid for the show in cash that morning. As we grappled, a lantern toppled from a bedside table and shattered. "Give us a hand here Camel," I gasped. The teenager was wiry and strong. Remembering a ju jitsu hand-hold I had learned years before, I folded his palm inwards and pushed hard on that elbow in the opposite direction to which it was meant to move. The James Bond treatment did the trick. He collapsed face down on the bed. A sleepy Camel, joined me. It was all over in seconds.

I frog-marched the artful dodger to the manager who tried to dissuade me from alerting the police as it would earn the boy a police record. I initially bought into this. As time flittered on, stories changed like a woman's whims. My inbuilt bullsh*t detector started beeping. The police arrived. The boy was related to the sitar players. I started to imagine conspiracies. Did they work in together, the sitar players drawing punters away from the rooms while the boy raided them? Or was the boy merely being a lone wolf opportunist?

If I let the law take its course, I would have to remain a month for a court hearing. I settled on a refund of the sitar show money and an apology. Some punters commented that they liked my dramatics much more than the puppet performance.

Driving, accidents and breakdowns

It took me less than an hour of driving to realise that **Indians are *really* good at *bad* driving.**

It takes a brave ... or perhaps a foolish man ... to drive on Indian roads. Even in a substantial Lodekka, coach or four-wheel drive truck. Tony Wheeler hit 'the nail on the head' when he wrote "Indian roads are pure hell to drive on with traffic, animals, bikes and suicidal trucks to contend with." (p11. 1979)

Westerners have three things to consider on Indian roads. The first is the condition of the roads, the second being the volume of traffic and the third being the attitude of those using the roads.

Westerners' ideas of road rules and the locals' views are polar opposites. The locals don't think of 'your side', 'my side', a centre line, *western* notions of courtesy and giving way. They think of getting to their destination in the fastest way possible. Getting there using imaginative ways. Taking risks is part of the fun. Livens what could be an uneventful day. They are spontaneous opportunists. They're gamblers.

Indian roads are narrow for the volume of traffic using them. Maintained well? Nah. Rough and uneven. Unusual cambers. Potholes. Often *large* potholes. Some states spend more on their roads than others.

Indian roads are crowded with humanity, thousands of people—walking, cycling, carried by creaking groaning ox and bullock-drawn carts, riding donkeys, on trishaws, on camels and at times elephants—from before dawn until after dusk. The bitumen roads are as wide as a Lodekka and you are continually moving onto a dusty berm to allow oncoming, aggressive traffic to pass.

Two wheeled transport—bicycles, mopeds and small motorbikes—are unpredictable. Sometimes a bicyclist would trundle along slowly completely oblivious to a monster truck breathing down his neck. I smiled at one distinguished-looking, elderly Sikh, cycling along as if he was in an English country village. White turban, long white beard, short sleeved woollen jersey over a long sleeved traditional white shirt with tie and tapered pants. Other vehicles swerved past him, their wind trail buffeting him. He cycled on bravely, seemingly oblivious of the dangers.

Mopeds and motorbikes often have two, three or even more passengers and undertake vehicles as one found out to his detriment.

Pip was preparing dinner late one afternoon whilst *Lemming* was 'on the move'—peeling, chopping and dicing apples, mangoes and bananas for dessert. She was single-minded, totally focused. The last time she had glanced up, *Lemming* was pitching along a country road. She hadn't registered that we were now edging into a populated area. With her mind on autopilot, Pip hurled the content of the green plastic bowl of peels and skins out the open back door.

Unfortunately a young couple—he in jeans and a sports coat, and she in a colourful sari—on a moped, chose *that* particular moment to *undercut* the bus. They ended up wearing the scraps. In the absence of helmets, their heads were now covered in apple skins resembling long curly ringlets.

Pip gasped a giggle, "Whoops!"

Or as Maxwell Smart would have said "Sorry about that …"

There are long drives in India. Long and slow. You have to concentrate—for your sake and the passengers. If punters weren't in the cab with me, music kept me focused.

A dog's life

On each overland tour we struck at least three traffic jams. A two-hour delay was lucky. There was a four-to five-hour delay on *Befa*.

On Casper, with Rags and Boogie in tandem, we hit a traffic jam that delayed us hours. Cars and trucks stretched away as far as the eye could see. In front and behind. Loxley, Trevor and Steve piled out to have a heated, very animated and colourful discussion with the local drivers. Language differences were no barrier. Their voices rose a few octaves ... and decibels.

Much energy was expended, arms were waved about furiously like the sail arms on a windmill, fingers were jabbing the air, globules of spit caught the light in the air, faces turned pink and the air turned blue with expletives! I didn't join in. No point. The solution to the traffic jam was well beyond our control.

The others were in their element in this 'abuse-fest' and needed no help from me, a mere kiwi. I didn't see the point. Indian drivers weren't going to move for us. I would be adding to the numbers of enraged white men but not to the quality of the spectacle! After all, they were Aussies and, if their '70s cricket teams were anything to go by, were seasoned masters of sledging. The rev-up of the locals didn't ease the traffic jam but it obviously felt good to the participants!

The Grand Trunk Road was described by Rudyard Kipling as "a river of life that exists nowhere else in the world". It stretches across the sub-continent. Ever present are silk cotton trees and Banyan trees. I like the Banyan, India's national tree. Gnarly. Knotty. Distorted. A fig tree beginning as an epiphyte that grows on another plant enveloping and ultimately killing the host tree. Huge, stocky banyan trees are a photographer's delight. The shapes. Like gargoyles. You can see faces in some.

They have far-reaching overhangs. High above us, trees on one side of the road intertwined branches with trees on the other side. Together with the silk cotton trees, they provide long avenues of shade stretching away into the distance. Foreign invaders have marched long distances in this shade.

The Banyan's shade is cooling for pedestrians but the sun filtering through their branches is broken up and, being split and dappled, plays havoc with a driver's vision.

Low-hanging branches from the trees on both sides of the road reach down like triffids to snare and scrape the bus.

Branches screech along the paintwork like my fingernails once did down a classroom blackboard. Or languidly slap the side mirrors. Sitting upstairs at the front, punters often duck involuntarily at low-hanging branches.

Lodekkas compete with suicidally-driven Tata trucks, game cyclists, mopeds and low-powered motorbikes, overladen bullock carts and oxen, stately elephants and even plodding camels for a relatively narrow strip of uneven bitumen. Tata trucks were the bullies of the roads. Belonging to a wealthy Indian automotive conglomerate (now worth US $35 billion) they often barrel along at breakneck speeds towards you in a deadly case of 'chicken' and 'brinkmanship'.

They don't always win.

I saw five variations of smashes: Head to head, head to tail, up a tree, in a ditch, truck v pedestrian. At semi-regular intervals we found Tata trucks immobile. Most often they were welded together, head to head. Less often they were welded together head to tail as though the front truck had stopped abruptly and the one following had barrelled into it. Sometimes they were wrapped around trees, or in a watery shallow ditch or flat on their sides blocking the road. They were often overloaded. Running repairs were done anywhere. Put a ring of rocks around your vehicle and begin (photo below). Sometimes there were unequal contests. Truck versus one very dead, flat, splattered and scattered pedestrian.

Loxley on Casper loathed Tata trucks. With a vengeance. After discovering leftover fireworks in the cab, he scrunched down beside me. Lighting a fuse to a Varanasi 'banger', he paused while the fuse fizzled and spluttered, then propelled it like a dart at an approaching Tata truck. It exploded behind us and he cackled long and loud like a wizard preparing a toxic brew. A maniacal laugh.

Every cloud has a silver lining

It's unreasonable to expect to travel for extended periods without having breakdowns. With Top Deck I had few serious breakdowns despite *Casper, Befa* and *Lemming* being built in the late 1950s.

I started as a tour leader with Tracks in Bedford J registration coaches. On two of three European tours we had mechanical troubles. One challenge when breakdowns occur, apart from getting the problems fixed asap and maintaining punter morale, was to make the best of a bad situation. When you are in an unexpected negative situation, look for positive opportunities.

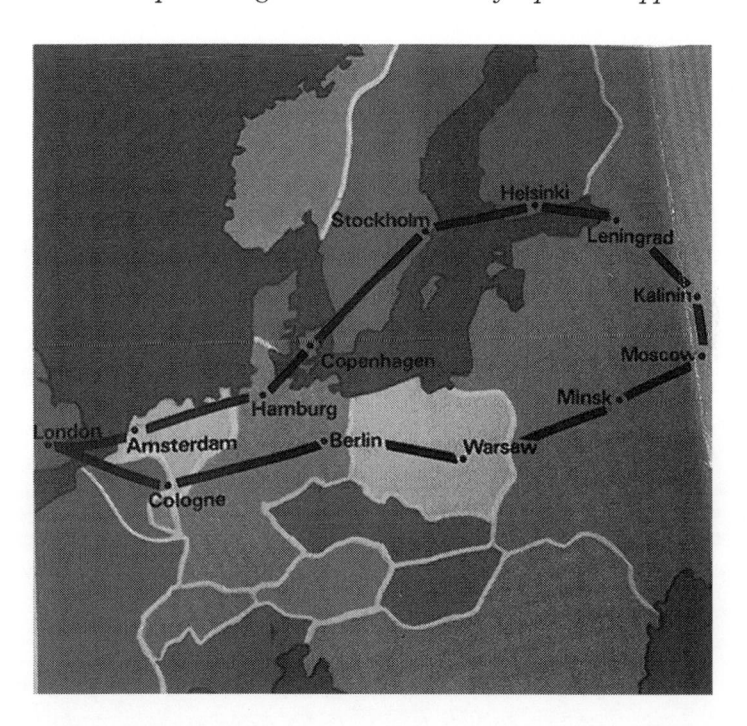

My first breakdown was on my training trip, a three-and-a-half-week Russian/Scandinavian. On route to Kalinin, a wayward stone smashed a hole in the coach's radiator. Hours later, thanks largely to the resourcefulness of our Intourist guide, we were delivered to Moscow's 'Mozhaiski' campsite.

Our coach followed. In addition to the hole in the radiator, a piston had blown. Tracks' London HQ were contacted. We needed spare parts.

Their initial reaction was "No! No spare parts".

What? Refusing to act on the advice of experienced crew? Should I work for this company?

The saga dragged on. Three punters left by public transport. They had planes to catch. We were stranded in Moscow for ten days before replacement parts were eventually sent and the coach became operable.

With so much extra time, I made the best of a bad deal and with each additional day, ventured off the beaten track. Travelled by the local concertina buses. Shopped in the markets. Ate in local cafes. Went back for a closer inspection of St. Basil's Cathedral. Stood in the middle of Red Square where the Soviets hold their annual May Day parade of Soviet Military might.

Earlier, I had passed on entering Lenin's tomb as there was a huge queue. Now I had the time. I was fascinated by the locals, all formally dressed. Their fashions were at least a decade behind the west. Polyester was in. They took Lenin seriously. Sunday best clothes. Suits. Ties. Formal clothes and hats for women. Lenin looked like a waxwork mannequin beneath his glass viewing dome. Unsmiling. Shiny. He had certainly changed Russia and its satellite territories. For the better? Communist theories were enticing on paper but in reality? Some of our punters were turned away from his mausoleum by guards as they looked too casual. Shorts. Flip-flops. Not respectable enough.

The extra time in Moscow enabled us to go to Moscow s Central Bolshoi Theatre on Karl Marx Prospekt. It has been home to the Bolshoi Ballet and musical performances for over a hundred years.

They put on 200 performances per year to full houses. Our box seat was stage left. The programme was a selection of iconic pieces from Sleeping Beauty, Swan Lake and The Nutcracker. Very athletic. I had been to a ballet once before. The Kirov ballet in Leningrad.

A dog's life

Now ... the Bolshoi. The icing on the cake.

The theatre was a five-tier auditorium with magnificent crimson and gold velvet curtains, chandeliers and gilt edging to the box seats. Acoustics were fantastic. At the interval, some of the audience congregated in the buffet room. We consumed Russian beer and champagne, fresh French loaves, red caviar and smoked fish. The Caspian Sea caviar was salty. Nothing to write home about! However the smoked fish, champagne and chilled local beer were a different story!

I loved mixing and mingling. Communist locals and capitalist westerners. We had both been conditioned by our respective governments and media to see the other as the 'bad guy'. They looked normal to me.

I had two more memorable interactions on the way out of the USSR. The coach pulled over on the main highway south to allow Intourist guide Lora and supercook Linda to haggle for potatoes and spring onions from an elderly trio running a small roadside stall. They looked like anyone's grandparents. Two buckets of large firm potatoes tempted. I had discovered in Moscow days before, that edible potatoes cannot be taken for granted. These vendors were farmers. The boss, the wife, wore an aged but colourful cotton sleeveless dress and a white headscarf. The husband wore last decade's weathered flat cap, a long sleeved checked shirt and, several inches below his stomach, dark brown corduroy trousers (I doubt he could see his toes) and plastic sandals streaked with dust. His ample stomach strained at his shirt, strongly hinting he ate plenty of carbohydrates. He looked as though he had recently dug up the potatoes as his hands were dusted with dirt. They were presided over and supervised by her mother – slimmer, white scarfed, slightly taller, high cheek-boned and with shoulders squared. Dressed in clothes better suited to the city, she exuded a dignified, regal ... supervisory air.

Further south, on route to Smolensk, Belarus, the day brightened when we visited a weathered, stone-clad country village store. Like a down-under local dairy. Out front sat two green Russian motorbikes with sidecars, 1930s style. They didn't have the performance of the Japanese bikes I'd ridden but they did have a seriously comprehensive toolkit which helped them last for ages. The store had food, souvenirs, clothes, ornaments and cloth hats – all with labels of indecipherable Cyrillic writing. Russian boiled sweets were liberally passed around to encourage us to chat and buy.

A dusty farm truck pulled in for refreshments. The back was packed with giggling peasant women returning from work. They had all been poured from the same mould short, stocky, ample-bosomed with cherubic faces. Not thin, flinty and disagreeable as I sometimes found in the cities. Especially the hairdressers. Their countenances were adorned with colourful scarves and sported irrepressible grins accompanied by infectious titters and chortles. They looked like western women bound for a bingo evening. Punter Chris and I climbed into the back of the truck to 'converse' with them and soon found we were all laughing and giggling together. Way to go. Unity between disparate nations.

Always look on the bright side of life

I got into London one day and was off the next on a Central European 4.5 weeker. £215.00 pp plus £40.00 food kitty.

All smooth running for 2.5 weeks until we left Rome for Florence. First a tyre blew. Then the coach overheated, followed by the starter motor jamming. Two hours of trial and error tinkering by the roadside.

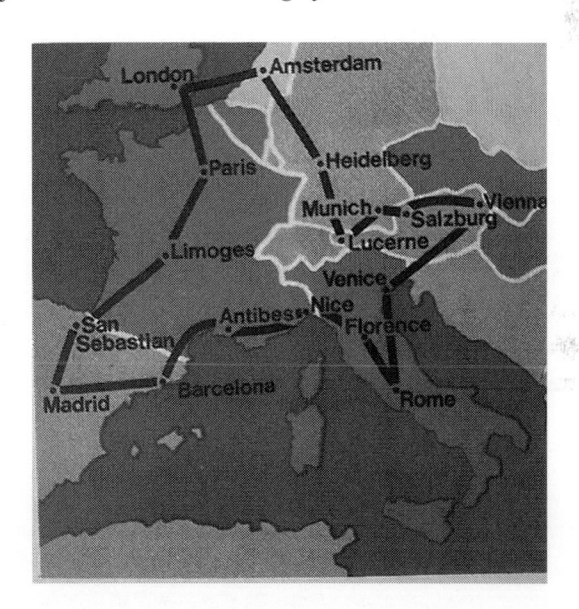

Approximately two days later, Antibes bound, the brake line fractured.

Two days after that, driving to Barcelona, the coach overheated and blew a gasket. Driver Geoff and I found a Spanish garage whose foreman Joseph, via very limited English but unlimited sign language, assured us that his mechanics could fix the problem.

Overland with Top Deck

I tried to turn that breakdown into a positive experience. Enjoy the sunshine, relax and meet the locals. We camped that night and the following day in a field opposite the garage. Couldn't have picked a better spot! A hot sunny day. Not a cloud in the sky. Time to wash clothes, catch up on diaries, go for walks. Rolling hills were broken up by hedges and rows of trees on one side and on the other were fertile fields of varying shades of yellows, oranges and browns.

Local shopkeepers and farmers rallied around. We had a barbecue in the grounds of foreman Joseph's house. It was accompanied by music and generous amounts of local Spanish rough red, purchased from wife Marie's shop. That evening we mixed with local people, all poorer than us and much less travelled. I savoured the experience.

The coach was ready by 8.00 p.m. the following evening. One day behind schedule. The mechanics made out a docket for Tracks and another for us. The 3000 peseta difference paid for the beer I shouted the mechanics. A 'win-win'.

We departed for Barcelona where, for two days, I showed the punters the sights of Barcelona including the Ramblas and the Montserrat mountains. In order to 'spoil' the punters after three successive breakdowns in six days, I successfully arranged a national meal and a sangria evening. The rejuvenated mood was snuffed out a day later as the coach drove towards Madrid. A brake pipe leaked and jammed on. With smoke pouring liberally from the tyres, we limped back to La Bella Allegre, the Barcelona campsite.

Combined with those frustrating breakdowns, I spent an inordinate amount of time visiting European banks chasing tour funds and being given the brush off. In Rome, I rang Tracks requesting the remaining tour funds. Director Andy said they would be forwarded to Cannes. "Could we last until then?"

A dog's life

"Could we last until then?" I muttered. Grrrrrr.

In Cannes: "Your funds aren't here. Try Madrid. The Banco Centrale." After waiting in a queue at Madrid's Banco Centrale I reached the top of the queue to be told, "Your money's not here." I was redirected to their International Division a few blocks away.

Twenty minutes later. Standing in another queue behind ten others, I reached the front again … to be told that the funding had not arrived. Geoff drove me to Madrid's main post office to ring London. "Sorry you can't ring London from here but you should be able to from the telephone exchange three blocks away." I eventually got through to Director Andy who insisted the money had been sent to the Central Bank.

I didn't believe him but … back I went again.

No luck so … back to the telephone exchange again to ring HQ.

This time the big chief, Bill—'ol blue eyes' himself, the 'chairman of the board'—answered icily, "Ian. What is the purpose of this call?" I took a deep breath, dropped my voice an octave and, added my own frost, "The purpose … BILL…is to bring this tour back to London safely. You want that. I want that. The punters want that. But in order to do that, I need trip funds for petrol, tolls, food …"

Bill arranged to have money wired to Paris but suggested an alternative if those funds weren't there.

Some punters were waiting outside my telephone booth. They heard the sarcasm, not to mention the volume. I started with a reasonable John McEnroe imitation "You cannot be … serious?! You want me to borrow off PUNTERS to get this tour home?"

Once word got around, that was the death knell of the tour. Morale disintegrated. Ernest Hemingway wrote about Spain. 'For whom the bell tolls? It tolls for thee'. Very appropriate. It was tolling for me alright. The drive from Madrid to Paris and then onto London was filled with punters' grizzles, groans and gripes. An ugly situation. They got 'down' and couldn't be kidded out of their funk. Tempers frayed. I felt like a fireman—putting out a multitude of scattered fires as soon as they flared up!

Tracks 4CE10 limped into London on September 14th. Punters were spent by the successive mishaps. Most were fed up, collected their bags and disappeared. No goodbyes. I didn't take it personally. Half the punters had completed their appraisal forms. From their mutterings they were going to give the company an earful. The remainder screwed the reports up.

I entered 'Adam and Eve Mews' at 165 Kensington High Street wearily and warily climbing the stairs to the Tracks' office. Stairway to heaven? Hardly. It was like approaching the OK Corral. Where were Burt Lancaster and Kirk Douglas? The Dimitri Tiomkin film theme was playing in my head.

There was a very strong possibility of a clash with a director. But I ... had an edge. I no longer cared about keeping the job. I was prepared to walk. I had a Plan B—Do ten-week overlands during the English winter.

Senior Director Bill met me. I liked Bill, more mature than his younger, brasher, status-conscious colleague Andy, a product of his country's apartheid era. To him everyone had their place and as co-director, he was further up the status totem pole. Bill was older and seemed less concerned about his status, was professional, organised and well spoken.

Reading the tour reports, Bill initially seemed happy. But then he hit the 'home truths'. The speed wobbles. I smiled to myself as his reading slowed down like one of his coaches struggling through thick cloying mud. "Here it comes," I predicted. He demanded "How would the punters know you had run out of funds?"

I am a product of a '60s upbringing. Scottish grandparents. Strong work ethic. Respect for elders. Robust sense of right and wrong. But no siblings.

Little experience in confrontation. Normally I am (too) respectful towards superiors.

But I don't like being 'put upon' unfairly.

Bill and I were <u>both</u> seconds away from finding that out.

Taking a deep breath and using those precious seconds to marshal my thoughts, I shook my head in frustration. Staring defiantly into his pale blues, I dropped into sotto voce and added my own menace. "There were no funds waiting for me in Madrid as you promised. It was you who told me to borrow off punters. Fortunately for you, BILL, because I didn't think it was a good look for your company, I ignored your advice and didn't ask them."

The company was operating on a shoestring budget. Multiple tours operating at once. It was common practice not to give full tour funds up front. But at least with Top Deck the funds arrived at the intended bank on time even if the Operations managers, either Dave Reed or Dillon O'Sullivan, thinking they knew better, or being skinflints, trimmed my requests.

A Mexican stand-off. Cue the quintessential Ennio Morricone western theme. 'The good, the bad and the ugly'. Which one was I? I was doing a passable imitation of 'Angel Eyes'/Lee van Cleef. I squinted my eyes threateningly.

Being a student of history, I recalled Secretary of State Dean Rusk say during the 1962 Cuban missile crisis—"We went eyeball to eyeball and I think the other guy just blinked."

Bill had blinked. He didn't apologise or admit any wrongdoing but his rhetoric softened. He didn't belabour the point. He redirected. Offered me another job. A choice one. The Oktoberfest and the Greek Islands. I grunted and stood up. I said I'd get back to him.

Goodbye to Tracks' J Registration Bedfords.

Smooth running

What was I thinking by turning to Top Deck?

Was I thinking?

I was leaving Tracks because of the constant coach breakdowns. But the Bristol Lodekkas were even older than Tracks' J registration Bedfords. *Casper* was YHT 953, *Befa* PDL536 and *Lemming* PDL518. A 19,300 kilometre route. Asian 'roads' are incomparable to European roads. Hardly the routes and conditions the Lodekkas were designed for.

But surely they couldn't be as bad as the Bedfords?

Was I lucky?

Definitely.

'My' Lodekkas proved reliable. I often had to spend time and buy numerous spare parts to prepare them beforehand but on the road they were brilliant, helped along by excellent driver/ mechanics. Fortune was smiling.

I was the cause of two dings on my first tour on Casper. After the Bremner Pass ding, I had another five weeks later. I drove Casper into the sprawling suburbs of Tabriz in Iran's east Azerbaijan province. Large city. Bustling, vibrant traffic. Their pace was hectic. Cars and motorcycles would pull out from the curbside or swap lanes with little warning. Punters gasped in amazement. I swerved to avoid an errant motorcyclist. The next second—thwhack! I had collected a portion of a broken metal fence, which was jutting out into the road. I gritted my teeth, grimaced, and started counting down from ten. By the time I got to seven, I heard Mr. Cranky curse.

Two dings on a 12,000 mile journey. First-time driver. Drove at least a quarter of the way, maybe a third. Not bad going.

Casper, Befa and Lemming were all reliable. Prepared well for the tour. Maintained well on the tour. They all had punctures, dents and broken windows which needed repairing. Window mounts had to be replaced so that rain or dust couldn't get in. Roof panels were adjusted to keep rain out. Engines overheated. Dust got into air filters. Screws were jolted lose and cupboards had to be tightened. Spare parts were sent from London. All the mechanical issues seemed to be within the drivers' mechanical or creative, 'number 8 wire' capabilities.

If drivers needed a hand, locals were only too happy to assist, usually with 'technology' our grandparents and great grandparents used. On Befa, in Lahore in February 1980, Iain and I hailed an auto rickshaw to have a brace bent and shaped. A few wheel nuts were determined to stay where they were. Once he knew what we wanted, the rickshaw driver also made it his problem. He located a forge where the job was done in front of us. 20 minutes maximum. The 'forge' consisted of a brick oblong three feet by two feet. The blacksmith got the coals burning, the coals soon glowed orange and yellow, our brace was placed in the centre and the embers piled in a mound over it. I was expecting him to use a hand bellows to keep the heat going. Too much like hard work! Instead he had an electric fan leading to the gorge and within minutes the metal was pliable enough to bend to our required shape. This was 'number 8 wire ingenuity' that the average kiwi would have been proud of! Priceless.

When the auto-rickshaw returned us to camp, Ian McKinnon climbed out with his wheel brace and Ray Clarke clambered in. "Lahore Airport, Driver". Our spare parts were difficult to locate. We wandered up and down aisles with an assistant for thirty minutes. There was no set section for each airline or record of the date they arrived. London HQ had not helped by not sending a weigh bill.

Stories abound on the 'Top Deck buses crew and punters' website of crew not requesting spare parts but discovering and inventing all manner of ingenious 'Heath Robinson' and 'number 8 wire' adaptations to keep the buses rolling. And having willing assistance from locals.

A dog's life

Doug Foskett recalls he and Colin Carter on *Tadpoles* had the main leaf spring on the rear left snap 50 kilometres from Varanasi. "I can't remember the actual arrangement but I recall it involved a block of wood and a length of wire … and a pair of scissors and a hammer. Whatever Colin did, worked, and we limped very slowly to the Dak Bungalow in Varanasi. As we pulled up in the field there, the arrangement gave away completely…"

Brian Langbein writes of the generosity of local tradesmen. He had a breakdown on the way from Adana to Dogubayazit "… the driveshaft of *Woftam* started rubbing on the underfloor. We stopped at a roadhouse, whipped the front off to see the shattered front engine mount bracket loose and broken. Within a few hours the locals had made one out of half-inch steel plate. Cut, welded and drilled. We got enough bolts in to get out of there and all the way to Pakistan without further problems from it."

Jess Skepper had a similar experience with helpful locals who often made the crews' problems *their* problem—"May '78. Camping Londra. Istanbul. The big ends were making their music again… Moose had had a guts-full at that stage … I grabbed the tools and ripped the head and sump off. No big end spares left, so I took a taxi into Istanbul, to the market place where all things can be found. Rows of shacks devoted to clutches, bearings, wheels and whatever you wanted. But no specific big ends for us. However, I found an old bloke, who took my shells, got his little burner out and with a saucepan, melted some white metal in it, and relined the shells. He came back to the bus with his callipers and got the correct dimensions, then back to his shack, where he turned out the bearings. Magic!"

Hak Howell adds "…the radiator on *Snort*. The top and bottom tanks were in at least 50 pieces. The tuk tuk driver found the metal worker who had a cobalt/oxygen torch. Over a period of 7 hours he fused the pieces together … filled them up layer upon layer, a master craftsman … he let Johno Wellington and I sleep in the workshop while he toiled.

I reassembled the radiator, filled it up and it leaked like a sieve. All of the rubber grommets had perished so 2kg of black pepper sealed her up and got us back to London."

Murray Dunlop learned from locals—"… a leak in the fuel tank in Iran. In Balutichistan we found some straw, chopped it up fine and shaved a cake of soap, moistened it and made a paste, covered the leak, lasted until London and beyond. An old desert man told me about that."

Like bees to a honeypot, locals came to inspect us whenever we stopped.

After the two dings on Casper on my first tour, I had just one other ding. That was on Befa in February, 1980. No dings on Lemming and I drove a lot on that tour. Befa's damage was a scratch to the left front mud guard.

But like my two motorbike accidents—the injuries were minor but the manner in which they were achieved was, to some extent, dazzling. Being somersaulted

A dog's life

right over a car (even if it was a Fiat Bambina) or over a car's bonnet when colliding on a motorbike has a certain 'wow' element.

Punter John 'Motorboat' Hutcheson on Befa wrote up the incident in his diary. John and girlfriend Jo-Anne had started the 20-week tour the year before with the Sydney to Perth leg. John was 'earthy', a lean redhead with curly hair, full beard, a grin on his face, a cheeky quip on his lips and an expensive camera usually slung over his shoulder. His humour was somewhat on the 'blue' side. I am guessing the 'motorboat' tag came from his snoring. Jo-Anne complemented him being reserved and quiet. Her well-practised eye rolls at his comments were often so subtle, John didn't notice. I told him she was a "keeper". Hang onto her. They are still together 43 years later. No doubt the eye rolls continue. He's incorrigible.

Driving Befa through the outer suburbs of a sprawling industrial city, I was confronted by two Tata trucks, side by side, bearing down on me. They looked like two demented enraged elephants racing each other. One JUST managed to pass the other. As one overtook the other, I was forced onto the gravel berm. I felt the rush of warm grit-laced air as the truck swept past.

However my left front mudguard just clipped the edge of a pedal rickshaw's awning sending it sprawling. I jammed on the anchors, skewing to a halt in a swirl of dust. Hastily bailing out, I received a torrent of abuse from an irate soldier. "Who are you?" I wondered.

Whoops. The rupee dropped. The rickshaw's passenger!

I apologised to driver and soldier. The soldier's eyes were as cold and grey as the gravel he had just picked himself up from. He thought nothing of my regrets and proceeded to berate me at full revs. After a few more seconds of inspecting the rickshaw and its driver, I climbed back into the cab. The soldier climbed up beside me and clung onto the outside of the door. He continued to read me the 'riot act' still blustering and delivering a tirade of Shakespearean quality. No doubt some of his Hindi vocabulary was colourful. Blue?

> Anyone get the no. of that bus!!!

I gave him a few more seconds to get his problems off his chest. Then I considered I had been patient enough. I heaved the door back ... with soldier attached ... grabbed him by his khaki tunic and hauled him around to show him the scratch on the black mudguard that I ... err ... Iain would have to repair.

All the while, I was conscious of punters Jo-Anne, Motorboat, Ric, and Charles' noses pressed to the windows grinning and chuckling. Their breath was fogging up the glass. Not the professional look I was aiming for—the tour leader bowls over a rickshaw and gets into a scuffle with a soldier!!!

My audacity left the soldier momentarily bewildered. Me too on reflection. Would never argue with a soldier 'down under'. I re-entered the cab and drove off. Looking into the rearview mirror I could see him chasing after me, shaking his fist furiously as though hammering loudly on a thick door. Still mouthing abuse. His progress was abruptly halted when his beige canvas shoulder bag looped around the handlebars of a cyclist going in the same direction but at a slower pace and, in true Buster Keaton slapstick fashion, he was jerked off his feet.

A classic pratfall. Flat on his back. By the time he scrambled upright and dusted himself off, I was gone.

A dog's life

Tony Wheeler writes "An eye for an eye is how the victim and his relatives are likely to view it, whether you are right or wrong. Don't hang around to ask or answer questions!" (P13.1979). The soldier wasn't interested in the aggressive driving of his countrymen. By being sent scrawling, his ego was dented more than Befa's mudguard. He wanted revenge. That dish would have to wait and be served cold ... if at all.

On the other side of town, the shrill sound of a train whistle pierced the air. Warning bells started to clang and a railway barrier pole swung slothly down in front of me. It wasn't a passenger train with freeloaders sitting on the roof. A diesel locomotive rumbled past, hauling a seemingly endless sequence of carriages, hammering and juddering, straining and grinding. The rounded rear end of a silo car was the last as the train rumbled away ... clackedy-clack, clackedy-clack.

The barrier remained down for several minutes. Why the delay? A one-man corrugated iron shed was diagonal to us within which a partly obscured railway official was on the phone. His body language looked nervous, furtive and shifty. In due course, four punters of reasonable size and bulk—Ric, Charles, Paul and Motorboat—ambled over to determine the reason for the hold-up. Shifty's eyes stopped darting. He fixated on the impending arrivals. His eyes widened, his hands moved rapidly and the barrier suddenly rose. I engaged gear, the bus thumped and bumped across the railway tracks. We were gone.

Later I wondered if my earlier collision with the rickshaw was linked to the police being informed by the aggrieved soldier and an attempt made to retain us.

Diesel was hard to come by, especially on my Casper and Befa tours, because of the Iranian revolution causing fluctuations in oil production and distribution. Everyone, including tourist companies, had to apply for diesel permits. Tourists got a bigger daily diesel allowance than local truckers (seventy litres).

Overland with Top Deck

Applying through official channels on <u>Befa</u>, driver Iain was given a forty litre permit. That wasn't going to cut it. Our tank held three times that—120 litres.

Leaving that official's office, 'Light Fingers McKinnon' deftly 'liberated' the official permit stamp. Once in our hotel room, he placed it in front of me with a theatrical flourish. "How did you acquire that?" I asked in disbelief, when I read its label. "Don't ask!" was sneak-thief's haughty reply. I copied the official signature on similar paper, stamped it and we were in business for 120 litres.

In Delhi, a Rotel* crew told us that the police were looking for the Top Deckers who had forged diesel permits. Their search wasn't very thorough though. We were in the country for another ten days.

* Das Rollende Hotel were a German outfit for an older, affluent demographic, Rotel meaning 'rolling hotels'. Behind their red-painted coach department they had a further detachable unit of the same size and dimensions—twelve metres—which had three levels of about twenty-five (total) bed pods into which passengers crawled at night. You couldn't stand up in them. When punters uncoiled themselves in the morning, they resembled caterpillars emerging from cocoons. At the end of the second detachable unit—left behind in camp while the front portion went touring as a normal coach—was a small compact kitchen unit with a fold-down platform from which food was served.

A week later it was highly ironic that a diesel attendant didn't initially accept the legitimate permit for 100 litres that I handed him. Had the 'jungle drums' been beating? Iain and I were at the pumps but the attendant walked us back into his office where, retrieving his spectacles from his desk, he squinted long and hard at our paperwork. His lenses were as thick as the bottom of milk bottles. I chuckled to myself. Fought back a smile. What goes around, comes around? The permits are kosher. Look at this innocent face! Completely trustworthy.

Our tank still had diesel in it so probably wouldn't take 100 litres. Iain suggested we fill up the tank. Then pay. No, that would be too logical. "We ... might ... not ... need ... one ... hundred ... litres," Iain enunciated, being from the 'speak-slowly-and-deliberately-and-they-will-understand' school of international communication.

No! The attendant had a system. He stood his ground with fists planted on hips and lips pursed. Shaking his head vigorously he insisted that we pay for the full 100 litres ... beforehand. I reluctantly paid it, cooled my heels while he laboriously hand-crafted a receipt, returned to the pumps and filled up the tank. Eighty-five litres. We went back inside to the cash register where I received change and another laboriously bespoke receipt. I rolled my eyes, shook my head and shot the attendant my best "I told you so" glare. Iain grinned, patting me gently on the shoulder "Down, Dog, down. Easy boy". My subtle protestations fell on the blind and deaf. At birth he must have fallen out of the obstinate tree and hit every branch on the way down.

The British Raj had bequeathed to India cricket plus a good infrastructure including a sound road and rail network... and ... BUREAUCRACY! Endless rules and regulations, red tape and triple and quadruple copies of forms.

The Taj Mahal

It was smooth driving to Agra on *Lemming*. The Jumna River flowed alongside us, wide, brown and peaceful. A fertile, prosperous farming region, strewn with small holdings.

Agra's 'Laurie's Hotel' had the feel of the British Raj. Staff wore pressed starched uniforms and were eager to please with tea, snacks and cold drinks. Queen Elizabeth and Prince Philip had been guests here and their 'thank-you' letter was proudly displayed in the foyer. Punters bought numerous drinks, both alcoholic and otherwise, as they lounged around the hotel's swimming pool.

I disagree *strongly* with colonialism. One country plundering another's people and resources. It is intriguing both as an era and an error in history. Arriving in India in August 1600 in the form of one Captain Hawkins representing the East India Company, English influence grew immensely over the next 250 years. Economically and militarily. In 1857, following the 'Indian Mutiny', control of India transferred to the British Government. After the mutiny, 10,000 British officers, 60,000 British troops and 200,000 Indian army troops controlled over 300 million people.

Reflecting on the Raj, I imagine an archetypal English middle class 'gentleman' officer: with superior attitude, speaking with a 'plum in his mouth', who attends polo matches, drinks 'sundowners' of whiskies/sodas or gin/tonics, participates in cricket matches and tiger hunts, visits the North West frontier and the Khyber Pass, knows members of the 77th Bengal Lancers and sits down to formal dinners served by subservient indigenous people.

The 'Befa Winter Overland' group. Late January, 1980. 'Motorboat' back row, fifth from left, in between Charles and Ric. Front row. Jo-Anne fifth from left in front of him.

India represented adventure and challenge to England's young lower middle class men. (The 'grunts' were working class). They arrived in their late teens/early twenties, raw and naive with 'bum fluff' still on their chins. They returned to 'old bighty' forty years later, their bodies scarred by disease, bullet and sword wounds, by tigers' claws and broken bones from polo accidents. By then their faces were ravaged by age, by sun and too many whiskies and sodas. But they had lived a part of a romantic legend called India.

While punters were orienting themselves at Lauries, I searched for a guide. In February, I had enlisted an experienced guide. MA in Indian History. Thinking I was a teacher on a 'travel sabbatical' with a History degree, he invited me to lunch with his wife and family. Spicy vegetar-

A dog's life

ian fare with naan bread. On his walls were a collection of celebrity photographs taken with the likes of Hafez al-Assad of Syria and James Callaghan of the UK. Alas this time he was away visiting relatives.

With another guide, away we went to see the world's most famous mausoleum. White marble gleaming in the sun but changing in colour at different times of the day and night. Now it looked milky-white.

The best time I ever saw it was the first time. Under a full moon. Glowing golden. Romantic.

Being a shutterbug, I advised fellow photographers that they 'capture' the Taj from different angles. The Taj has the main arched gateway, the gardens, the mosque, the mausoleum and the rest house. Photograph the different components from different angles, from varying distances, in different lighting conditions and at different times of the day. Take close-ups of the intricate inlays of semi-precious stones and intricate designs, often floral. Look for miniature poppies, irises, lilies and tulips. They are intricate/ Moguls loved flowers, symbols of paradise to them. Much of the exquisite Arabic calligraphy are Koranic verses.

Shah Jahan built the Taj in 1630 in memory of his favourite wife, Mumtaz Mahal, who died in childbirth. He assembled the best architects, draftsmen, masons, sculptors, craftsman, calligraphers as well as a multitude of skilled and unskilled labourers from across the Indian sub-continent, Persia, the Ottoman Empire and Turkey. The architect, of Persian descent, incorporated Asian, Islamic and Persian elements into the design. Shah Jahan argued with his son Aurangzeb who imprisoned him in the Agra fort. He died in 1665 in a cell from which he could gaze out at the Taj.

My visit to the Taj on Casper in November was marred by a dose of 'Delhi Belly'. Steve Pyatt on Rags was suffering too. More so than I. We had met my first day with Top Deck. I was upstairs on Casper figuring out how to replace the front window sashes when Steve asked me to come purchase the groceries in Acton for the two buses. He was a competent driver and mechanic. Intelligent, quiet, thoughtful and considered. We had often conferred together on the tour, especially in Iran, on driving routes and times.

The following incident played out like the 'Fortunately/fortunately' drama game I have had kids play at school. The class sits in a circle. One begins a story with the word fortunately. The next continues the same theme with unfortunately, the next with fortunately... and so on.

Steve pulled in besides me at the Taj's South Gate and let the passengers dismount while he repeatedly clenched his buttocks and smiled valiantly at them, wishing and willing them to depart faster.

Unfortunately he was in some discomfort. When the last of the stragglers had finished faffing about and disappeared, he grabbed a loo roll from under his seat, climbed from the cab, and walked stiff-legged and briskly towards a low stonewall.

A dog's life

Fortunately I could sense he was about to vault the wall and thought "This is NOT going to end well!"

Unfortunately, everything seemed to grind down into slow motion and my "Nooooo!" was straggled in my throat. It was both funny and woeful at the same time.

Fortunately he vaulted the wall and cleared it easily.

Unfortunately, landing with a thud on the far side, he lost control of his clenched muscles.

Fortunately no-one was around and in private behind the stone wall and amongst the low hanging branches of a banyan tree, he cleaned himself up! I fetched him a bucket of water and a towel.

Not long after, I was horrified by Rags' punters at a loo stop. In the long grass well away from the buses, the guys were measuring and photographing their poos! Long broken ones were regarded as the best and received the highest rating. What happens on tour stays on tour! Those photos were probably viewed months after the incident. Thank goodness this was well before the era of phone cameras with instant recall.

Earning a living in India is a HUGE challenge for the millions of uneducated and poor. Although it is annoying to tourists, the way locals 'get in your face' to make a sale, I realised they had to do that, to be a tout, hawker or hustler and get noticed. The survival of the fittest.

I did my Don Corleone imitation. The masseuse comes to me to recommend his massages, the hairdresser to promote haircuts and shaves, someone else for manicures and pedicures or to read palms. I stroked my moustache thoughtfully, with index finger in an upwards motion, Marlon Brandon/Don Corleone style.

Mr. Grange and myself outside Laurie's Hotel, Agra.

In early 1980, notebooks were being produced by rickshaw drivers. If they were helpful to you, they would get you to write a recommendation which they could show other people that they were reliable. Not everyone who spoke English could read or write it. I wondered how many who produced notebooks, knew what had been written.

I got to know Mr. Grange, a pedal rickshaw driver based near Laurie's Hotel. He pedalled me around Agra helping me find items like camping gas or fresh meat. It was a 'quid pro quo' dynamic. You scratch my back and I'll scratch yours. He was a bit of a rogue but he knew how to look after himself and his family. I paid him for pedalling me around but he also earned 20% commissions from the people he took me to. His tourist commentaries as we passed places of note, were free.

He realised the value of tour companies. He kept a notebook in which satisfied customers wrote recommendations. By 1988, he was a regular 'fixer'. In 2020, I posted the photo of Mr. Grange and I outside the Lauries Hotel on the 'Top Deck' website. To my surprise, Ali Moveen wrote "That's my dad!" I gasped ... but he wasn't referring to me. He meant the rickshaw driver.

A dog's life

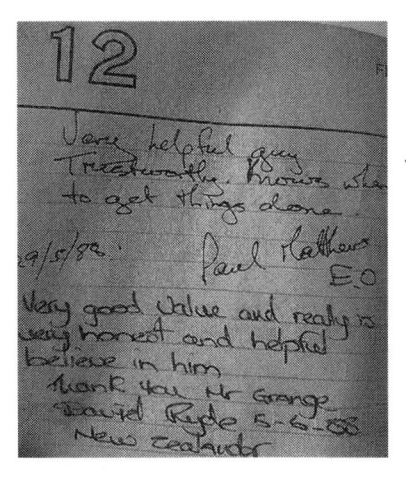

His father passed away in 1998 but his son has proudly kept his notebook. He also carries on the same type of business for 8-10 hours each day. This time in an auto rickshaw. In 1980 an auto rickshaw driver hired his for 50 rupees a day and needed another 50 for living costs. Inflation had hit by 2021. Ali wrote back to me, "I hire a rickshaw ... for 350 rupees a day. I have to pay for fuel ... what is left is my daily earnings around 200-300 rupees per day." He must have done OK. Grange's son is married with a son and three daughters. He has owned a home for twenty years. I was chuffed to catch up with the son of a contact 40+ years before.

Jaipur

The Highway drew *Lemming* into arid Rajasthan. Rajputana, the Land of Kings. I was in a 'Beatles' mood so played 'The Long and winding road'. Appropriate. I talked punters out of the 400 kilometre journey to Khajaraho. Capricorn P33H thought it was a letdown. The friezes on the Jain-like temples, circa 950 AD, are infamous for their soft porn carvings. Some positions needed exceptional suppleness to achieve. All the women depicted are voluptuous. Did breast implants originate here in the tenth century? Jules Skinner observed in the Trip book "Erotic carvings? I've seen more erotic carvings on the desks of the school I used to teach at!"

I had been to Jaipur on Capricorn P33H in early 1979 but not on *Casper* in late 1979. Jaipur hadn't been on Top Deck's 1979 itinerary. Skroo seemed interested in Jaipur when he drove me to the workshop to meet fellow crew. Did I help instigate a route change or did Skroo note other companies going there and decided to follow suit? Unfortunately management sometimes added extras onto itineraries but didn't delete anything. That meant 'the boys' often did night drives to keep to an overly-ambitious schedule. Fortunately 'the boys' also did their own editing. In three Top Deck overlands, we never did get to Khajaraho.

As we neared Jaipur, we found ourselves in Thar Desert territory. Sand dunes, tussock, desert scrub. A few scattered villages. Shepherds herding their flocks of black-faced sheep. The clouds overhead had blackened considerably. Tensed up. Humidity was high. A tropical steamy heat hung in the air. You could smell it.

The rains came suddenly. No build up or warning. The heavens just opened. Furiously. Roads were awash with rivers of rushing water. In the cab, sheets of rain lashed the bus creating a jungle drumbeat on the bus' exterior. Camel couldn't see more than a few metres ahead. I hailed a motorised rickshaw to direct me to Khetri House.

In the short interval it took me to scramble from bus to auto rickshaw, I was drenched. Warm rain. The waters swirled back from the advancing bus as waters do from the prow of an advancing ship. *Lemming* sluiced valiantly through the flood waters leaving a widening wake. The scene was chaotic especially when the bus slipped into a drain. Somehow Camel skilfully manoeuvred *Lemming* out of it.

Khetri House, an ex-Maharajah's house was a three-star, heritage hotel, situated at the western Moon Gate. It has sixteen bedrooms, several with en suite and four-poster beds, alcoves, dining rooms, lounges, drawing rooms, smoking rooms, wooden panelling, ornate internal arches and ceilings, chandeliers, carpeted stairways, internal mezzanine balconies, gilt-framed paintings, Afghan rugs and heavy drapes. A grandfather clock added to the elegance of a by-gone era.

Maharajahs were warrior princes dating from the Second Century. Through conquests, strategic marriages and financial manoeuvres, they amassed considerable wealth. The title ceased in 1950. Maharajahs received compensation for loss of income. The majority of Maharajahs retained possession of palaces and estates, some converting them into tourist accommodation.

The Maharajah of Gwalior liked to impress dinner guests with a working miniature train set assembled across his dinner table. Dishes were carried to and from the kitchen via the railway. He controlled the delivery of each dish to his quests, on occasions even depriving an out-of-favour guest of his dessert by sending the carriages hurtling by. At one banquet, the control panel short-circuited, the train sped up and wouldn't stop. Careening around the table at breakneck speed, it flung chicken, gravy and the contents of assorted dishes into the laps of startled diners.

In each city I insisted punters write down the campsite address in the (usually highly unlikely) event of their getting lost. As some mellowed out on plush sofas and armchairs in the lounge, Kathy, Cress, Angie and Heather 'took high tea', Gary and George had haircuts, massages, manicures and pedicures. Jeff played cards. Chris had his palm read. We could hear the intermittent piercing screeching of the blue Indian peacocks outside. Dark iridescent blue head, spiked crest, blue shoulders, white body and stunning green tail feathers.

Shakespeare wrote some very wise words like … "Hell has no fury like a woman scorned". *Lemming's* punters dined in the elegant dining room at a long table with white starched tablecloth, white napkins folded into little steep pyramids and high-backed padded chairs with padded arms. Attentive waiters attended to their every culinary need. Rajasthani food is tantalising. Vegetarian dishes included vegetable korma, red beans, black lentils, vegetable curries. For those who like their protein, the fiery mutton Laal Maas with plain white rice, chicken in curd and cream with cashew nuts and Bhuna Kukda—chicken in Rajasthani spices and coriander.

Later, punters watched a vibrant animated puppet show in the lounge. Beautiful costumes and background scenery. Commendable production values. Camel and I were ushered into the manager's study. With so much competition for tour groups, managers needed to spoil 'the boys' and earn return visits. The book-lined study had an aroma of fine, dark walnut wood, cigar smoke, cracked ageing leather … and whisky. My kind of study. Camel and I settled back into winged, dark leather armchairs, and discussed the tour over a few drams. I savoured the slow burn of a Johnnie Walker. The manager offered us cigars. Imitating Roger Moore (my least favourite Bond) with the raised eyebrows and the supercilious sophisticated look, I unwrapped it, inhaled the smell appreciatively (as though I knew what I was doing, which I didn't) and snipped off the end. I lit it whilst revolving the cigar slowly so that the flame caught evenly. All the while trying to imagine the youthful bronzed Cuban thigh that it was rolled on.

A dog's life

At 11.30 p.m., an attractive punter knocked on my door and entered. I hadn't talked to her all evening. She usually wore jeans and a T-shirt thus hiding her figure. Now she was clad only in black. Black bra. Black lacy knickers. They weren't very substantial items but she filled them out admirably. Curves. Wow. They were all where they should be. Lascivious smile. I suddenly had a hard time thinking. Her voice was a study in seduction—husky, inviting, intimate.

She had started the spadework down-under but I rightly sensed she would be a formidable foe if I got on the wrong side of her. The aforementioned whiskeys had clouded my judgement. My gut instinct was saying "Noooo." Another part of me was pleading "THAT'S the right direction!"

When later I did not wish to establish a relationship, I was snubbed for the remainder of the tour. I knew I was going to have to let *her* let *me* know how p*ssed-off *she* was. We co-existed under an uneasy truce. She often speared me with a withering wintry glare when others weren't looking. When others *were* looking, she smiled a tight smile. The kind of smile cats conjure up just before they dine on mice.

Some of her friends also withdrew speaking rights in sympathy. This included the 'lady' who had tried to crawl into my bunk on the first night of the Aussie trip.

I bet *she* didn't confess *that* to my seductress!

I *should* have resisted. Being inebriated was no excuse. I said farewell to receiving a glowing end-of-tour report. Or Christmas card. I sympathised with Clint Eastwood after he has a one night affair in 1971's 'Play Misty for me'. Jessica Walter as Evelyn Draper was deserving of her Golden Globe nomination.

Charming, flirtatious then brooding and menacing. I checked the duty roster. When was she next on cooking duty? When might she have scissors or a sharp knife in her hand? Preferably dicing up vegetables. Not me.

"How's your diet lately Dog?"

"Either lashings of tongue or cold shoulder".

Time out. In the dog box … again.

Jaipur's Amber Fort

In Jaipur, Camel came down with the 'trots' as I had on my first visit to Jaipur. He slept it off. Rice and yoghurt for the next forty-eight hours was a nurse's recipe that had worked for me.

I drove *Lemming* through parched hills to the **Amber Fort,** thirteen kilometres from Jaipur beside Lake Moata. We passed men walking camels, numerous vintage Royal Enfield motorbikes and water buffalo lazing in the sun in the gorge. From the car park at the bottom of the steep hill, some walked with me up the steep incline to the main gates whilst others took the journey atop an elephant.

Punters climbed up a wooden tower. Two by two they gingerly clambered onto each side of the long wooden bench straddling the elephant. I watched with interest. It's easy to take these events for granted when you've done them a few times. But look at the punters' faces! Laughing. Giggling. Elation. Like kids on their first elephant ride. There's a child in all of us. I was touched by their childlike innocence. Long may it continue.

The mahout straddled the elephant's neck and gave it instructions, occasionally with the encouragement of a wooden stick. They swayed and lurched from side to side for more than twenty minutes as the elephant plodded determinedly up the steep hill. Punters snapped off photos of the breathtaking views.

The elephants carried them into the fort via the Sun Gate and deposited then gently down in the garden courtyard.

The Amber Fort had panoramic views of the area on a day when the sky was a very pale blue, with a scattering of very high cirrus clouds shaped like wispy horses' tails on the outer reaches of the sky. The Palace inside the fort is a striking example of the opulence enjoyed by the maharajas. The Palace of Mirrors has high vaulted ceilings covered with thousands of little convex mirrors. The walls are also covered with green, orange and purple glass. Painstaking work over many, many hours. Our guide had an excellent command of English but with a heavy accent.

It was wickedly hot. Many passengers slumped against the walls or tried to catch the prevailing breeze.

Shortly after, we were ushered into the Hall of Pleasure. I wondered what kind of pleasures maharajahs got up to here. Cress, Flo, Kay and Angie were thinking along the same lines judging by their smirks and their furtive glances at each other. The doors were inlaid in ivory and sandalwood and the finely chiselled lattice stonework allowed in the prevailing breeze.

A dog's life

The Palace of the Winds

Jaipur, 1980. The road where the Palace of the Winds is located.

Back in Jaipur, *Lemming's* punters had a thorough tour with the experienced, knowledgeable guide Eugene Pram—used by Top Deck, Capricorn and Sundowners. Free time was spent browsing bazaars including the Siredeori Bazaar specialising in jewellery shops selling gold and silver. Women walk past wearing colourful saris and skirts, their wrists weighed down by serious jewellery. Some Rajput men are flamboyant in colourful pastel-coloured robes and turbans with well-groomed 'soup-strainer' moustaches. In the middle to late 1800s, Jaipur's population grew and went beyond the old city walls. From then on, a new city developed around the old city.

The five-storied Palace of the Winds, Hawa Mahal, was built in 1799 and dominates one side of the thoroughfare with a huge range of bazaars, shops and stalls around it and opposite.

It has 953 small intricate honeycombed windows to catch the prevailing breeze. The 'court ladies 'of years past could peer through the stone-carved screens at life in the busy streets, seeing without being seen. It's an elegant façade being only one room thick. I once went to the top of the building and caught stunning views over the Main Street and the City Palace complex behind it.

The Palace behind the Hawa Mahal. Where the courtesans came from to peer down on the plebs in the streets.

Jai Singh II followed astronomy, believing he was a descendant of the Sun Dynasty. The Janitor Mantar observatory was fascinating. The sundials measuring time were very precise. So too were the instruments measuring seasons and the signs of the zodiac. Impressive for 1727. Our guide was informative and well worth his hiring. However after 40 minutes, the passengers' glassy eyes and yawns revealed their attention spans had gone the distance. Flo twitched her eyebrows north. Let's go.

Time to go Ian?

Reading their body language, I gathered everyone up to return to the hotel. I looked around for the main exit. It was some distance away but I spied a nearby alleyway that would give me a speedier exit. With me at the helm, I then squeezed *Lemming* through the narrowest archway imaginable with, what felt like at the time, just inches on either side of the bus.

In anticipation, the passengers disembarked to take photographs, elbowing and jostling their way through curious locals who had materialised to watch my impressive feat of driving skill and acumen.

Photo: Morris Tanner. I may have inadvertently started a photographic trend. Jaipur wasn't on Top Deck's itinerary in 1979/1980. Is there a photo like this before July 1980?

I twisted around in the cab and shouted "All aboard?" Gary went off for a head count and I eventually heard "Yeah Ian, all accounted for."

Away I drove, leaving pint-sized Sabrina still elbowing her way through the crowd. She was only missed by her best friend Jenny back at Khetri House. Subby arrived back later in tears in an auto rickshaw having remembered that the hotels' name started with a K. I apologised to her.

We had a pair system for occasions like this with the person you did duty with. I thought Jenny had her back.

Grumbling from a usually supportive corner came from the cooks when they used the last of the camping gas. The full bottle of gas stored under the stairwell had a Greek fitting, not the Jordanian type we usually used. Unexpected. From a cursory glance, I couldn't tell the difference. Dark storm clouds formed above the punter's head, he turned all doom and gloom and bellyached darkly "Well breakfast is going to be rather bland." … grumble, grumble, gripe, gripe, mutter, mutter. The muscles in his jaw flexed like biceps. Revealing my tiredness, I retorted "Ah hell, if it's going to cause too many hassles, I'll do it." He gave me a death-stare. Stomping off, he spat out, "We need another tour leader" as if a bug had crawled into his mouth. On the road too long perhaps at twelve weeks!

No big deal. I quickly asked the chef to boil up eggs and make toast. The cold-shoulder treatment would last a few days. Led by the aforementioned seductress of the night before, there was a queue of sulkers developing.

Bustling New Delhi

New Delhi was a 300-kilometre drive from Jaipur. For *Lemming*, motoring was smooth. No protracted traffic jams but .... a puncture at Delhi's outer limits prevented us getting to the campsite by midnight. Ten minutes after Camel and I wrestled on the spare tyre, aided by punters with torches, another was ruptured. Disgruntled and weary, we pulled over to the curbside for the night.

Gingerly and prudently, we drove into Delhi at first light. Another puncture. Three in one night. *Lemming* limped very slowly into the campsite an hour later, some of the passengers walking beside the bus and getting an education on poverty as they zig-zagged their way past skeletal sleeping dogs curled up amongst piles of roadside rubbish, three puppies getting breakfast from their emaciated mum, yawning beggars with amputated limbs and the homeless sleeping under large cardboard sheets.

The campsite on Jawaharlal Nehru Marg, a kilometre from Connaught Circus, was well-appointed. A café. Money changers. Perhaps most important ... dependable hot water. Punters made a bee-line for showers. They'd had a sweaty interrupted night.

The campsite had several beatniks/hippies/bohemians. After all, this was either the start or tail-end of 'the hippy trail' very popular in the mid-'60s to mid-'70s. Finding spiritual awakening and enlightenment was not as fashionable now as it was in past eras. A different mindset to mine.

Photo: Iain and Ray replacing a window on *Befa*.

Dusty, battered 'magic buses' heading east or west were all around us. VW Kombi Campers contained couples and small groups. Travellers who wanted a 'heads up' on the areas we had been to, sought us out.

I considered the 'Top Deck experience' was a Kombi van on a larger scale. Punters and crew became friends, agreeing, disagreeing, bickering like a van's group.
Two distinctions were that Top Deck had a tour leader and a set itinerary which reduced some potential disagreements.

The most convivial and rewarding way of travelling is *'en famille'*, as a family, a group of friends.

Opulence, wealth and poverty live cheek by jowl in Delhi. Indeed throughout India. I walked punters around Connaught Place. Named after King George V's paternal uncle, it radiates out from the central circle of Rajiv Chowk. Many grandiose buildings show the wealth of the British Raj. Delhi's shopping malls comprehensively cover India's regions. Each government emporium seems to represent a state. Shops sell Kashmiri carpets, small furniture and papier-mâché. Others sell Rajasthani linen, puppets, kites and paintings. Shops representing Uttar Pradesh sell gems and marble inlay work.

Distributing Tourist Office maps, I suggested ways to get around: walking, hiring a bicycle, a pedal rickshaw or a motorised rickshaw. Travelling by local transport was entertainment. An experience. A must do.

By now punters were used to being hassled. If a repeated "No" or "Jow" doesn't work, stare straight ahead (the 1000 yard stare) avoiding eye contact. But as I'd said before, keep all hassles in perspective. India has a massive population. They like sex. Birth control is not a priority. This is survival for them. They need to put food on the table. The most persistent are *not* on a fixed daily wage. They are the less educated, the less skilled and the most desperate. On or below the poverty line.

I reflected on the 'accident' of birth. Where one is born. And to whom. I am fortunate. Irish great-great-grandparents who survived the 1845 Irish potato famine, great grandparents married in Derry in 1875, moved to Glasgow in 1890 for a better life and in 1907 they and my maternal grandparents moved to NZ. I imagined a 'better life' for them meant a steady job, house, food, education … and equalitarianism. A society where everyone is treated equally and there is no class system as they experienced in 'the mother land'.

Punters gasped, shaking their heads in disbelief at the driving tactics in Connaught Place. Chaotic. Not unlike circumnavigating the Arc de Triomphe in Paris. Cars dodge and swerve avoiding each other. While drivers lean on their car horns, touts and hawkers scream and shout trying to attract attention. Music blares from shops. A scrawny dog barks. Car fumes, incense, spices, putrid open drains, urine and body odours assault the olfactory senses. Punters wrinkle their noses.

I frequently used motorised trishaws. A fun means to an end. Often my destination was an embassy. After negotiating a price, the driver would take me to my destination through a knot of bustling streets, wait for me whilst I went in, then return me to the campsite. 100 rupees secured the driver's loyalty and attention for two hours. One fare can sometimes provide a normal day's earnings. Saves him from repeated hustling.

Drivers cut abruptly and riskily across several lanes of traffic, zip around stationary/stalled vehicles, and sometimes go down narrow alleys—often the wrong way!

Ah, well. When in Delhi …

I sat back and savoured every moment. How often in life do you get to do this?! You have to have nerves of steel, and faith that the driver knows what he's doing and can 'read' the traffic, and clean undies back at camp!

I loved these two stroke machines and wanted to drive one. They throbbed away endlessly—tuk, tuk, tuk tuk—in a cloud of two-stroke vapour. A distinctive smell. I had ridden two-stroke Suzuki and Yamaha 350cc motorbikes for ten years. I was young and had quick reactions. Unfortunately this dream was not to be.

The trishaw had the handlebars, clutch, gear change and 150 or 200cc engine of a Vespa motor scooter with the back-end adapted so that two people could sit side-by-side with two more facing them on bench seats covered by a canvas awning. One trishaw driver, Ranjit, couldn't afford a new 1980, 50,000 rupee vehicle so he rented for fifty rupees a day and needed an additional fifty rupees on top to feed his family. A twelve-hour day.

A dog's life

Ranjit knew all the embassies, the major government buildings and hotels. If he didn't know the exact location of a small lodging, he would head in the general direction then ask other auto-rickshaw drivers along the way. You scratch my back and I'll scratch yours. Often as they waited in traffic, Ranjit shouted out an informative running commentary to me whenever we passed a structure of note. I had to lean forward, straining to catch his words as they could have been easily lost in the vehicle noise, honking, tooting, bell ringing and general din around us.

Telexes were sent confirming the Srinagar houseboat arrangements. I searched for camping gas with a fitting that would work then arranged Irani visas for a few.

Camel had the three tyres repaired. The tyre repairers took the wheels apart and repaired, reassembled and reflated them in the time it took us to drink a chai. Back at the campsite, I assisted Camel in dropping out a piston. Working with objects rather than people. Pays to have a competent, patient mentor who knows what he's doing. I made sure I had plenty of grease over me to let others know I was doing 'real' work.

Nick Duce arrived in *Woftam* and 'the flier' mid-evening. *Woftam* already looked the worse for wear. It was good to catch up with Nick again. Plenty of laughs over a Kingfisher beer …

Shopping in local markets was a quintessential part of the overland experience. Indelible memories. Amusing. We quickly gained a sense of how much fruit and vegetables were by haggling. We became creative with our communication and thespian skills—flapping our elbows and clucking to imitate chickens if need be. Even pulling imaginary objects from our butts to indicate a hen laying an egg.

We usually got the message across. As well as cracking up fellow punters … It wasn't unusual to have bystanders with red flushed cheeks and tears in their eyes. Some locals must have thought we were 'a sandwich short of a picnic'. Seeing what locals were purchasing, we often asked them how to cook that vegetable. Locals were supportive. They wanted a sale. Punters often came back from shopping 'buzzing'.

Fresh fruit and vegetables supplemented and complemented the tinned and dried supplies purchased in London. Meat was available in Nepal, India and Pakistan. You didn't always know exactly what you were getting. Buffalo, ox, horse or goat? Chickens were usually identifiable by their shape but were often scrawny and chewy. They needed plenty of time in the pot. And quite a few herbs and spices.

Morris and Trish went shopping for fresh meat and vegetables for *Lemming* using an auto rickshaw. Despite having that 'girl-next-door' persona, Trish could switch on her feminine wiles at will. She would produce a disarming smile and a 'fluttering of the eyelashes' which could turn auto-rickshaw and stall owners into the equivalent of slobbering Labrador puppies. Much to the vexation I'm sure, of lesser genetically endowed punters.

At a butcher's, Trish asked for chicken mince. She was instead sold chunks of sinewy goat strewn with bone fragments. Morris added a small packet of curry powder. Once the brew was bubbling away, it smelled *far* too spicy. They drained off the liquid, washed the meat and started again. Even then the meal was inedible.

Jammu and Kashmir

Before leaving for Jammu, I began a tussle with London HQ regarding being sent adequate tour funds. Having been jerked around by Tracks on my last tour, I didn't *need* the same hassles with Top Deck. Multiple fob-offs. Waiting in queues. Going back and forth to numerous venues.

Dillon, the Operations Manager, didn't know that history. I might have overdone my forthrightness with him. He didn't appreciate it. *C'est la vie.*

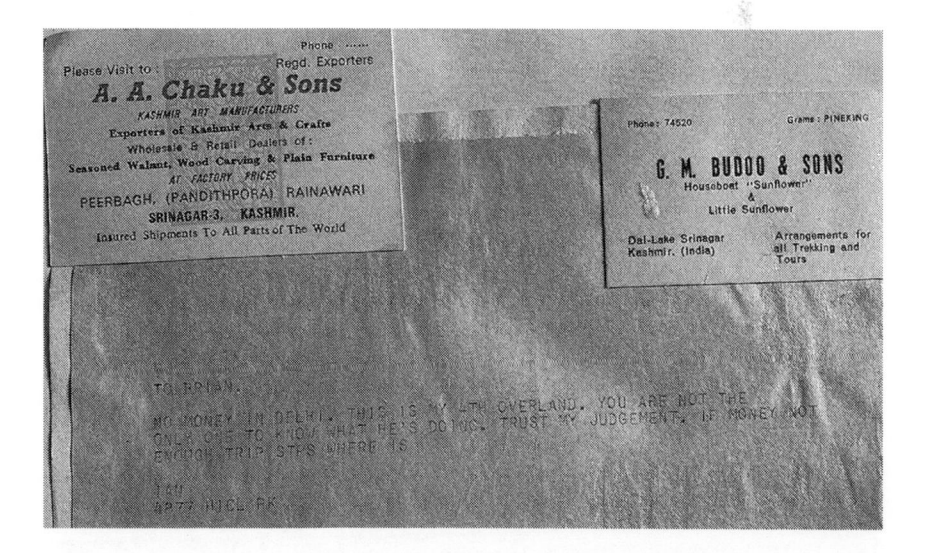

Two factors were in play here. The first was that the last time he'd seen me was *immediately* after the *Casper* tour. I was then the 'new kid on the block'. After the tour with domineering Mr. Cranky, I was browbeaten. Bruised. I lacked confidence and kept a low profile.

I had learned from that experience. My 'normal' confidence had returned. In addition I had confidence in my skills and judgment as a tour leader. I was on my third Asian overland as tour leader. Fourth

Overland with Top Deck

overland in total. Sixth tour as tour leader. Camel was predicting needing spare parts. I knew how much we still needed for the food kitty. And there was always the unexpected. Expect the unexpected.

Secondly, Dillon was no longer 'one of the boys' but middle management. Different responsibilities and allegiances. What he once boasted about as a crew member—ie: getting a tour in several days late—was no longer acceptable as a 'boss'. Hoist by his own petard?

En route to Jammu, air in the diesel lines caused *Lemming* to splutter along erratically. I crawled into the cab beside Camel to chat about solutions. As a result, I perched myself on the bonnet to be shaken about and bled the engine as we progressed. Hot work. I regularly doused myself under water pumps at service stations.

The Punjab is a fertile state with a largely Sikh population. Once baptised into the Sikh religion, men have the last name Singh and the women Kaur to announce the equalitarianism of their religion. The names were based on a powerful 17th Century warrior and wife who conquered the Punjab. Sikhs are opposed to caste distinction, pilgrimages to rivers like the Ganges and the 'suttee' practice of cremating widows with their husbands.

Sikh men have five practices known as the '*Kakkars*': *Kesh* for uncut hair and beard; *kanga*, the comb in their hair; *kacha* the soldier's shorts; *kirpan*, the ceremonial dagger and *kara*, the bangle around one wrist. The *Kara* became the rage amongst overland crews and male punters as they were excellent beer bottle openers. Wearing the *Kara* meant you had done the overland. Sikh women are distinguishable from Hindu woman via subtle clothing differences. Sikhs are energetic and enterprising individuals and seem to favour occupations such as taxi and bus drivers and airline pilots. They are also strongly represented in the Indian army and as skilled farmers in the Punjab.

On my last tour on Befa, en route to Jammu, driver Iain came down with 'Delhi belly'. I like to drive so wasn't worried. However... after free-camping on the side of the road, I awoke to find an ever-expanding diesel stain under the tank.

A dog's life

From his 'death bed' (I suspect he was hamming it up and suppressing a wry grin), Iain groaned and wheezed instructions on how to connect a hose to the engine and through the front window to a plastic diesel container on the front seats. The photo shows the tour leader extending his range of skills. His hands are dirty. NOT as rare as the majority of drivers, would have you believe. Unlike me, Tour Leader Yvonne Grisaffe could fix engines but like me she knew the need to project a certain image, "I'm sure I would have got a lot of engine grease on me to make it look like I knew what I was doing!"

I drove gingerly to Ludhana where I located a garage and accommodating Sikhs dropped the diesel tank out, had it welded and reinstated in no time.

At the Jammu Lodge, I encountered the tall, bright-eyed and very bushy-bearded form of Merv Lapwood, the third driver of Capricorn P33H. As always, he looked lean, fit and healthy and in a jovial mood. As we shared recent adventures over a cold beer, he laughed when he saw the grease stains on my hands and clogged dirt under my fingernails. "I thought you tour leaders always kept your hands clean!" he teased. Maybe with Capricorn, I mused. Top Deck's a different matter. I can't remember tour leader Greg Marks getting his hands dirty much on Capricorn P33H.

Lemming discovered the hard way that the Northern Punjab has bone-crunching, teeth-jolting and brain-rattling roads. "Shaken not stirred!" Trainee Jeff drove for two-hours. He needed more than one stiff drink afterwards.

In Jammu we unwound. Jammu/Kashmir is the most northerly state. The subject of three Indo-Pakistani wars pre-1980. I don't wonder. Its snow-capped mountains, lush green meadows and bountiful lakes make it a top tourist destination. Tourists = money. Jobs. Souvenir hunters.

I confirmed our houseboat arrangements with a telex. Punters showered and freshened up at the Jammu Motor Lodge. The evening meal of mutton from Jammu's markets, fresh salad and rice was tasty. Sated, punters retired to the lounge to recline in deep chairs and sofas and chat and relax.

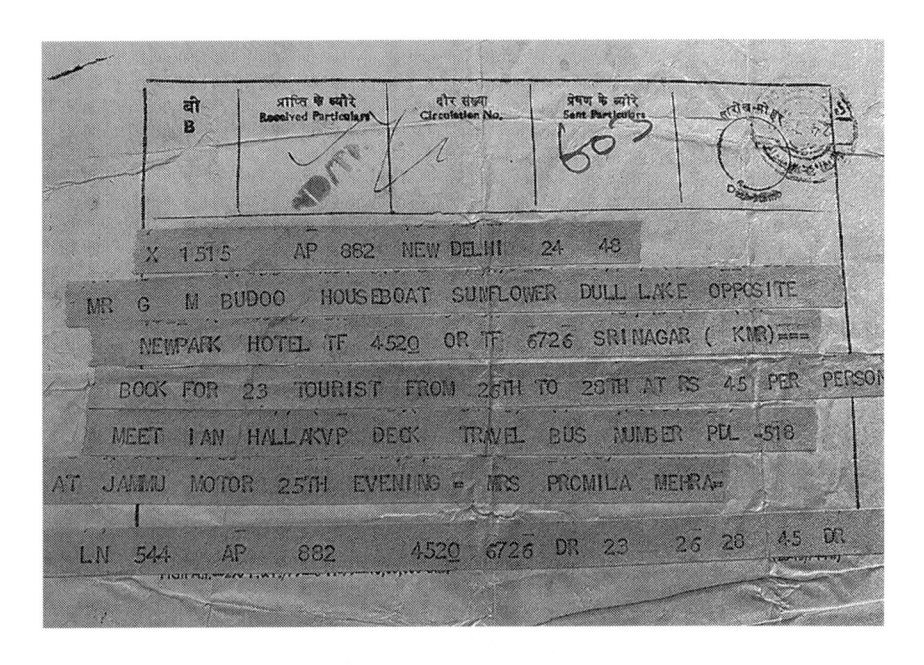

After seven o'clock, the bus was cleaned and prepared for our return. I booked local buses that could fit through several low narrow tunnels en route to Srinagar. The rooms were two-and-a-half star quality. Getting between clean sheets after a refreshing hot shower and a shave was very welcome indeed. The simple things in life are often the best. The sheets were thin but had that freshly washed and air-dried smell. Just nodding off after eleven-thirty, it was irritating to receive a knock on the door. Kathy did the 'fluttering of the eyelashes, I know you'll do anything for me' thing that women practise with cops when trying to avoid a traffic ticket. All to get a late night shower.

The next morning I had the Jammu Lodge equivalent of a full English breakfast—bacon, omelette, beans, hash browns, tomatoes and sausages—at the 'all-you-can-eat' buffet. I hoped a GP was on stand-by with a defibrillator. All the major food groups satisfied in the one sitting! Protein, carbohydrates, fibre! I got stuck in like the lead character in the 1975 movie 'Jaws'. I would need it. It was going to be a long twelve-hour day.

Plus a caffeine hit was essential. The filtered black coffee was fresh, hot and strong.

The scenery en route to Srinagar comprised steep, serrated, jagged mountains towering before us, lush, green native bush, precipitously perilous gorges, vertiginous inclines, fast turbulent rivers and white water rapids, serene and placid rice paddies, brilliant multi-coloured flowers and brightly-hued birds. The scenery distracted us from the arduous journey. The landscape had a primitive primeval beauty. What impressive engineering to get the road around and through mountains to Srinagar. At times we encountered landslide debris on the road. Looking down to the gorge far below, we saw gigantic boulders from rockfalls. Stopping at intervals for fast food, the more adventurous, usually males, tucked into deep-fried, golden vegetable samosa triangles, fried lentil balls and spicy potato patties.

I chuckled at the signposts forewarning us of treacherous bends and steep plunges to rivers far below. The sign writers had a 'gallows' sense of humour: Beep, beep, don't sleep; Drive like hell and you will get there: If married, divorce speed; Drive don't fly; Hurry make worry; Be soft on my curves. Lower your speed, a curve is near.

Camel and I travelled by taxi to Srinagar. Morris, who was severely weakened by the 'runs', accompanied us. He was still trying to sulk after the Jaipur no-camping-gas incident. I made it my day's mission to make him smile and bring him onside.

It was a long day for punters. As soon as they got off the coaches I intended to greet them, assemble them, dispatch pre-organised groups in shikaras to their houseboats. Their houseboys would welcome them on board, conduct a brief orientation then serve dinner within an hour.

Smart Mughal Emperors journeyed to Kashmir to avoid the stifling summer heat on the plains. So did British Raj officers. The shrewd local Maharajah wisely passed laws to prevent foreigners buying land.

Necessity is the mother of invention so some bright spark had houseboats built, Victorian in design and scrumptious in style and detail. After the 1947 partition and the end of the Raj period, some English went home selling their houseboats to locals who converted them into guest houses.

A dog's life

Houseboats range from Class A at 100 rupees a night (8 rupees = $US) per person through B, C and D to Unclassified. *Lemming's* punters were in Class C judging by the price of 45 rupees a night pp. It's like being in a 'time-warp'. In the Victorian era. When passengers see the houseboats after a day's travel, they are ecstatic. Living room with comfortable furniture. Pot-bellied stove. Stacks of wood in wicker baskets nearby. Heavy velvet drapes. Chandeliers. Indian kilims and carpets. A small library of paperbacks left by previous visitors. Rooms with en suites. The *'coup de grace'* was the empty whisky bottle which was later filled with boiling water and used to warm your feet at night.

I got acquainted with houseboy Assiz. Diminutive in height, lean, tousle-haired, good command of English, ever helpful. My 'go-to' person. He had a secure 24/7 job which must have been a plus at his age. No doubt family members benefitted. He earned 300 rupees a month (NZ$40.00). He confidentially admitted to me that he got up to 20% commission on sales of chocolate, cigarettes, biscuits, fruit, tampons, etc. when shikara sellers paddled by. The commission on more expensive items—leather. antelope hooves, precious stones, carved wooden and bone chess sets—was an added bonus but rare.

Once oriented, punters were served that night's meal in comfortable high-backed arm-chairs at a long table, white starched tablecloths with napkins and attentive waiters. I was impressed on my first visit and on subsequent ones. Over three days on the houseboats we were treated to dhal soup, naan, chapati, dum aloo (fried potato with yoghurt and spices), paneer shaman (cottage cheese sprinkled with cardamom), hot chicken curries, tandoori chicken, minced meatballs in a fiery red curry and rogan josh, a reddish coloured mutton curry.

The following day dawned chilly. I led punters on a wander through Srinagar. Two-and three-storied houses are packed close together. Once prestigious architecture, many now ramshackle. Some dwellings have been well maintained. Others had plaster cracked and flaking off. Like dandruff. Thin, torn, worn transparent curtains hung at windows. Chickens cluck noisy greetings on the corrugated iron roofs of sheds which house mountains of firewood for winter warmth. Bedraggled kids look forever optimistic and cheerful.

Several areas had a shanty-town vibe with rows and rows of washing hanging out windows and on makeshift lines to dry. Along the waterfront there are houseboats that locals live in, a far cry from the quality and comfort of our houseboats. Just a basic narrow boat with few windows and none of the intricate carvings on the tourist houseboats.

One morning, after a leisurely breakfast, I sat on a cushioned bench seat on the front verandah, viewing the every-day flow of life. People watching. I looked at the stunning snow-capped mountains. Not enough snow to go skiing at this time of year.

On February's Befa tour, myself and three punters hired a taxi to get to Gulmatg, 'the meadow of flowers' and local ski area. The slopes weren't steep but the snow was thick and powdery. We had a fun day skiiing. Throwing snowballs. Inhaling the crisp air and scenery.

The sun was strong. From my verandah I saw a new house-boat taking shape nearby. Assiz hailed a shikara to paddle me over for a nosey. There were two craftsmen. The elder was dark skinned, wore a white skull cap and was dressed in a loose white shirt and baggy trousers. Holding it down with his bare feet and toes, he shaped a structural support with hammer and chisel.

A dog's life

The younger man was dressed in striped baggy trousers and a long-sleeved, checked shirt. He hammered out ornate designs for a beam for above an entranceway. With chisel and a block of wood. A hookah bubble pipe sat nearby. So did a transistor radio which belted out local tunes.

There was a strong pleasant smell from the fresh wood shavings strewn around. They informed me that a Delux Class A three-bedroomed houseboat in 1980 costs in the region of £18,000 to £20,000 UK sterling.

Tour leading was a brilliant but temporary interlude in my teaching career. 'How people live and meet their needs in other lands and other times' was a major part of the NZ Social Studies curriculum. Hence my observations.

Top Decker Doug Foskett commented on my observations and in doing so came up with the perfect Tour Leader's Job Description—

"Crikey Ian Hall, I don't know how you managed to notice all that stuff and think at the same time. All I remember is worrying about today's meals, the next diesel stop, somewhere for the punters to have a piss, is the kettle on, is the driver ok, is the bus ok, what day is it and where should we be according to the itinerary, can we squeeze an extra day in on the houseboats if we do a night drive in Iran, have we got enough water on the bus, where are we stopping tonight, and... oh yeah, are the punters all happy?"

The next days were spent soaking up the unique ambience of serene Lake Dal. The Pir Panjal Mountains were reflected in the lake.

I arose early to visit the dawn floating markets. Dozens of shikaras laden with vegetables sell to the chefs of houseboats and individual locals. Fascinating to watch the haggling. The early morning blue light gave the scene a paint-like artistic quality. Almost eerie.

A tour of a papier-mâché factory was always informative. The papier-mâché work was intricately and painstakingly done in very basic rooms: grubby walls, woven mats on the mud floor, no heating. There

A dog's life

was a production line in one room. A teenage boy sat on a mat, back against a wall, dressed in long-sleeved cotton shirt, woollen v-necked sweater with no sleeves, grey tracksuit pants and bare feet. By him was a large wooden bowl in which was the papier-mâché—waste strips of paper, old cloth strips, rice and sulphate—ready to be shaped into a variety of moulds.

Once the outer cask dried in three days, a boy of eight in a checked pheran and warm beanie on his head, carefully cut the cask in half to get the original mould out. He then sand-papered the exterior with a stone to achieve a smooth finish. Glue is applied, more tissue paper is applied and rubbed smooth again. A teenage boy, also in a pheran, scarf and beanie, applied the first outline of a design and a coat of basic water colours.

The only teenage girl in the production line, sat squatting against a wall, her knees drawn up to her chin under her pheran, applying intricate designs of many colours using oil paints.

A variety of tools of the trade lay on the floor around them: A tumbler of water to clean brushes, blocks of tissues, 2-3 strips of sandpaper, small cans of glue and lacquer, towels to wipe their hands, wicker basket in which was a clay bowl and hot wooden embers—whether as a heater or as a tool, I couldn't fathom.

I bet the artisans only got a very small percentage of the total profit made, yet they are the ones with the skills. How long does their eyesight last? I bought two sets of coasters. That won't set the local economy alight but it was a contribution.

I still have them 40 + years on. They have stood the test of time.

The green and gold colours still seem as bright now as when purchased. I marvel at the intricacies of the artwork more now than I did in 1980. With age comes perception and wisdom. As well as … wrinkles.

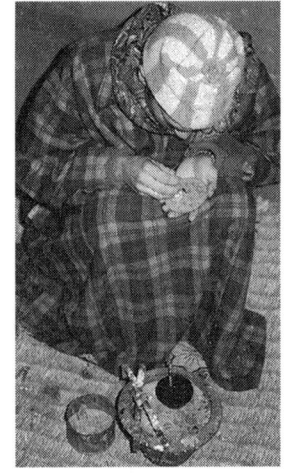

A tour to see craftsman carving furniture was popular with both the guys and gals.

I was tempted by a stack of four intricately carved stacking coffee tables for UK £100.00.

Plus …a walnut chess table with carved chess pieces consisting of Moghul warriors, elephants, camels and horses. UK £120.00. Superb craftsmanship.

A dog's life

Most evenings, punters would mellow out in the houseboat's lounge. Comfortable couches to sink into. Heat from pot-bellied stoves. A few tipples.

I was partial to a double-rum and coke, Triple X being the best of the Indian brands. The local gin was also well worth a try. With tonic water. Tonic water contains quinine which assists in the treatment of malaria.

I can lay claim to only ever having one puff on a joint, and that was on a houseboat in Srinagar. Like William Jefferson Clinton, I didn't inhale … much. It seemed to have the same mellowing affect as alcohol. I wasn't impressed enough to keep smoking. As a boy I had grown up with an alcoholic stepfather. Seen alcohol's negative effect. Arguments. Food being flung about during a drunken stupor. I determined that I would control alcohol, not alcohol control me. I regarded drugs the same way. I had seen people spaced out. Drugs were more powerful than alcohol. Ian, don't even start.

Morris got over the 'runs' but not before an embarrassing moment or two. One included farting whilst on a shikara, oops. That was a 'liquid' fart. Departing the shikara he left a brown skid mark on the cushions. Camel had a similar incident at breakfast when he 'quietly' let rip as he arose. Sheepishly he muttered "Oops! That was a mistake!" He shuttled off in a bow-legged John Wayne walk (as though he had been riding a horse) to change his clothes.

On my winter Befa overland in February, houseboats were a haven from the cold outside. Punters got bargains in town while others got value buys when persistent hawkers and tenacious trades-people paddled over to the houseboats. Hawkers could be heard calling across the still waters—'Chocolate, Coca Cola, biscuits, coffee, tea, tampons, the pill …"

Then in quieter, deeper tones—"You want marijuana Mister? Hashish? Good price!"

I was measured for a pair of sheepskin-lined leather boots. Unfortunately they were too small and I rejected them. I did buy a dark-blue, winter-weight, good quality pheran. A knee-length poncho. Locals tuck their arms inside to clutch a woven rattan or rope basket containing a clay bowl which in turn contains hot glowing embers of cubed charcoal. These are stirred to circulate heat. Brilliant idea!

When in Kashmir …

One evening at a party on a houseboat, petite Canadian Rita, more than a few tipples inebriated, declared she would jump in the lake for 200 rupees. Ray took her up on it, not expecting her to follow through. Before we could stop her, she was submerged! I hastily wrapped her in a towel and told her to have a hot shower immediately. Raw sewage flowed into the lake. As she was showering, I passed her a couple of stiff whiskeys through the shower curtain. To chase down and kill any germs she might have swallowed from the lake.

I later volunteered to jump in for a week's wages, but there were no takers! Cheapskates!

Later that same evening, while Ray was chilling, I balanced on the narrow wooden landing that ran along the side of each houseboat and heaved a solid block of firewood into the water, immediately calling out for help. I watched, hidden from view as people came running outside. Ray started to strip off to dive in and search for me. The prank almost turned sour because I was laughing so hard my ribs hurt. I couldn't speak and I was almost too late to stop him from taking the plunge!

He was <u>not</u> amused.

The journey back from Srinagar to Jammu for *Lemming's* punters was a different experience in summer to what it was in winter.

In February, on Befa, snow fell continuously throughout the day and the frigid interior of the bus reeked of waterlogged, squelchy clothes. I snuggled down into my pheran, pulled my muskrat hat down over my ears, hugged my arms around me and tried to doze off. I tried to ignore my numb toes that could have been 'as snug as bug in a rug' in those fur-trimmed leather boots.

We had three 'comfort' stops to stretch our legs, relieve ourselves and descend on the Indian equivalent of fast-food shops.

At one, I quaffed Dahl, a thick lentil soup, accompanied by hot naan. Tasty. At another, golden vegetarian samosa triangles and gol gappa, puffed bread with a spicy filling, quaffed my appetite. Both smelt and tasted good. Some vendors pre-cook their food then drop them into a wok of boiling, bubbling oil to crisp them up. My theory was that deep fat frying would kill off any evasive germs.

We navigated the steep and winding Banihal and Batote passes smoothly but in the late afternoon became ensnared in a prolonged traffic jam. Two Indian drivers adamantly refused to give way to each other. Sometimes this is due to their having simple brains, a lack of road courtesy, sometimes it is religious and sometimes a good road rage just spices up the day. I've noticed on more than one occasion that Indian drivers can be pretty obstinate, intransigent and unyielding but ... nobody wins.

At one stop, our bus slid slowly, surely and steadily over the road's ice-encrusted surface towards a stone retaining wall, the other side of which was a gorge. Where was the driver? In a boxing/wrestling match with his opposite number. Fisticuffs. Getting stuck in. No Queensbury rules here.

I tried to push Rocky Balboa and Apollo Creed back to their respective corners. No luck. I yelled to punters, "Shore up the bus. It's sliding on the ice". Several passengers jammed rocks under the tires. Rocky was nonplussed however. He later had the cheek to ask me for a tip when we eventually arrived at Jammu. He was baffled when I refused. Miserable westerner!

Two Indians fighting in the snow whilst our bus slides over the cliff.

Amritsar

From Jammu to Amritsar, the Punjah's capital, the site of an infamous massacre of innocents by the Brits under one trigger-happy, Acting Brigadier General-Reginald Dyer in 1919.

Indian street food. Takeaways. En route to Amritsar.

Amritsar is the ancestral home of the Sikhs and base to their powerful 17th and 18th century empires. Home to the holy Golden Temple of the Sikhs, the dome, cupolas and turrets of which are said to be overlaid with 750 kg of gold. It is a magnificent edifice from a distance. Even more so close up. The temple is accessed via a walkway around the mirror-like 'pool of nectar' in which swim large red carp. The temple shimmers in the water. The sun's rays ricochet off the gold dome and the water. Blindingly bright. We walk slowly because of the fractured light and because the white marble walkways are slippery through constant wear. Everyone had removed their shoes as per the Temple's requirements.

The surroundings are sumptuous. Lingering sweet fragrances of incense sticks hang suspended in the air. Committed devotees bow their heads in prayer. One of the Sikh principles is 'inclusiveness and oneness of mankind'. Every day volunteers feed thousands of pilgrims. Their kitchen is a hive of industry. Machines churn out thousands of chapattis a day. Volunteers handed them out along with bowlfuls of soup. Pilgrims waited patiently.

As I awaited the last stragglers touring the Golden Temple, I noticed billowing, anvil-shaped clouds over us. Almost imperceptibly they glide across the sun snuffing it out altogether. About five minutes later, the heavens demonstrated the ferocity of a monsoon downpour. The last punter was boarding the bus. It bucketed down. The street around us was awash, the torrent tugging gently at the bus. As the waters started to subside, Kathy, Kay and Jan seized the moment for an impromptu splash about amidst the swirling waters. I leaned out the cab's window "Be careful of the undertow. Don't be swept off your feet". At least it was one way to clean the streets. The air smelt clean, fresh and smog-free in the wake of the downpour. As though the impurities had been momentarily sucked out.

Monsoons are a double-edged sword. The rains come in June after months of searing heat has baked the earth. They continue until September. In summer, the monsoon wind changes direction and brings rain from the sea. Villagers love the rain and they pay homage to Varuna, their god of rivers and oceans. Monsoons are important to India's agriculture and economy but they are also destructive. Landslides engulf roads and villages, topsoil is washed down hills and rivers often break their banks.

Skinflints. *Back in February on Befa one evening, Jo-Anne and 'Motorboat' decided to experience a Bollywood movie. Taking my suggested bargaining strategies way too seriously, they negotiated a rock bottom price to get from the campsite to the cinema. The rickshaw owner was old—"ninety in the shade"—according to 'Motorboat'. Hours later, when they came out of the cinema, he was waiting patiently to cycle them 'home'.*

For a pittance! No tip either.

A memorable rickshaw incident *with Tim Oliver and Russell Facer occurred on the Casper tour. November 1979, our three buses travelled in convoy from Dogubayazit to Amritsar. Three bus loads were on Casper and Boogie. Rags was off somewhere. Boogie's punters complained about overcrowding. A bit petty. Be patient, it won't last long. Tim, Russell and I hired a pedal rickshaw to venture off to arrange additional accommodation. We clambered onto the vinyl bench seat behind the pedlar just as dusk was fading to night.*

Not long after, the rickshaw's chain came off. Then ... again ... and again ... and again!

Tim took over pedalling. The rickshaw wallah jogged beside us, a worried expression on his face. Not wanting to challenge us but concerned about the future of his rickshaw, his livelihood. Tim struggled up a bridge over a railway line. I jumped off and pushed.

Russell stayed glued to the bench seat, his chin up and arms folded imperiously in front of him as he shouted out 'advice'. Read that as inane and unhelpful. Hilarity ensued. Tim paid the rickshaw owner.

I added a tip as I'd had so much fun.

For all my hard work pushing him on the rickshaw, I didn't make much of an impression on Tim Oliver.

After he saw my 2020 Facebook posts, Richard Hewitt wrote "Myself and Tim Oliver, over a few beers in Pattaya, can't figure why we can't place Ian Hall. Tim was out that way and I did 11 overlands from '79. Great stories though!!!"

I posted a photo to Richard taken by Russell Facer showing Tim and I sitting opposite each other at a meal put on by Uncle and Aunty at the Withies after we arrived there in convoy on December 12, 1979.

A dog's life

Tim also forgot the photo taken of himself with Dog and Doug at Trevor Carroll's book launch in Sydney, June 2017.

Lahore

The 'Beating the Retreat' ceremony is held each evening at the Indian and Pakistani customs which oppose each other at Wagah/Atari, a dusty cluster of roads, custom buildings, fences and barriers. It is *quite* the performance. Soldiers from both countries, each in army dress uniform and elaborate headgear, march in synchronisation to bring down their respective flags. They execute elaborate complex manoeuvres involving quite some flexibility in joints and limbs. Impressive high goose-stepping is included. An opposing soldier stands at attention, each side of the iron gates.

As the sun sets, the gates open. The two flags are lowered simultaneously. Flags folded, the ceremony ends with a retreat involving elaborate marching steps and handshakes between opposing soldiers. The gates close. Both sides take it seriously. I found it so 'over the top' it was hilarious: the ridiculous synchronised high-stepping moves are all done with a flourish. As was the twirling to turn ninety degrees. The Indian soldier finished his manoeuvres seconds before his opposition and had a glowing smug expression to which he added an arms up, bicep displaying pose. "Beat you that time! His opposite held the muscle displaying move a fraction longer.

Indian customs at Wagah, near Amritsar was cleared smoothly by *Lemming*. On the Pakistan side, Sabrina didn't have an official stamp in her Health booklet. That earned her a serve from me—my well-practised admonishing frown. She volleyed a sheepish grin back. Pakistani customs can be strict. I wondered if encouragement would oil the wheels of progress. I cadged cigarettes of one punter and a 'Penthouse' magazine from another. This booty was slyly passed to the clerk with a 'nudge, nudge, wink, wink' manoeuvre. It saved the day. It is a way of life in Asia dating back centuries. It brightens up their day and puts a little extra-something in their pocket.

Enforcing prohibition. Thirty minutes later, an officer approached me. Tall, moustachioed, tight smile, bone-crunching handshake. All business. As he was checking the passenger manifest, he let his voice sink a few octaves, quietly enquiring if I had 'bootleg whisky' on board. Having had plenty of practice, I did 'innocent-looking' pretty convincingly.

I replied indignantly "No." He repeated the inquiry twice more as he checked the chassis and engine numbers. "Nick," he said "was caught last month with whisky hidden under the stairs. He's in jail. Do you want to join him? Do *you* have hidden whisky?" His eyes were like searchlights. They doubled as lie detectors as he glanced at my lips, observing my body language and reactions for any signs of falsehood. Don't glance to the right. Don't twitch. Don't show nerves.

"No" was my unflinching reply. He had me worried. He knew about the compartment under the stairs. He knew Nick Duce's name! Nick was on the 'flier'. Was he in jail?

We could be in for trouble here! More precisely and concisely, *I* could be in trouble here!

The formalities over, he said "Come, let's have a look under those stairs!" We approached the bus, me with trepidation, trying to keep my nerve and bluff him out. Impassive, unworried and upbeat was the image I was aiming for.

Abruptly he halted, turned, chuckled, clapped me on the shoulder and strode back to the customs office.

What was that all about? Having a little fun at my expense? Trying to scare me?

It certainly worked!

Incident in no-man's land. On Befa's entry into Pakistan in February, we had an official 'carnet de passage en douanes' for Nepal and India. Not for Pakistan. Whenever there was a problem, Top Deck would find a way around it. In Delhi, a different set for Pakistan and beyond was delivered *to me by Dillon. Iain painted up a new number plate so, when we had completed Indian customs, we drove into 'no man's land' and pulled over, out of sight of both customs buildings.*

Punters suddenly felt an insatiable, irresistible need to brew up a cuppa and milled around the front and back of the bus. Iain and I crawled in amongst their legs. Many female legs were tanned, muscular and lithe. We unscrewed the old number plates replacing them with ones that matched the paperwork. A few handfuls of dust thrown liberally over each plate gave them a suitably weathered appearance. The obligatory cup of tea over, we trundled into Pakistan.

I like Pakistan and Pakistanis. Many people I met were dirt poor but friendly, welcoming and helpful. Being Islamic, they were generous to a fault, frequently sharing what little they had. Some travellers *rush* through Pakistan on their way east or west but I find it fascinating.

Wealthy, historical, icon-filled Lahore. Centre of Pakistan's famed agricultural Punjab region. Then the northwest frontier and Peshawar. Mountainous and rugged Kashmir. I especially like the southwest. From Lahore to Quetta and then Quetta to the border at Mirjaveh/Koh-i-Taftan, the 'frontier region'.

Four thousand years ago it was the Indus civilisation's centre, ruins of which are at Mohenjo Daro and Harappa in the Sind. Clay brick houses. Roads. Agriculture. A writing script. Greeks, Persians and Turks have all invaded. When the Moghul Empire became paramount in the 1500s, their influence ultimately stretched from Afghanistan across Pakistan to Northern India.

The decline of the Moghuls coincided with the rise of the British East India Company and the British Raj. Indian sub-continent troops fought bravely for the Raj in WWII.

In the post WWII era, Hindus and Moslems wanted pay back. Independence. New English PM Clement Atlee wanted to grant independence. By January 1947 he wanted the British gone by June 1948. He dispatched Lord Mountbatten to achieve a result in mere weeks.

How would this happen? The subcontinent was predominantly Hindu but ruled by Moslems for centuries. The favoured option was to split the country into a central India and two Moslem sectors. The very influential and charismatic Mohandas Gandhi wanted the country to stay as one. As did Viceroy Louis Mountbatten. Pandit Nehru, the Indian National Congress Party Leader firstly wanted the country split but if it was to remain one, he was prepared to be responsible for the Hindu sections with Mohammad Ali Jinnah's Moslem league in charge of the Moslem Sectors. Mohammed Ali Jinnah argued for a separate Pakistan. If the others around the negotiating table had known he was dying of cancer, they may have pushed harder together for unity. Independence was achieved at midnight on August 25, 1947. Ali Jinnah died just over a year later in September 1948.

In the end, India got the better deal in terms of territory, natural resources and iconic monuments. Pakistan comprises the NW Frontier, the Punjab, Sind and Baluchistan inheriting rival tribal factions and a troublesome border with Afghanistan.

Because the partition had to be achieved in a very tight timescale, little thought appeared to be given as to how to move people to new areas without widespread bloodshed. People of different faiths were widely scattered. Millions of Hindus living in the newly designated Moslem areas had to move east. A similar number of Moslems had to move west. Four million people were on the move in September 1947.

We settled into the International Hotel in Lahore. *Lemming* carried punters to the 1757-built Kim's gun, the magnificent Akbar the Great inspired Mughal-era Lahore Fort and the 1673 Badshahi Mosque with a capacity for 100,000 devotees. Flooded streets from yet another torrential downpour did not deter us. Rudyard Kipling, a Lahore journalist was both a promoter and a critic of the British Raj.

Scenes from John Huston's 1975 film "The Man who would be King" show soldiers of fortune Danny Dravot and Peachy Carneham, (Sean Connery and Michael Caine), meeting Rudyard Kipling (Christopher Plummer) in Lahore. The film captures the feel of the period well. The *cavalier* attitude of Dravot and Carneham was not unlike that of

Overland crew I knew. Adventurous. Risk-takers. Always optimistic and resourceful.

The half-dozen bottles of Indian whisky that I'd bought for $12.00 a bottle were sold for US $40.00 a bottle at the International Hotel. I felt like putting the price up and charging him 'danger' or 'stress' money as a result of the border incident. I didn't usually actively seek to make extra money on the Overlands. Anything I needed was cheap enough as it was. Akram was the exception. He produced a wad of used greenbacks and peeled off a few Andrew Jacksons and Abraham Lincolns for me. He was able to pay me half of what he owed. He would have the rest for me 'next time'. Whoops! There very likely wasn't going to be a 'next time'.

As an alternative, he offered me a carpet displayed in his show window. Pakistani carpets do not have the same 'name' as Turkish, Afghani and Persian carpets. This one was predominately oranges, yellows and reds and looked distinctive. I gave it the once-over. It appeared well designed, few obvious design mistakes, the knots on the back numerous and close together. I still have it 43+ years on. It has worn well. No doubt Akram got the better end of the deal but I am more than happy.

As we drove away from Lahore, I thought of my most memorable encounter in that city.

A riotous incident. Mid-November 1979. Casper and Rags had arrived via Iran. There were anti-American protests in Tehran after the 52 US diplomats had been taken hostage by students on November 4th.

Around two o'clock, I accompanied Trevor and Steve on Rags into central Lahore. They were picking up their punters from the Badshahi Mosque. I intended to book a tandoori-flavoured national meal somewhere for that evening.

At an intersection, we encountered a surge of irate civilians. It took nanoseconds to scan the placards and realise that this was an anti-American demonstration in sympathy with the protests in Iran. There were hundreds of people moving past, faces flushed and contorted, eyes wide, mouths open, chanting, shouting and waving placards. There was a blunt vanguard of a few men then a wide base behind them fanning out to our left. The herd instinct was operating. They were worked up. The situation was potentially explosive. Who knows what could set them off? If someone started getting destructive, the others would follow. Blind mob rule. They wouldn't question or challenge the act, they would just repeat the action. In a crowd such as this, you were anonymous, not accountable to anyone.

A handful of youths saw us, abruptly changed direction, raced over and reached for Steve in the cab, grappling to pull him out. Trev reacted ultra-fast, shouldering past me and out the back to grab two of them, pushing them away from the cab. Another local angrily demanded. "Are you Americans or Jews?"

"Australian!" roared Trev and after climbing back on board, Steve engaged reverse gear, Rags shot backward, rear tyres squealing and smoking. Steve hauled hard on the steering to turn the front wheels around. With the reverse gear whining, he deftly turned Rags, engaged first gear and accelerated away as quickly as he dared.

Were the three of us scared? No. It all happened so fast. You don't have time to consciously analyse the situation. You take in the ball game in seconds and react how our ancient ancestors did.

Fight or flight?

Flight! Let's get the hell out of here.

That wasn't the end of the dramatics for me. After leaving Rags, my nose followed exotic smells into a restaurant where I consulted the menu. Over a courtesy chai, I negotiated a group discount for a group banquet. Just as I hailed a motorised trishaw to take me back to the hotel, a mob suddenly appeared. They fanned out across the dual-carriage highway blocking our access to the hotel. The trishaw owner bundled me out. On the edges of the mob. He worried because he was carrying a westerner and could be a target.

He hadn't delivered me to my destination yet still wanted payment! I hastily thrust a handful of tattered rupees his way. A fraction of what he was expecting. He exited the scene in double-quick time!

As the mob didn't notice me, I threaded my way through the low, leafy bushes on the raised median strip and set off at a measured pace. I didn't want to draw attention to myself. Not running. Not ambling either. I kept calm. Never expected to be caught up in a riot. I aimed for a circuitous route back to the hotel and safety. Sense of direction, don't fail me now!

As I glanced back to see if I was being followed, three army lorries swerved abruptly towards the kerb, their brake lights flared red accompanied by a squeal of brakes. Soldiers disgorged quickly, promptly forming up into a ragged line to confront the mob. Dressed in black with helmets and plastic visors, their clear plastic riot shields were linked together. The first part of the Roman 'tortoise' formation without the shields covering their heads. They meant business!

Back at the hotel, bottles and wood were strewn around the carpark. Police were setting up a perimeter around the hotel. Passengers, other guests and hotel staff were standing in small groups in earnest conversation. They looked shocked and bewildered. Being scared they sought solace together. It's not every day that you get tangled up in a riot. The rioters had visited just minutes before. Punters were worried. "Where have you been Ian?" I caught up with my driver on my way down the corridor to my room. "Thought the rioters had got you. Glad you're back. Didn't want to drive the rest of the way by myself."

Isn't it nice to be needed? His social skills were improving.

When I included that story on the 'Top Deck website, Gerard Butler wrote "Ian, you could tell that story to people who've never been there and they'd never believe you. Those of us that have, know just how volatile and crazy situations can get and all of us have had similar experiences".

The North West Frontier

If I had been doing the *Lemming* tour eighteen months before, I would be driving northwest from Lahore, Pakistan's second largest city to Karachi to Peshawar and then into Afghanistan via the Khyber Pass.

In late February 1979, Capricorn P33H was one of the last tours to journey that way. With Afghanistan closed, and after the April 1980 disaster of 'Operation Eagle Claw', the attempted rescue of the US diplomats in Iran, Capricorn and Sundowners' overland groups flew from Karachi to Istanbul to collect a second coach and continue.

From Lahore, coach RNA 696J took all day to drive the 480 kilometres to Peshawar. Peshawar is fascinating, the dividing line between the Indian sub-continent and Central Asia. Every conqueror passing this way—Alexander the Great, Darius of Persia, Genghis Khan—had to 'take' this town.

I knew of its reputation from my youth: The northwest frontier, the tribal area, Pathan tribesmen, bandits and brigands, thuggees, Rudyard Kipling, Gunga Din, the Khyber Pass. The English comic named 'Victor' of my youth often had stories about the British Raj and the northwest frontier. They weren't my favourites but I read them. Something had sunk in.

Peshawar is a city divided—the original city and the British cantonment. The old city was once a heavily guarded citadel consisting of high walls. Only remnants of these original walls remain. Most of the houses are constructed of unbaked bricks but many are distinctive with ornate carved wooden doors and latticed wooden and iron balconies. Craftsmen had been innovative. Attention to detail. Examples of old architecture can still be seen in the old city and bazaars. There are numerous bazaars. Some with a multitude of different shops, some specialising in niche marketing—shoe making or pet birds. As I later found in Quetta, pet birds in cages are the 'in' thing and are very popular. So are gardens and fountains.

As an amateur film maker, I was in my element: interesting architecture, great character studies of weather-worn Pushtu tribesmen wearing turbans and bandoliers and carrying rifles, curious youngsters wearing caps which designated which region they were from, locals sifting flour and making naan bread and pastries, locals cooking mouth-watering kebabs, weaving flax, selling birds, mending shoes, selling fish and fresh vegetables and making pots.

A highlight was a forty-five minute drive through tussock, scrub and desert to **Darra**, *a small village famed for its bazaars packed with gunsmiths and weapon manufacturers and sellers.*

A dog's life

The town is only one street lined with multiple shops, with side-alleys containing gun workshops. A wide variety of firearms are produced including rifles, machine guns and anti-aircraft guns, all handmade by individual craftsmen using traditional manufacturing techniques, handed down from father to son. Guns are regularly tested by test-firing into the air.

The ramshackle houses and 'shops' were of shanty town quality, square with flat roofs, high narrow windows with no window panes and with high walls surrounding some houses. The visit was fascinating. Rob and Barry were particularly intrigued by the range of weapons available. My favourite armament was a small pen which fired a .22 bullet. I considered buying one—that would be useful in an unruly class—but I didn't think I could get it through customs. Others loved the 'walking stick' gun. Darra also sold hashish for A$5.00. A similar amount in Australia would cost A$25,000.

On March 3, 1979, our early morning departure was delayed when the coach broke a spring soon after leaving the Park Hotel. Once fixed, we eventually departed for the Khyber Pass. The pass crosses part of the Spin Ghar mountains to connect Pakistan with Afghanistan.

As part of the ancient Silk Roads, it has long been an important trade route between Central Asia and the Indian sub-continent. Because of its location and design, the Pass has been a military choke point for invaders. The lowest point is at Jamrud in the Valley of Peshawar and the summit of the pass is five km inside Pakistan at Landi Kotal.

A dog's life

The younger P33H punters were excited. The older demographic were worried. The place had a reputation. Pashtun tribesman with handmade rifles and bulging bandolier belts seemed to roam the province with impunity. Tourists only have access through the pass in daylight hours and anecdotes of bandits, smugglers and hold-ups of tourists, whether true or false, abounded through the tourist community.

Whoever drew up the boundaries of Afghanistan and Pakistan used rulers as Sykes and Picot did in 1916 creating Syria. No recognition of ethnic and tribal affiliations. The Afghani Pashtun tribesmen refer to the Pakistani side of the border as 'Pushtanistan'. There is a fort at Jamrud with crenulations and turrets and towers. How many times had that had been won and lost over the centuries? The start of the pass is marked by signs that declare you are entering 'tribal' territory. Where ethnic loyalties surmount National affiliations. Self-governing tribal enclaves exist where local chiefs administer a communal concept of a conservative 'law' enforced by the Kalashnikov. Legend has it that these tribes are the descendants of the lost tribes of Judea. I sensed that the government has limited control in the north.

The Khyber Pass and Kabul

The scenery along the fifty kilometre pass lived up to expectations—desert terrain, jagged cliffs, shingle, shale, varying shades of red, brown and orange, vast plateau and deep valleys cut through by rivers and lakes. The buzzing, bustling market town at Torkham precedes the border. We waited before a one-lane bridge as three Afghani shepherds herded their flock of thirty-something goats. White coats, black faces. Colourful Afghani trucks passed. These ones had many references to Islam and carried wool and skin, dried fruit, nuts and barley, wheat and corn.

P33H entered Afghanistan after a three-hour stint at customs. Towards late afternoon the midday pale blue skies became darker as cumulus clouds knitted together. The cumulus-nimbus became more water-laden, gloomy and threatening and gave the whole scene a dramatic foreboding appearance. Very appropriate for such a place. We stopped for photos. The whole journey was a photographer's nirvana!

The Kabul Pass was more spectacular. The Kabul River cuts through the Kabul Gorge 25 kilometres east of the capital. The road was financed by funds from both the US and USSR. Afghani governments of different political persuasions play one off against the other to secure funding. The road, with concrete block barriers to prevent cars tumbling into the abyss, ascends, twists and turns dramatically, turns backwards and forwards on itself many times before climbing up a plateau and then descending.

Khyber Pass Postcard. 1979.

Plenty of time to settle back and soak up the view. I had read James A. Mitchener's 'Caravans' as homework. Set after WW II, the protagonist, at Kabul's American embassy, is assigned to find a young US woman who has disappeared after marrying an Afghan. During his search through Afghanistan, he understands Afghan life at a much deeper level than previously, its complexities, subtleties and nuances.

The 1978 film 'Caravans' was B grade. Inane dialogue. Even Anthony Quinn, as Afghan tribal leader Zulfikar, could not save this film. One redeeming feature was Mike Batt's haunting instrumental theme. Ingrained in my memory through repeated playings, I replayed violinist Vanessa Mae's version in my head.

A dog's life

Snow sprinkled the roadside as we approached Kabul. With each passing kilometre, snow drifts got higher, thicker, heavier. The lights of Kabul were twinkling in the distance when we were flagged down by three Afghan soldiers who came aboard. Young and fresh-faced, not surprising with the temperatures outside. From beside driver Carl Capstick, they did a cursory inspection. We beamed back benevolently. They did not understand English. Driver Carl Capstick gave them the twice-raised eyebrow treatment (a la Tom Selleck as Magnum) and with a faux smile said "Hi guys! How's your mother's chooks? Keeping well? Fine!" Courier Greg Marks shook his head and chuckled. Rosemary, Tineke, Barb and Jude snorted, stifled giggles while hiding their mirth behind the seat in front.

Kabul lies in a narrow valley between the Hindu Kush Mountains, 6,000 feet above sea level. Legend says it to be over 3,500 years old. On an ancient Silk Road trade route.

King Zahir Shah was deposed in 1973 and the monarchy replaced by the Republic of Afghanistan. In April 1978, Afghanistan's government was overthrown. One political faction, not representative of all tribes and ethnic affiliations, sought increased liaison with the Soviet Union. The others didn't. This was civil war. The government launched attacks on anyone who opposed it, and began widespread land and social reforms.

However the reforms were resisted by ethnic Afghani as well as Muslim and anti-communist populations. Revolts grew against the government by a tribes calling themselves the mujaheddin.

These rebellions prompted Soviet intervention for the communist sympathisers. Outside intervention in Afghan affairs was not new. The Russian Empire and British Raj had sparred over Afghanistan. Russia wanted to extend its empire, the Brits wanted Afghanistan as a buffer to their 'jewel in the crown' India.

When P33H was there in March 1979, Soviet troops were gathering on the borders. Thousands of Afghani refugees fled over the border to Pakistan.

By December 24, when the USSR invaded, they numbered 50,000. Over centuries, Afghanistan has seen off Alexander, Persians, Mongols, Genghis Khan, Timur the lame, Muslim Arabs, the Mughals, the British East India Company and the Raj.

The British Raj and the Russian Empire drew up Afghanistan's northern border in the late 19th Century without any consideration of ethic and tribal considerations and the Sunni/Shia faiths. The Raj eventually found it economically unviable to have troops in Afghanistan while based in India. Ultimately the Soviet economy too, as well as their military, was stretched in maintaining a presence in Afghanistan. Hence the country's reputation as 'The graveyard of Empires'.

In Kabul we stayed at the Plaza Hotel. 175 Afs per person. Exchange rate =36 Afs to 1 US$. Kabul was freezing. I didn't have appropriate woollen or leather clothing so wore three layers of what I possessed. Plus the Cossack-style hat I'd purchased in Kashmir.

Our group wandered down 'Chicken Street', window-shopping. I absorbed the ambience. The rugged, gnarled faces of the Pashtun tribesmen were riveting. A country's history etched into a face: furrowed foreheads, long grooves running down the face emphasising high cheekbones, greying wispy beards. Their blue-eyed stares were piercing and defiant.

Kabul had a range of shops from the high-end plate glass boutiques selling genuine antiques, furniture, samovars, embroidery, jewellery, the latest electronic gear to dingy, dimly-lit gloomy 'hole in the wall' shops with no heating. I chose the latter. I purchased portraitures by renowned photographers Roland and Sabrina Michaud of craggy Pashtun tribesmen. One had a small bird of prey perched before him. Another was of a turbaned gentleman with long wispy beard squinting and looking thoughtful while holding a rose. His lined face and pock-marked nose hinted at an eventful life.

A dog's life

Six years later, Steve McCurry's photograph of twelve-year-old Sharbat Gula, made her the unwitting posterchild for tens of thousands of Afghan refugees. Sharbat Gula, the 'Afghan girl', had piercing green eyes which stared directly at, into and through the camera. An instant icon, she was orphaned at age six during the Soviet invasion and trekked to Pakistan with her siblings and grandmother.

McCurry made a name for himself with that photo. In contrast, Sharbat Gula disappeared into obscurity. McCurry tracked her down 20 years later and found her, like her battered war-torn country, somewhat weather-worn.

Looking around the streets and alleyways of Kabul was adsorbing. 'People watching', a favourite pastime coupled with photography. Women walked past us enveloped in long black chadors with only a narrow rectangular slit to see out of. This ancient custom of 'purdah'—seclusion of females—was beginning to end in '79 but tolerance fluctuates with the government of the day.

Broad-walks and pavements are cluttered with people selling everything imaginable—cigarettes, chocolates, watch straps, sweaters, socks, trousers, shirts. It is difficult to get past. Once you step down from the raised wooden broadwalks, the short area to the next broad-walk can be swimming in cloying clinging mud. Sometimes iced-over mud. Near a building site, a man had set up his shoeshine equipment and was hard at work polishing a customer's brown boots. He was on a roll. The weather and mud were pushing customers his way.

Locally made shoes are readily available and for 450 Afs appear of a reasonable standard. From what look like long tea trolleys, youths sell knee-length, knitted socks with leather soles. They look warm and are great value, their soles needing an application of linseed oil or dubbin before wearing. I smiled. Like the pheran/hot clay-pot innovation in Kashmir, locals find unique, ingenious ways to dress to suit the conditions. On the next corner, a turbaned, bearded man looked out of place as he sold women's bras.

Men-only tea houses are gathering places. Ornate brass samovars brew up tea or chai which is usually served syrupy sweet. Sugar cubes are always close by.

Makeshift barbecues are set up on any spare inch of broadwalk. The sight, sound and smell of lamb kebabs sizzling on hot coals attracts attention. You can't always see the barbecues through the throngs of people pushing past but a cloud of grey smoke waffles by and alerts you. The smell of the meat cooking is heady, aromatic and tempting.

For lunchtime, we had a meal in 'The Steakhouse'. Free soup is provided then you can choose between beautifully presented kebabs for 30 Afs, huge wiener schnitzel for 35 Afs and cordon bleu for 40 Afs. The veal was usually accompanied by a potato salad. The French sisters were discerning eaters, often sending food back if it was not up to their gourmet standards. Their classic complaint of all time was uttered at 'The Steakhouse'. "This ice cream is too cold." Followed closely by "Dog! Don't you dare draw that in the Tripbook."

A dog's life

The main room had a mixture of tables and chairs and little tables where you sat on cushions and stretched out on Afghan carpets. In a garden area there was a giant chessboard with outsize pieces you physically shuffled about.

The restaurant was the haunt of "Okky Dokky", a glib motor-mouth moneyman. He had a computer-like mind able to rapidly figure out different exchange rates. I tried to avoid dealing with him because, like one of those shell games where you try to guess which cup the money is under as they are deftly moved about, the knowledge of international exchange rates at any particular moment was in his head only. There was bound to be a gulf between what he claimed was the truth and actual reality.

Courier Greg announced that morning that our coach and driver Carl Capstick were going no further. The political situation in Kandahar and Herat was volatile. Civil War. In Iran, the situation wasn't any better.

Ayatollah Khomeini had returned from Paris. There was a distinct anti-American, anti-western mood as fundamentalists demanded the Shah face trial.

P33H and a Sundowners group arrived at Kabul Airport to catch the 9.00 a.m. flight to Istanbul. Security was tight. An orange in my shoulder bag was squeezed, an aerogramme was opened and I was thoroughly frisked. The solid air hostesses didn't know how to smile or how to give friendly helpful service. As the plane was over-booked, Brian Mockler and I sat on the floor near the Emergency Exit and played backgammon. Brian was going to London to catch up with his brother Laurie who worked for Capricorn/ Sundowners. Maybe get a job there too. He was intelligent and athletic. Breakfast consisted of cheese or luncheon sandwiches and tea or coffee. One of the Frenchies didn't appreciate the sandwiches and muttered, "Yuk, I can't eat this sh*t. Give it to the Dog." Barb shook her head at them in despair. We peered through the windows and the cloud cover to see jagged snow-capped mountains and green valleys far far below.

'Off the beaten track'

900+ kilometres. Lahore to Quetta.

I was eagerly anticipating the journey to the Pakistani/Iranian border. Why? The challenge! In summer it was going to be tough. Expedition territory. Venturing where few sane westerners had explored before.

As in India, roads teemed with humanity. Bullocks, elephants, camels and donkeys became common. Bullock carts were in plentiful supply, piled high and wide with hay, the animals labouring along docilely.

Julia caught my eye and asked "Ian can we ride a camel?" I recalled their previous unabashed pleasure and euphoria with elephants. A delight to see. Why not? This was their 'once in a lifetime' overland.

Julia and Trish apprehensively laughed and giggled but hung on for dear life the few paces the camel took them. It looked as though they were an itch on its back it couldn't scratch. Curly, who was still trying not to talk to me after Khetri House, swung her gaze at me, yet again like an artillery piece seeking another target. I got the message. Lazy-eyed Curly and Jenny clambered aboard. These camels are one humped dromedary camels which make up 94% of the total camel population. The two-humped kind make up 6% and the wild Bactrian camel, found in the Gobi desert, are almost extinct. Applying anthropomorphism, Camels appear haughty. I love the way they look down on you imperiously. As a University professor might look at a naïve first year student questioning an assignment. You can't seem to hurry camels. They will move at their own pace thank you very much!

On the Befa tour, we had pulled into a layby to finish off the cooking begun 'on the run' and to eat dinner. Purely by accident it was opposite a two-storied sugar mill. The manager ambled over to the double decker. He had a conflab with Iain in the cab and offered him a tour of the mill. Iain, ever the opportunist, told the punters that this was pre-arranged. This little hoodwinking backfired because the tour, though well-intentioned, became too long and boring. The manager liked the sound of his own voice. First I saw passengers'

yawns, secondly their eyes starting to glaze over and thirdly I was the target of "the glare" from Estelle. Despite being petite in size, Estelle's 'look' was not to be ignored. I had already experienced it at Jaipur's Observatory. "Let's move along Ian." I informed the manager we had a schedule to keep to and departed.

Gradually, imperceptibly, the landscape changes from lush green and fertile to burnt-out pale greens, arid yellows and whites and cracked desert terrain parched of water. Crossing several muddy brown tributaries of the mighty Indus River, we followed the main drag to Multan where we turned southwest and headed towards Sukkur and ultimately Quetta. We crossed over the arched Sukkur Bridge. Evidence of the 4000-year-old Mohenjo Daro civilisation is to the south of Sukkur. Advanced for its time, it had criss-crossing streets laid out in a grid pattern, indoor baths and wells and an elaborate sanitation system. The Indus people appear to have been organised and clean.

In Sind province, gradually moving from the civilisation of Lahore, and the Punjab towards the Baluchistan 'frontier', the mighty Indus flows 2000 miles traversing the subcontinent. If coming from the west, the Indus marks the beginning of the Indian subcontinent. It is known here as the Sindhu River, hence the province's name, fed by snowmelt from the northern mountains. In 1932, the British built a dam at Sukkur which irrigated the desert and extended arable farming lands. Sluice gates feed seven irrigation canals that eventually take water to three million acres that were desert before. Farming has been hit hard by monsoon rains from time to time.

Psychedelic painted buses and trucks rattle and rumble past us. Pakistani trucks are painted a variety of paisley designs. Very sixties, early seventies. They are festooned with strings of neon fairy lights allowing them to glow like mobile Christmas trees in the dark. Other embellishments include garlands of flowers, good luck charms and effigies of gods. These dazzling, 'busy' works of art, are a Pakistani icon. Each truck or bus is hand-painted and designed to tell the owner's unique story—his home region, his ethnic origin, personality and interests. Islamic calligraphy plays an important part of the overall design and is indeed beautiful.

A dog's life

Lemming stopped regularly at *dhaba*, roadside stops, for punters to stretch their legs, consume water and buy vegetables and fruit. At times the trees around the *dhaba* are festooned with nosy parrots. At one stop, a wizened, leathery-skinned turbaned man came up to the cab. As I climbed down, a little rigid and inflexible in the joints from several hours driving, he grabbed me tightly by the forearm and lead me firmly and paternally over for a chai. He seated me on what looked like a bed frame, a string bed—a *'charpoy'* (The seated guy in the last photo is on one) and plied me with hot, sugary, black tea brewed nearby in a battered black kettle over a small kindling fire. He seemed to be urging me, the driver, to rest. I was grateful. Some *dhaba* have stalls that sell dhal and roti that truckers wolf down voraciously as we would a mince and cheese pie or a kiwi hamburger. The *charpoys* are for long distance truckies to sit on or stretch out on for 'forty winks'.

Lemming bounced, gambolled and ricocheted her way into the evening on the A2. The southern edge of the Thar Desert. We negotiated floodwaters. The heat was sweltering, searing, stifling. The road's washboard corrugations juddered and jiggled us. Some potholes looked shallow to begin but then threatened to swallow us. The driver had to concentrate. This wasn't 'mind on autopilot' country.

Preparing dinner whilst on the move was a feat of gymnastics and perseverance. The cooks were concocting a rice and chicken curry. The accompanying salad didn't have to be tossed by the cooks as the road was doing that for them. For brief times we were driving in fourth gear. For extended times in second. Around 1:30 a.m. we pulled over for the night. The only bunk available was in the middle upstairs. Stale air. Body odour. Light snoring. No thank you. I figured I wouldn't be getting any sleep in that heat.

I slumbered outside atop a long earthen levee.

If the temperatures were in the forties in India, they were nudging fifty degrees Celsius as we moved west. The punters were handling the heat well. We still had shade from trees.

Prickly beads of sweat ran down my back pasting my T-shirt to my skin or to the vinyl driver's seat. We drove ever on the look-out for water pumps where we liberally doused ourselves, savouring and cherishing our time under the water. Our clothes didn't take long to dry! Water containers were filled to the brim and water purification tablets dropped into them for safe keeping. All on board were tempted by the availability of imported Coke, Fanta and Lemu. But sugary drinks made dehydration worse. Drink bottled water or piping hot sweet tea. British Raj soldiers had discovered that this was the best hydrator. The coolest part of the bus was usually either the cab or the area immediately behind it but now a warm breeze assaulted our skin and dried our eyes. *Lemming's* punters were stoic and uncomplaining. Discomfort was part of the adventure.

Dinner that evening was tinned beef goulash beefed up by goat bought in a village at midday. And a horde of fresh vegetables. It was devoured in a desolate isolated spot with only a few mud or dried-dung huts with thatched roofs scattered about us. A handful of our guys wandered over to a rough lean-to in order to purchase drinks. A tight knot of locals were clustered around a black and white TV set, earnestly watching the 1970s' American motorcycle cop programme 'Chips.' I grinned. What a contrast to their way of life. Surreal! That encounter really stood out for me.

We were later escorted by police through 'brigand country' and once in relative safety in a compound, we dragged our sleeping bags outside to sleep.

The Bolan Pass

The morning was cool and crisp in the dark. I brewed myself a black coffee and let *Lemming's* engine idle, my mind initially fuggy. No one stirred. I snapped out of my reverie and, by the cab's light, with the back flap behind the driver pulled down, I estimated that day's kilometres on the map. A few centimetres on the map translated into a day of driving. Interesting journey today.

The dark is an all-encompassing stage curtain that is slowly hauled up heralding a new 'production', a new day. Pale stretches of dawn light started showing, coming in low and horizontal. The land slowly brightens to reveal the stony, pitted, craggy terrain. The world began to take form again, all the way to the horizon. The rising sun bathed the sky ochre and silhouetted saw-toothed hills in the distance.

I headed off early as the distant hills turned salmon pink. The sun rose higher and higher. The terrain looked very much like the 'south of the border' terrain in western movies. Therefore I thought it fitting to dig out an Ennio Morricone 'spaghetti western' tape. Energetic, uplifting, upbeat music. Morricone changed the sound of western film themes as typified by Jerome Moross' 'The Big Country' (1958) and Elmer Bernstein's 'The Magnificent Seven' (1960). Morricone used traditional guitar combined with voices, whistles, wind sounds, duck calls, scratching and unusual sound effects. I flicked the switches so that the music could only be heard in the cab and motored along, lost in my own cinematic world.

'For a few dollars more' was Morricone's best theme in my book followed by 'The good, the bad and the ugly'. His style rubbed off on others. Jerry Goldsmith's 'Rio Conchos' (1964) was a classical-styled western theme. Again for Mexican settings. But by the time Goldsmith composed 'Bandolero' in 1968, he was incorporating Morricone-like affects including whistling, a Jew's harp, harmonica and banjo. In 1975 he went back to the classic western theme with 'Heartbreak' Pass.

The road west was dead straight until the heat on the horizon broke it up into a shimmering, shapeless mirage. We seemed to drive … and drive… and drive. Continuous forward motion without much visible progress. After two hours, Camel clambered into the cab with an enamel cup full of black coffee for me. He scrutinised the map, his brow furrowed in thought. When we spotted a narrow, clear stream running parallel to the road, we stripped off and washed with soap and shampoo. Ahh, the pleasure of small things.

The position of the sun directly above told me it was nearing noon as we wound our way through the Bolan Pass. The road surface was reasonable tar-seal. The Pass stretches 80-odd kilometres from Kolpur to Rindli and rises from 200 metres to around 1800 metres above sea level.

On the Befa tour we spotted a train of 20+ camels—plus a few donkeys and a small herd of sheep intermingled with black faced goats—weaving their way along the rock-strewn craggy gorge. As their ancestors had done. Nothing substantial has changed for centuries. Kids sat astride camels. Youths walked. These were Kochi nomads heading from their summer pastures near Kandahar south for the winter. They keep sheep and goats. They get meat, milk, make butter, cheese and spin wool from their herds. This produce is part exchanged or sold along the journey to purchase grain, vegetables, fruit and other necessities. As a result of their movements, networks of trade and exchange have developed along the routes annually followed by the nomads.

Yet again, I felt I was in a time machine. What a gift.

A dog's life

John Hutcheson's Bolan Pass Photo. *Befa* tour.

Over the centuries the Bolan Pass had its fair share of nomadic traders, invaders, armies and travellers. In the two Anglo-Afghan wars, British troops marched through the Bolan Pass to Afghanistan. In January 1842, the garrison of 4,500 British troops in their crisp red and white uniforms, and 12,000 camp followers, marched out of Kabul to retreat to India. They came under attack from the hill tribes who launched raids and picked them off.

One person reached Jalalabad's safety.

Rudyard Kipling wrote "When you're wounded and left on Afghanistan's plains, and the women come out to cut up what remains, just roll to your rifle and blow out your brains, and go to your god like a soldier". That would have been good advice to Soviet soldiers occupying Afghanistan in the 1980s.

Sandy escarpments rose up on our right and dropped away on our left to a tributary. It had been narrower than a one-lane road most of the way. Now it was football field wide.

My cotton T-shirt was sticking to my skin. Time for another splash! I pulled into a layby and, in shimmering heat, descended to explore the stream. The air was as dry and tough as sandpaper.

Thinking "Dog's got the right idea. He's going dog-paddling", this time punters followed me *en masse*, scrambling exuberantly down a reinforced block retaining wall and gambolling across the shingle bank to splash and soak. The stream was flanked by vertical cream, orange and brown cliffs. A few small dark-green trees, well spaced-out with flattened tops and bowed over by the prevailing wind, were scattered along the banks. Their leeward side branches seemed to reaching out like arms to steady their imminent fall. The stream's depth fluctuated between ankle-and knee-deep and was refreshingly cool. Punters gasped in near ecstasy as they lowered themselves into its depths. The shadowed darts of small fish quickly scuttled away from us to wriggle themselves into the mud. The water smelt clean and fresh.

We stripped to our underwear. The girls returned to the bus to retrieve soap and shampoo. Several like Heather, Ces, Cress and Kathy wore light cotton wrap-around dresses from SE Asia to immerse themselves in. Some wore panties and bra. The girls bathed in small groups, the guys a discreet distance from them. Decorum and manners in the

Baluchistan desert. Subby and Jenny took turns to shampoo each other's hair. Bolivian Ces and Gary looked on bemused. Pop was his own isolated desert isle, a pale, tight volcanic mountain rising sheer from the water around him.

After the searing heat of the sun, the water felt like a cleansing balm. How good is this? We didn't want to leave. We spent an hour there luxuriating in the cool waters. Local trucks trundling past on the road nearby bleeped and beeped at us. Those westerners have been out in the noon-day sun *far* too long.

Quetta

I keenly anticipated Quetta, a photographer's paradise. It has a distinctive Peshawar-like 'vibe'. 70% + Pashtu. Tribal. In the 1990s, it became an Al Qaeda base.

5,000 feet+ above sea level, Quetta was a busy, bustling metropolis of 156,000 people in 1980. Its name derives from '*kwata*', the Putshu word for 'fort' and as the capital of Baluchistan province, it protected the roads to India, to Kandahar in Afghanistan and to Persia.

Known as Pakistan's 'fruit garden', Quetta is a fertile oasis set in a natural amphitheatre surrounded by barren, stony desert. It became significant when the Brits entered the scene around 1876. The museum dedicated to 'British Raj Military History', is housed in the former bungalow of Field Marshal Bernard Montgomery, he of El-Alamein and D-Day fame. Quetta has been rebuilt after being largely wiped out by an earthquake in 1935.

Quetta is multi-ethnic. You can see it in the clothes. Afghani pushtus have rugged, leathery-textured faces. Their skin has worn dark by years of exposure to the relentless sun. Clothes are hues of grey, brown or blue. Often a sleeveless waist-coat would be worn over a baggy-sleeved top. Their bodies are somewhere inside loose-fitting, baggy, drawstring trousers which, combined with a long front buttoned jacket or shirt, forms the shalwar kameez. Looks surprisingly comfortable and designed to catch a breeze. Heads are usually wrapped tightly in turbans.

Others wore chitral caps from further north beyond the Khyber Pass. Hazaris. A few had the fur-trimmed, winter hats of Tajiks and Uzbeks. Punters stared out in amazement. The locals returned our gazes with curiosity and bemusement.

I came to Quetta in November 1979 on Casper from the west. Ours was an impressive entry as it coincided with the arrival of a long camel line, plodding along in a rocky, tussock-flanked ravine alongside the roadside. Forty camels, several with riders, the adult camels laden up with wicker baskets, wooden poles, tents, utensils and provisions. A handful of spindly-limbed, skittish camel calves scuttled along with their parents and intermingled with horses, donkeys, goats, dogs and puppies.

A dog's life

In 1978, Top Deck had travelled Herat, Kandahar, Kabul, and onto the NW Frontier. Since that route ceased, the only way to Kathmandu was south through Iran and into Pakistan. The condition of the Pakistani 'Highway', indicated that not many had been this way before. Trucks and local buses maybe. Not tourist vehicles.

Against the backdrop of arid, steep, dwarfing hills, the camel caravan belonged to another millennium. Travelling one of the network of roads, repeating their ancestors' tracks. Punters were speechless. Awestruck.

This scene was imprinted indelibly in my memory banks and has prompted a lifelong fascination with 'the Silk Roads', a label given by 'the Red Baron', Ferdinand von Richthofen's cousin in 1877.

Cue Mike Batt's haunting 'Caravans' theme from the 1978 film.

In Quetta, we located the Lourdes Hotel in Staff College Road, a rambling bungalow-style hotel harking back to the Raj. How many thousands of overlanders have recharged their batteries here? The spectacular tree in the front of the grounds with huge spreading boughs like an octopus' tentacles was a favourite retreat out of the heat. I directed passengers to the *poste restante* where many received mail.

The bungalows of the 'Lourdes Hotel' have an old-world ambience, complete with well-tended manicured lawns and bright, colourful flower beds. A dark iridescent-blue peacock with distinctive Mohican crest uttered a shrill, piercing cry whilst strutting its stuff. It haughtily soaked up the ohhs and ahhs from photographers. Rooms are faded and jaded but are clean and well-swept, beds are comfortable and hopefully bug-free, the sheets, although thin and almost transparent, smell washed and the showers become hot after a while with adequate water pressure. The white towels have lost their fluffiness eons ago and are thin and slightly sandpaperish.

I booked two rooms for punters to use the facilities. They had to be accurate with their timing if wanting hot water. Not too fast. Not too slow. Too hasty to have a shower and they might be waiting ten minutes for hot water from the distant heating system to stir itself. Too tardy after everyone else had been? At best you could be standing under a tepid dribble. At worse, in a stone-cold puddle. Males needed to be fast. Females have a reputation for spending time in the shower.

Tribal affiliations, rules and laws reach back through generations in Quetta I wondered if grievances and disputes go back a long way too. Tribal and village loyalties take precedence over the influence of central government. Closer to home, women in pairs, walked by in burqas or shrouded in light cotton hijabs. Males were curious and asked where we were from to practise their English. Fruit and vegetable stalls abounded. The cooks stocked up for several days. Shop owners squatted effortlessly on their haunches in their doorways sipping chai.

Some took leave of their bartering to beckon to us enthusiastically. Shoe-shine boys observed us with curious interest, their eager expressions vanishing when they saw jandals or sandals Quetta had an industry around weaving. Flax and carpet weaving. Men deftly weave flax baskets whilst keeping one anchor strand between their toes.

Elsewhere are huge piles of rugs, kilims and carpets, blankets, shawls, cottons and silks, clay and brass bowls. Several shops sell a range of birds including quail and parrots. Pottery, mats, bicycle repair shops, shoe shops, kebab stalls—all these sights, sounds and smells assaulted the senses.

When I pointed towards my camera and via sign language asked if I could take photos, the locals broke into big beaming smiles, nodded and obliged.

The entrepreneur in the next photograph sat cross-legged in front of his huge frypan, intently stirring its varied and multi-coloured contents. I smiled at the basic simplicity of the kitchen of his takeaway shop. Large well-seasoned, cast-iron, black pan with handles. Eggs. Spices.

At a small bakery nearby, a bearded turbaned man sitting cross-legged, crafted the dough into a long naan shape, placed it on a small cushion and then reached down to slap it on one side of an underground earthen oven. In less than two minutes it was ready. Behind him in a darkened corner, squatted a skinny teenager, kneading the dough balls with one strong sinewy hand whilst holding an ancient set of scales in the other. The dough rattled very briefly in the scales and was then sent hurtling off like a thin, wobbly frisbee in the direction of his father.

Meat was available in Quetta. The hygienic conditions it was kept under was questionable. On all my tours in Quetta, eating out was *so* inexpensive and delicious that we dined out often. Local chefs would slow cook and tenderise the meat for us.

Punters could eat cheap tasty snacks during the day. The Chinese restaurant in Jinnah Road could dish up a huge meal for just over 1£.

On one visit, I consumed a very generous bowl of chicken and sweet corn soup. That was followed by sweet and sour beef and vegetable chow mein.

On Befa, our 'national meal' evening ended on a sour note. I was in my room after eleven just sinking into a deep sleep. A punter rapped urgently on the door and demanded I come. While Estelle went to the toilet, Nadine had waited patiently outside. Nadine accused the security guard of 'getting fresh' and painted him as aggressive. I asked him a few questions but he didn't have a strong grasp of English. He looked confused, not aggressive. I pushed him towards manager Ivan's office.

Iain, often hot-tempered and more than a little impulsive, appeared on the scene. I protected the guard from Iain, making sure I was sandwiched between them. Manager Ivan was short and solid. His eyebrows had a mind of their own reminding me of an out-of-control blackberry bush. His nose was bulbous like actor's Karl Malden's but was covered in thin spider webs of blood vessels. A heavy drinker. All in all, a swarmy individual. He heard our story, said he would ring the guard's superiors and have him replaced. The guard remained quiet and bewildered. He didn't defend himself. The following afternoon, Ivan informed me that the guard had been jailed for three months. I thought that was too extreme. I had since heard Estelle's less melodramatic version of the incident. I asked the kind of searching questions I should have asked the night before but I was groggy with sleep and still waking up.

In the evening, I spoke to the police superintendent. It took considerable 'robustness' and cajoling on my behalf to get the 'sentence' reduced. The incident had been overblown.

As the tour leader, I had to take the complaint seriously and protect the punter. But I should have taken in the punter's personality and been sceptical of the first version of an incident I received to verify that version with others at the scene. When describing an event some people will sum up the situation reasonably accurately, some will underplay it and some will overplay it. The onus is on the tour leader to take diverse factors, including cultural differences, into account, play God, make a judgement and get it right! In four overlands, three as tour leader, this was my only 'sexual harassment of a punter' incident.

Lemming's national meal the first night was in the regally furnished 'Farah Restaurant'. This was the second time I had brought a group here. I wanted them to sample dishes with a Baluchi or Pushtu flavour. We had the choice of: chappati, naan, thick lentil Dahl soup, Moghul-influenced tandoori chicken marinated in herbs and garlic and cooked in a clay oven, chicken made with green masala and yoghurt, chicken biryani—chicken with orange-coloured rice and nuts and dried fruit and a superb Rogan Josh slow-cooked mutton.

I was acquiring a taste for chilli, cumin, cardamom, ginger and turmeric. Although a confirmed carnivore, I was also relishing vegetarian dishes. The flavour combinations! I was also trying to see whether my palate could distinguish between Rajasthani, Kashmiri and Baluchistani flavours. I still had a way to go.

A dog's life

That meal *really* impressed me. I can *still* see that scene, almost drool over that 'melt in your mouth' mutton 43 + years on. Just fell apart to my fork's probe. I sank back in my chair. Utterly satisfied. I scanned the faces in the room. Punters looked satiated. They should be. We were in Quetta. The Baluchistani desert. Tribal Pashtun country and we were dining like this. Just as good as I've had in London's Mayfair. Look at the surroundings. White starched table-cloths, padded throne-like seats, being waited on by nervous but ever-vigilant waiters, silver service ...

Ah, you can't beat *this* dog's life!

The road less travelled

On August 4th, *Lemming* crept out of Quetta in the chill morning air. "American Pie" was waiting to go on the sound system. Darkness was breaking. I knew this was going to be a big 36 hours. 670 km to Koh-i-Taftan. Desert. *Intense* heat. 'Roads' unworthy of the name. Punters would be *well* outside their comfort zones today and tomorrow. An odyssey.

Rows of serrated, bluish-tinged hills behind Quetta stretched away towards Afghanistan, 400 kilometres away. We had already loaded up the tank and plastic containers with diesel. *Lemming* continued on through a pass and down onto the dry, sun-baked plains.

Photo: John Hutcheson. Baluchistan desert. Befa tour.

Baluchistanis are proud and independent people—many are nomadic shepherds—who feel marginalised to Punjabi interests in the government in Islamabad. Hence the lack of road infrastructure, I surmised. There have been several insurgencies since independence.

The landscape on either side of the bus was barren, dry, inhospitable desert. Dusty parched brush stretched away to the horizon. You could almost hear the earth baking and cracking under the sun's intense heat. I half expected to look up and see vultures circling and tucking in their bibs for their next meal … us.

By midday, the heat was borderline crematorium. *Lemming* was a mobile oven. Punters' clothes were clammy and sticking to their skin. Riverlets of sweat trickled down my spine. The heat was wringing my vitality from me. The guys could get away with just wearing shorts. All windows were open but the breeze coming through them was sultry.

Photo: Morris Tanner. Water pump. George and Camel. Note the difference in skin colour and attire between the local and Camel.

A dog's life

I had noticed an old pump, bore and well by the edge of the desert last time and scouted for it now. It was marked on my map. The pump was hard not to miss. Huge. It looked like a one-wheeled tractor slumped on its side. One huge shiny wheel sticking up and connected to its engine by pipes and pulleys. It now had a mud brick wall around it. Most of the guys stood around it fascinated. How is this thing still working?

We filled a stone basin with cold water and, one by one, took turns to submerge ourselves in it. Slowly. Exquisite! Pop couldn't get in though. Perhaps when he was our age! We gave him a good splashing.

A mirage? Late afternoon, a worm of dust appeared in the far distance even though the 'road' we were on now was temporarily tar-seal. The thermals cause haze and shimmer. In 1962's ' Lawrence of Arabia', there is an outstanding cinematic moment when Peter O'Toole sees Omar Sharif for the first time, gradually materialising in black on a camel from a fuzzy ill-defined distant blur to take human form out of a shimmering heat wave. That was happening now. Our dust worm got larger. The waves of heat immediately above the blacktop distorted the images for some time.

Eventually the apparitions became … not one but two Top Deck buses—*Knackers*—and trailing by some distance—*Scrote*. I estimated that a dozen Lodekkas did the Kathmandu to London run each year with an equal number going in the opposite direction. Usually in tandem. I preferred going solo. I trusted my own wits and common sense. Peter Searle the tour leader and Gary Hayes the driver were on *Knackers*. *Scrote* had only a tour leader as the driver had fallen ill and left at the Turkish border. Punter Chris had volunteered to drive and for his initiative later earned him a Top Deck driver's job.

Peter Searle wrote on the Top Deck website "Ian I remember the contact with you because it was the first real contact with the *known* world we had since leaving Goreme, thousands of kilometres away ... We basically did a runner from Tehran to the Pakistani border (with a short stop in wonderful Esfahan), with Gary Hayes and I driving *Knackers* 24 hours a day. And after the Pakistan border, we had the hell drive through the desert road from Zahedan to Nok Kundi. There was a night curfew in Baluchistan, so we stopped overnight at Nok Kundi and then travelled at dawn along the road to Quetta, where we met you and *Lemming*.

I was SO relieved to meet a fellow Top Decker, 'cos it meant the road east was passable".

I muttered to myself 'when the going gets tough, the tough get going'. Well done, Peter and Gary. Plus punters stepping up. Teamwork. That's the overland experience.

Crews and passengers mixed and mingled, excitedly swapping experiences. We eventually departed. There is an unspoken bond and camaraderie between punters and crew. Like bikers nodding and acknowledging fellow motorcyclists as they pass. Peter accurately described driving on the 'Pakistani Highway' as "off-roading through the desert with vague suggestions of a 'road' in some places".

Adults will be kids. *As we neared Dalbandin, I smiled with the memories of two past incidents. The first was of Casper and Rags camping overnight on the edge of town in November 1979. Side by side in the Baluchistan desert. Around 9.00 pm there seemed to be a punters' meeting upstairs as most of the punters seemed to be heading up there. There was a lot of laughing and giggling, banging and crashing and huffing and puffing. Eventually a queue of red-faced pyjama-clad punters, both male and female, armed with pillows (they'd just had a practice pillow fight), came down the stairs to sneak across to Rags to engage their punters in an impromptu pillow fight. Minutes of hilarity followed. Love it. The kid in every adult is not far beneath the surface!*

Apparently the trigger for this was some of Rags' punters complaining that we were using too many inches of their clothesline and borrowing too much of their honey.

A local bus trip. *The second incident was when Befa ran out of diesel in February 1980. Armed with a large red plastic container from under the stairwell, I hailed a dilapidated bus rattling past! I was welcomed aboard, immediately offered a cigarette and via nods, chin pointing, raised eyebrows and grunts, was invited to squeeze in amongst three locals sitting on the engine canopy beside the driver. Only three out of five gears were working and whenever the driver did change gears the curved gear lever gave me a sharp whack on the shin. That was better than the gearshift lever hitting my scrotum. I had to swivel my hips suddenly, like doing the twist, to avoid that. The painful grinding and scrunching of gears prepared me for the incoming blow.*

Smoke from varying kinds of cigarette, legal and otherwise, drifted languidly around the bus, The passengers were Baluchi and Pashtun, the men in shalwar kameez and turbans, the women in black chadors. I was in shorts, T-shirt and jandals. They were accompanied by a veritable farmyard of animals—a dog, sheep, a goat, geese, a duck, chickens and quail in bamboo cages.

Several women of 'mature' ages in the back row had their black chadors pulled back to reveal their thick black hair streaked with grey, leathery, sun-scorched skin and yellow, chipped, uneven teeth. They didn't bother pulling their chadors on, as I expected, in front of this westerner. They were wailing loudly, completely immersed in a tune. Their beige, red-veined eyes and the distinctive smell from their clothes hinted strongly they may have been killing off a few brain cells prior to my boarding.

I don't smoke weed but I was settling into the atmosphere and inhaled a few breaths. When in Baluchistan ... It was free ... and potent. For a few blissful minutes I didn't have a flock to herd. Someone accompanied the singing loudly and enthusiastically on bongo drums. The chickens clucked, clacked, cackled and squawked their discordant contributions.

I closed my eyes, exhaled, smiled, shook my head in disbelief and just absorbed the whole experience. How further away could I get from a NZ primary classroom in fourteen months? Future Hertfordshire UK students like Tanya Page and Adrian Richards would comment favourably on my Overland 'stories'.

It was dreamlike. Surreal. Spiritual even.

So this is how 'the other half of the world' lives.

I was awakened from my reverie by the loud honking of Befa's horn driving past and ruddy-faced punters pressed against the windows waving and shouting, "Ian! See you in Dalbandin".

A dog's life

Or was that ... "You're not needed now Ian! Byeeeee!" 'Motorboat' was almost p*ssing himself with glee.

At Dalbandin I thanked the bus driver and skedaddled as the scrum of my new friends piled off the bus dragging their bags and possessions. Others shepherded their livestock. Not an easy task. Like herding puppies.

This photo of his wife Trish and the next of *Lemming*. Morris Tanner.

While *Lemming* refuelled at Dalbandin, we were surrounded by curious onlookers. The people were darker skinned than in the north. Kids were dusty, ragged little urchins, the boys dressed in long-sleeved shirts which covered their bottoms over baggy trousers down to their ankles. Bare-footed. Male punters dressed in shorts and jandals were quite a contrast. Trish and others were beckoned to climb up onto a donkey drawn-cart to have their photos taken with the owners and his kids. I felt sorry for the skinny donkey who didn't look up to the task.

The kids may have looked like ragamuffins but they were enterprising. They plied us with cold Fanta and Lemu that had been sitting in a Baluchistan earthenware pot containing cold water. Initiative plus entrepreneurship! We bought fruit from the orchards the area is famous for, then *Lemming* was away, humming along, albeit slowly. Twilight descended and soon disappeared. Beyond the bright ribbon of rough road lit up by the headlights, was nothing but pitch blackness.

Reaching Nok-Kundi by nine o'clock, I turned the motor off, dropping my hands off the wheel with a sigh. Whew. What a day. The silence in the cab was broken by the metallic ticking, dinging and pinging of the Lodekka's engine cooling. Several punters had migraines and were feeling chunderous. Needing to stretch my legs and get the kinks out of my back, I went for a wander. I asked if anyone wanted to come. You won't often experience this. I was tired but tried not to show it.

Befa. February 1980. Photo: John Hutcheson. Nok Kundi.

— 230 —

A dog's life

The frontier. Some streets were in complete shadow, others lit by pale yellow lights from lonely lamps. Groups of men with thick beards, their heads wrapped in turbans or scarves and bodies lost in baggy shirts and trousers, were standing around gossiping. Some cradled machine guns. '*De rigeur*' in this region. Despite being dressed in western clothes, we didn't attract a lot of attention. A few traders still squatted in their shop doorways, squabbling, bartering and negotiating bargains with bundles of tatty rupees in their fists. We soaked up the atmosphere. Like osmosis. So different to our usual world. Once again I slept out under the stars where it was cooler outside than in.

Off by five o'clock the next morning. The 'Easy Rider' soundtrack was on—"Head out on the highway! Looking for adventure. And whatever comes our way!" Very appropriate. Destination: the Mirjaveh/Taftan border post. Scribbles on my map from past tours indicated there would be no more water bores.

The road was rougher than my recall. In the first hour we crawled fifteen miles. The road was corrugated, furrowed and grooved. At times the hard-baked arid desert was smoother to drive on. On occasions we saw two parallel rows of oiled drums forming a funnel for several metres in the desert. These are 'drum roads' where the desert surface is better to drive on that the designated road. As an alternative to drums, small piles of stones in the shape of mini pyramids served the same function.

There were no other vehicles—private or commercial—keeping up with us. Or coming the other way. How were goods exported or imported? By plane? There was a rail line from Quetta to Koh-i-Taftan. 40 hours. No private cargo transporter would risk their precious vehicles on this stretch of 'highway'.

Nearing the border by nine o'clock, the sun was climbing higher and the pitiless heat made several squeamish. Pip and Ces were in tears.

Heather, Cress and Angie were sullen and morose. I tried to encourage them. "This is the last stretch. Almost over. No more roads like this. Tar-seal on the Iranian side. Civilisation. Hang in there."

Thirty minutes from the border I psyched myself into 'border crossing mode'. Find the bus papers. Count passports. Go through my mental 'To do' list. Anticipating. Predicting. Remind first-timer Camel of what to expect.

Abandoned oil drums, plastic oil containers, engine parts, rusted car skeletons, long shredded strips of tyres and assorted rubbish were scattered about. There were long rivulets of oil and diesel to step over, litter blowing in the wind, unknown pungent smells in the breeze, and … flies. Swarms of them. Blue. Noisy. Annoying. The place had a dirty, grubby feel. Numerous utes, most abandoned, were scattered about, all covered in dust with paint peeling, well used.

Mirjaveh on the Pakistani side/Taftan on the Iranian side, was isolated and barren, a small fly-blown, dusty collection of well-worn, breeze-block buildings with flat rusty orange corrugated-iron roofs. Inside the customs building, punters surrounded the available fans as eagerly as the Cheyenne circled George Armstrong Custer at Little Big Horn. We got through the official paperwork in under an hour. That compensated for the blistering, oppressive heat.

Crossing borders

Befa. Six months before, I foresaw Befa's crossing possibly having difficulties. I didn't have the intense heat to reckon with but three things could cause me headaches.

Health Certificate Issues. *First, in Quetta, I had asked punters to check their passport's health stamps. Work with the person you are on duty with. You check their stamps. They check yours. Are they current? If not, we will visit Quetta's medical centre.*

Despite my advice and 'systems', vague Cathy had 'a boy's look'. Only at the border did I find her health certificate had expired. Her duty partner, Nadine, didn't notice it either. As soon as customs pointed the errors out, I went searching for Lemming's two nurses. They were Canadian compatriots and successfully argued her case with officials. Cathy never appreciated how big a deal this was.

Other crew have argued that, since the punter was negligent, only she should return the 900 km to Quetta. Then under her own steam catch us up. Nah! Good in theory. This young blonde was lacking in 'street smarts'. She was a tragedy waiting to happen. And it did. Later, touring alone in Rome, she was raped. Her parents collected her. I groaned when I heard that news. She wasn't meant to be a lone traveller. She needed a group around her for guidance and protection. Sometimes a person realises they need other people to survive.

Sometimes they don't. Cathy didn't.

If her entry had been rejected, I wouldn't return to Quetta. A nightmarish journey. There and back for one person. Nah. This is the frontier. Officials would be open to baksheesh. I had a wad of American dollars to 'grease the palm', a millennium-old way of operating in this part of the world. I would ask Cathy to contribute.

Overland with Top Deck

Just love it when a plan comes together. *My second issue was that I had a bus whose engine and chassis numbers did not match those in the 'carnet de passsage', the customs document with the bus' details and which guaranteed that we wouldn't sell the bus whilst in-country. I had a plan and had already rehearsed a scenario with Iain.*

The customs officer was affable and thorough. As I hoped, he was dressed in a pressed navy-blue uniform, contrasting spotless white shirt with epaulets and regulation blue tie. He inspected the bus. On his clipboard he ticked off a list of requirements.

When he came to the chassis number, lanky Iain concertinaed himself to his knees in the dust, stuck his bum up and his head down to partially crawl under the bus to locate the chassis number near the engine.

In reality that was a pointless exercise. No amount of looking would have found the chassis number where Iain was. It was directly in front of you at eye height as you boarded the bus. Dammed efficient Lodekka builders. I had judiciously hung a jacket over it.

This was my plan. I was trusting the customs officer wouldn't want to dirty his uniform by getting down 'close and personal' beside Iain. Or ... get his hands and fingernails dirty scraping grease away to find a chassis number. Iain called out the chassis number (written on his left palm) then stopped ... "Sh*t!" I thought. "Has it rubbed off his hand?"

I was about to suggest the immortal words, "Do the numbers look like 765?" when, after more worrying seconds, he completed the sequence. The official ticked that off, beckoned me to return to his office where everything relevant was stamped.

A dog's life

"You scared me there! Forget the script?" I enquired as we drove away. "Well it would have been covered in grease and dirt. I wanted it to appear natural!" he mumbled with arched eyebrows and a know-it-all grin. And the Academy Award for method acting goes to Iain McKinnon! I hadn't reckoned him a Marlon Brando fan before.

This next photo was Iain on the first day of the Befa tour in Kathmandu when it refused to start. However he was often in this position throughout the tour. He was partly under the bus for this anecdote-head down, bum up, twice as dirty.

Michelin rated dining. The third possible problem related to nationalities. Three Canadian punters were on board. On January 28th, 1980, just a few weeks before, Canada found herself centre-stage of international news. The Canadian Embassy in Tehran had assisted six US Embassy staff to escape Iran. It became known as the 'Canadian Caper'. Ben Affleck's 2012 movie 'Argo' was based on CIA officer's Tony Mendez' memoirs. Was Iran still smarting from that? How might they retaliate? I opened all passports at the appropriate page to be stamped, sliding the three Canadian passports in amongst the Aussies/Kiwis. There were no problems. I successfully distracted the official with a stream of banal banter.

The Iranian side of the border was at Taftan. Deciding to cook dinner in the fenced compound before heading off, we occupied our time by having showers in the hospital-like Health Depot. We played volleyball outside. The cooking duo consisted of Cathy—of out-of-date medical certificate fame and Nadine of the 'fresh' guard incident. I was first alerted to her in Kathmandu when she quizzed me on what shows would be on in London when we got there. I suggested "The Rocky Horror Show" and "The Mousetrap" but that wasn't *good enough. "Rod Stewart?" she queried, "Will he be on? Where will he be playing? How much are the tickets? How about ..."*

This was the first time they had cooked. The last of the first duty rotation. Cathy had joined us in Delhi but by unwittingly teaming her up with Janine, I had teamed up two people, who thought 'outside the box' and marched to the beat of their own bongos.

They took cooking a <u>tad</u> too seriously. Producing something tasty in the 'cordon bleu' gamut, they in the process glowered, glared, and grumbled at anyone who attempted to move through "their" kitchen. I could see the 'writing on the wall' and promptly disappeared outside with a beer. Most of the guys picked up my non-verbal communication techniques—the Indian head bobble—and had my savvy to become scarce. The ladies were a little slower to cotton on to the impending theatrics. A narrow sliding window on the bottom floor slid back later and a feminine voice hissed. "Help, Ian, we're trapped in here! We can't get past them!"

When dinner was served, and it did earn 10/10, Janine demanded silence. I thought she was going to say 'grace'. Instead ... she commanded, "Now don't eat this too fast everybody! We've gone to a LOT of trouble here! Savour every mouthful!"

Amen! Three star Michelin dining in the desert!

Iran. November 5/6 1979

Camel drove *Lemmng* into Iran. His first time. My third. Revolutionary fervour still hogged the international news. The name 'Iran' had a danger/excitement element that other countries didn't have. How would we be received this time with a 'guard' for security? And just seven days to traverse the country. It didn't take much more than that when we had free rein. Wouldn't be able to get south to Persepolis though.

As we drove, I reflected on my first entry on Casper—November 5th 1979.

The day before—November 4th, 1979—is forever in the history books. Fifty-two US diplomats were taken hostage by revolutionaries in Tehran. There was discord, protests and chanting in the streets. Students burnt American flags, erected a gallows for the Shah and demanded he return from the Cornell Medical Centre, USA, where he was undergoing cancer treatment, to face torture, robbery and murder charges.

Nine months before, as a Capricorn punter, I had flown over Afghanistan and Iran. Were Top Deck the only ones entering Iran? What did they know that other tour companies didn't?

Tony Wheeler, in "Across Asia on the Cheap" writes "Until things have settled down and the current anti-foreigner mood dissipated, there is not going to be much over-landing through Iran." (1979, p. 259).

In contrast, a "TOP DECK STOP PRESS" declared, "In September '79 the situation in Iran and Afghanistan is fairly stable. If there are problems, contingency routes by-passing these countries will be used. No departure will be cancelled".

After the Turkish passport and health-card check, my driver and I elbowed our way through the throngs of Turks and Iranians to the Iranian passport check at Bazargan. The scene was shambolic. Shoulder to shoulder people. Drivers. Women in black chadors. Soldiers. Police. Children squished between their parents desperately holding their hands. Body odour. The stench of diesel on clothes. Stale tobacco breaths. 'Ripe' clothes.

During the jostling amid the mêlée, we learned that bandits between here and Tabriz had robbed tourist buses recently. Outside the building, money changers offered good rates. Once the paperwork was stamped, signed and fees paid, we drove to the gated police compound twenty kilometres from Dogubayazit for the night.

Whilst I had an Efes beer downstairs as the cooks prepared dinner, a tall, lean, moustachioed policeman poked his head around the door and inquired in halting English "Anyone play backgammon?" I raised my hand. Over a few games, using my new Venetian leather board, he informed me about the hostages in Tehran. Punters did a double-take when they saw the tour leader and a uniformed policeman talking first in hushed tones then later bantering and enjoying each other's company.

Word got around about my backgammon ability. Or perhaps the lack of it. An easy win? After dinner, an Iranian engineer with fluent English challenged me. Over more games I gleaned details about the hostages. More trouble in the cities than in rural areas. When he departed, I asked the antipodians on board for miniature Australian or NZ flags to tape to our windows. If challenged I hoped locals would know the difference between 'down-under' flags and the more well-known and now hated 'stars and stripes'.

The brilliant orange orb of the sun emerged unhurriedly over the silhouette of the blue hills to our left. It was six fifty-five. London East-Ender Mac sat with me. At one stage he left to find an extra couple of pair of woollen socks for me. It was sub-zero temperatures.

The cold had seeped through all my layers of clothing. My toes were numb, anaesthetised. The mountains beside us were varying bluish hues in the early morning light and the far-off ridges and valleys were cloaked in fine mist, some round like a halo above a monk's head. Mud villages surrounded by stone and mud walls with the occasional tower clung to the hillside. On top of many mud/stone houses were stacks of hay. If I was cold, how cold would those village inhabitants of be? Those images have stayed in my mind forever.

We made steady progress throughout the day passing through Tabriz and heading east and south. At 10.00 p.m. I took over driving duties. Canadian Theresa sat up to chat, the reprimand she had delivered in Florence long forgotten. She had become one of my biggest supporters. Bill James later read me a flattering comment from her report in which she said I really liked the punters and had their best interests at heart despite the domineering driver who bullied me.

We edged closer and closer towards Tehran. I wanted to bypass Tehran. Where was the bypass? Casper and Rags had been joined at the border by Boogie with Tim Oliver and Russell Facer. A 7 weeker. Our route minus the Middle East. We were in convoy stopping frequently for the drivers of that moment to confer. In the dark, huddled around Rags with torches and a map, Trevor, as our mentor commanded "Whatever you do, DON'T go into Tehran!" The capital was the hot spot. Sorry Trevor—but looking at the faces above their torches most of those on driving duty had already arrived at that conclusion.

After a period, I lost sight of the others. Never saw them until late the next day. I have never forgotten that evening. Embedded forever in my memory. I was in and out of the cab frequently to check battered and barely visible signposts. Most of the signposts in English had been painted out. Those remaining were in Farsi. Indecipherable.

Ultimately I followed a truck driver to a highway. He pointed me in a direction that I agreed with from my numerous map interpretations.

We were away. When we next encountered Rags, Trevor said he had the same problem with signposts and directions. He looked for bypasses but he did end up in Tehran.

Fortunately for him, the inhabitants of Tehran were too busy protesting to notice his orange double-decker.

I chuckled when I heard that. It immediately reminded me of scenes in 1963's 'The Great Escape'. Do as I say and not as I do. Potential escapees in Stalag Luft III in 1943 are rehearsing how to get through German police checkpoints. Senior British Officer Mac catches one out by abruptly switching from German to English. The escapee answers in English. "Don't be caught out by that one!" warns Mac. Later during the actual escape, Mac is boarding a bus. A Gestapo officer switches from German to English saying "Good luck". Mac replies, "Thank you." Caught!

Theresa stayed up chatting the whole time I was driving. At intervals she ventured back into the kitchen to make coffee. She was a godsend. Someone to bounce directional ideas off. By 6.00 a.m. the rising sun was striking us in the face. I wasn't tired. The tension of not wanting to make a wrong decision had probably caused a flow of adrenaline. Kept me sharp. I tilted the front visor and grabbled under my seat for sunglasses. The awakening sun fused the desert with a burnished orange tinge. When I pulled over for diesel at 8.00 a.m., Isfahan was just 123 kilometres away. To be expected, the price of diesel was the cheapest on the tour.

As I signed in at the marbled reception desk of the Isfahan Inn, I glanced around. The hotel's trappings were stunning, revealing opulence, high living, glitz and glamour. Money. The lifestyle the average Iranian would be a stranger to. No money had been spared. It had been worth driving through the night for this.

I was scruffy and unwashed, out of my league. But … I didn't look out of place in my trainers, jeans, T-shirt and two-day stubble. Why? There weren't <u>any</u> other guests. All had scarpered because of the revolution. No wonder the receptionists were happy to see us. I immediately saw this as a special treat. Make the most of this, Dog. This won't happen very often. If this is the doghouse, lead me to my kennel.

I procrastinated in the shower. My showers are usually short. Not this time. I lingered, digging the grime out from fingers and nails with a Swiss penknife I bought the year before in Lucerne. I scrubbed hard to get rid of the stench of diesel. Crashing exhausted into a luxurious bed at 12.00, I didn't wake until 4.00 p.m. I had a huge room with en-suite. A king-sized bed with clean sheets of 300 thread quality, soft mattress and pillows.

A dog's life

Ahh, Dog. Bath day. This is the life.

The Isfahan Inn was a very well-appointed 5 Star + hotel which was no longer frequented, probably because it was a symbol of the capitalist, decadent west. It had marble floors, glass walls, and gold finishing. Ornate Persian carpets, dark wood panelling, thick lush curtains, long curling balconies and stairways with intricately carved handrails, chandeliers ...all combined to give a rich, palatial impression.

I thought it was a real find and searched for it on later tours but it was closed. The hotel was featured in the 1974 film 'And then there were none' based on Agatha Christie's '10 little Indians'.

Iran. 1980. Summer

At the border, Camel and I completed *Lemming's* paperwork. An Aussie from Broken Hill was riding to Quetta on a much tinkered with grey BMW R75/5. He asked me about the 'road' conditions. Three Scandinavian guys overheard the conversation and came over to listen. They were cycling to Quetta. Lean as beanpoles. T-shirts, khaki shorts and trainers. Toned muscled quads and calves. A multitude of black bags balanced on the front, back and sides of their pushbikes. Wouldn't have been easy to ride. Narrow tyres. OK in Iran. The 'Pakistani Highway' would be challenging. I showed them on their map where the water and food stops were.

The formalities completed, I paid a deposit for the guard who would accompany *Lemming* through Iran. In seven days. I looked at my map and calculated the possible night stops. Doable. This was a recent innovation. Things had become stricter in six months. The girls were in their western clothes on the bus but in public in Pakistan had covered themselves well, reducing the amount of their flesh on display.

Customs instructed us to camp in Zahedan and return the next morning for the guard. We drove off on smooth tar-sealed roads. What a contrast to the other side of the border. With no bumping and rattling, you could hear yourselves think. We spent the afternoon at the Zahedan Inn simply relaxing in the shade or in the air-conditioned public areas, washing and drying clothes, writing letters or sleeping.

Returning to the border by 9.00 a.m., we were introduced to 'guard' Hussein. In civilian clothes. No uniform. Quiet and reserved. Limited English. Guiding him over the bus, I introduced him to punters. He looked around downstairs with a mixture of curiosity and incredulity. Welcome to Top Deck's world Hussein.

We also encountered an Indian named BJ. and his Japanese wife. Tall, lean. Full dark beard. Intelligent. Well educated. Articulate. He had a dilemma. BJ was returning to India from England in his Morris Marina. The Pakistani authorities wouldn't let him in. Was his paperwork incorrect? Or was this Pakistani/Indian rivalry? I said I'd get him to either Isfahan or Tehran to catch a flight to Delhi. He was forced to sell his Morris to Pakistanis for a pittance! His wife could get into Pakistan so decided to take a train and then public transport from the border to India.

He was likeable but soon grated on me. Loquacious. Garrulous. A 'know-it-all'. He had an opinion on everything. He tried to muscle in on my private conversations with Hussein and Camel. Unsuccessfully. The punters smiled at him sitting crosslegged meditating on the front seat with his wrists lightly on his knees and thumb and index finger touching. A poser. C'mon. Choosing the front seat. Back to the cab. Facing everybody. Show pony.

At a service station, we refuelled. I wandered over to see a sky-blue, triple-cylinder, Suzuki GT 750cc touring model I had lusted after in Aotearoa. Water-cooled via a radiator mounted directly in front of the engine. A first. Three Iranian youths joined me. The Iranian owner encouraged me to go for a burn. I politely refused. He was insistent. The bike responded with a powerful purr at low revs and I accelerated down the road. Within minutes, a tourist coach was bearing down on me on the same side of the road! Duh? We were in Iran. Unlike Pakistan, they drive on the right hand side of the road. American v English influence. I swerved to safety, did a few more kilometres and returned to the petrol station. I had been out of sight so the bike's owner thankfully didn't witness my misjudgment.

Shah Mohammed Reza Pahlavi was responsible for upgrading and maintaining Iran's extensive road network. The best Asian roads on the route, plus sustained economic development for a number of years. His father Reza Pahlavi was a military officer and politician who seized power in 1925 and was forced out in 1941. His son succeeded him and the country modernised and in the process made himself and his family and friends wealthy. But he forgot the common men and women. And the power and appeal of the clergy. These forces eventually caught up with and overthrew him.

A dog's life

Lemming made good time heading north-west. The cab windows were open and a muggy breeze provided reasonably pleasurable motoring. The sky was cobalt-blue with a few thin vaporous clouds kilometres high. Temperatures were well into the forty degree plus range. A few months ago it was under snow and minus twenty degrees! Judging by the mud adobes, locals lived in primitive conditions. How did they cope with extremes of temperature?

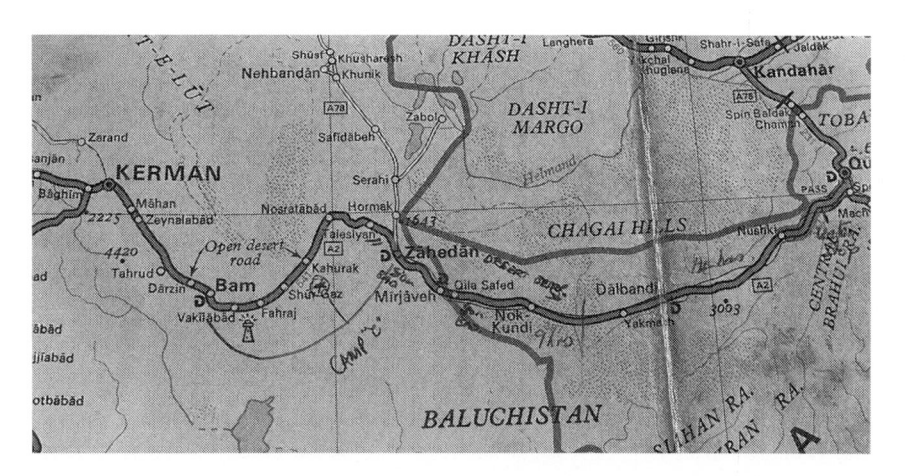

Driving towards Isfahan via Kerman, Rafsanjan and Yazd on the A2, I looked for 'Camp C', the British Marples-Ridgeway Civil Engineering firm. It was closed. Things were *always* changing. Like discovering the Isfahan Inn. A highlight on one tour, might not be there the next. Iran was in a constant state of flux.

Lemming passed through **Bam**, an oasis 1000 metres above sea level where the high central plateau gives way to the Sistan and Baluchistan deserts. The medieval citadel Arg-e-Bam, one of the largest structures in the world made of sundried mud bricks, sits atop a hillock above the township. I had visited Bam twice before for vegetables. Farmland is watered by underground water canals. Regrettably I didn't have the time to visit the citadel.

On Casper, I had been standing outside the bus awaiting the cooks' return, when I was approached by three youths. The US diplomats in Tehran had been seized a few days previously. "Are you American?" One demanded.

"*Why? Don't you like them?*" I replied. I immediately decided to dial back my unnecessarily aggressive rhetoric. "*No. Australian and New Zealanders,*" I said pointing to the many small flags I had displayed against the windows.

Lemming climbed higher and higher in altitude, passing from the southern sand desert into the northern salt desert. Sand dunes and more sand dunes. Irregular shaped tussocky sand dunes. Pebbly sand dunes. The terrain constantly changed and evolved. Scorched. Arid. Entrancing.

Eventually we reached the snow line. Just on dusk, I pulled over. Nature called. The air was thin and crisp. The sky a pale blue before darkness fell. Bright stars twinkled above me and I couldn't help but recall Don McLean's "Starry, starry night".

Looking past *Lemming*, the countryside stretched away endlessly for thousands of kilometres. I stood there absorbing it all. I looked over at the double-decker lit up both upstairs and downstairs, passengers cooking and conversing. An orange double decker was out of place, an alien in this landscape. The night air eventually chilled me. I climbed into the cab and drove off. I can still see that scene to this day, regretting not taking a few minutes to fetch my camera and capture it.

Isfahan, has been an important trading centre because of its central location on Itan's east-west and north-south routes. It is in a lush plain at the foot of the Zagros Mountains. It flourished from 1000 to the 1700s.

When Shah Abbas I came to power in 1587, he repelled the Ottoman Turks and was determined to make Isfahan a large and beautiful city. He succeeded. The Shah's reign ended in 1629, Isfahan's glory days lasted a mere 100 years.

A dog's life

When the decline began, the capital shifted to Shiraz and then Tehran. Isfahan is a beautiful city, renowned for its wide streets, arched bridges and ornate Islamic architecture. There are eight traditional elements to the city: spacious parks and gardens, porches, platforms, gateways, turquoise domes, arched chambers and minarets. The highlight is the King's Square, the Meidan-i-Shah, the focal point in the Square being the Masjid-i-Shah with its arabesque tiles, its dome and Safavid-style decoration. All of the inlay work in the Masjid-i-Shah is stunningly intricate. Islamic secular art is figurative as the Koran expressly prohibits icons and idolatry. The architecture's beauty is in the line, form and abstract pattern of the calligraphy.

The royal bazaar adjacent to the Mosque is recognised as the artistic and craft centre of the city. The craftsmen hammering out elaborately complex designs on silver and brass platters for which the area is renowned, were mesmerising to watch.

The work was painstaking and intricate and the craftsmen were totally focused on their work, not looking up to acknowledge me taking photographs. The two masters I watched were father and son and carrying on a family tradition going back generations.

One evening, a local invited me to a market at dawn the next morning. An illegal black-market operation. I had been here before on Casper and knew how it worked. We went without Hussein. On the shingle shore of a river, between two ornately arched bridges. Hundreds were there. With my olive skin, dark hair and thick moustache, I blended in. It looked like the Iranian version of a 'Sunday Market'. The weak sun had been up an hour but was obscured by clumps of cumulus cloud. A gusty fresh wind blew. Atmospheric.

People were selling clothes, caps, tracksuits, track shoes, jeans, watches, jewellery, sunshades, etc. I bought a pair of sunnies, a 'knock-off' of a name brand. I was approached by money-changers and, after haggling, got a decent rial-dollar exchange rate. I flicked through the banknotes I received carefully. Were they all the same denomination? Any folded in half? I wondered how long it would be before the Shah's face on the notes would be replaced by Khomeini's. Must keep a note as a collector's item in the future. I smiled. Americans were despised but their currency lauded. My guide was twitchy and nervy, forever on the lookout for police. At any sign of the authorities, there would be a loud warning

A dog's life

cry from a 'spotter' and everyone would grab their gear and scarper. I was reminded of the illegal, knock-off merchants in Montmartre, Paris. You'd be looking at items on display. A loud shrill piercing whistle blast would rend the air. Traders would scoop their wares into plastic bags and be off before the *gendarmerie* arrived.

On *Lemming*, Hussein helped us out on several occasions, most notably when an official stumbled across playing cards displaying completely naked girls with their legs akimbo. The cards' owner kept quiet. I stumbled for words and discreetly hid them in a back pocket. Hussein distracted the guard.

Observing Ramadan, he didn't eat anything from dawn to dusk. Ramadan moves around each year in conjunction with the appearance of the crescent moon. I chatted to Hussein a lot, trying to learn about his culture.

Tehran. We camped by the roadside and found the all-important camping gas before descending from the plateau into Tehran's congested sprawling streets in search of the Syrian Embassy. The streets were jam-packed with people, mostly men but a few women in black chadors over western clothing. Soldiers with machine guns slung over their shoulders. Iran's capital has been shifted around many times over the years with Tehran only being the capital since about 1783. It is situated 1000 metres above sea level.

Photo: The dog catching a few *zzzz* as we passed Qum.

This was my first visit to Tehran in three Top Deck tours. Anti-foreign sentiment was said to be still active. The fifty-two American hostages were captive in Tehran but were now in small groups and were being moved around every few days to foil another American rescue attempt like April's 'Operation Eagle Claw'.

Peter Searle, whom we'd met on *Knackers* on the 'Pakistani Highway' had accidentally 'found' a group of the hostages. He writes on the Facebook page, "We had a hellish trip through Tehran … being held up at gunpoint/Uzi submachine guns by the Revolutionary Guards when we stopped at a school in Tehran which was apparently where the American hostages were being held. All the punters were scared shitless."

The atmosphere was tense and I was glad Hussein was here. There seems no real distinctive centre of Tehran but, using Hussein's knowledge of Tehran we located the Syrian Embassy. Unfortunately we were told that we would have to wait seven days for visas. Instead we decided to seek them again in Ankara. We dropped BJ off on a bus route to the airport. He gifted Camel his tool box.

On the way out of Tehran, Hussein directed us to a modern dual carriageway. Camel put the foot down on the accelerator. Suddenly there was a squeal of excitement and someone yelled at me "Ian, look, look!" The passengers were pointing at the Shahyad Monument, the huge Arch de Triomphesque monument, tower, built by Shah Reza Pahlavi nine years ago to mark the 2,500 anniversary of the Persian Empire. SLR Shutters worked overtime.

That evening a roadside café on the fringe outskirts of Tehran, was our dinner stop. Hussein hungrily scoffed down a huge bowl of rice topped with butter and vegetables. We camped for the night in a police compound in east Azerbaijan province.

I set off at six o'clock the next morning on the main drag northwest. "Slow Train Coming" by Bob Dylan, his 'Christian period', was on the sound system to be followed by Carole King's "Tapestry", and my all-time favourite, "Up on the roof". An eclectic mix. The sky was light-blue and the scenery absolutely captivating—craggy hills, winding valleys, narrow fast-flowing streams and line upon line of poplar and cedar trees. In the distance, lines of white snow veined down from summits of the mountain range. Quite a contrast to the sand and salt deserts in the south. What a difference in terrain within the confines of one country!

A dog's life

The cooks bought vegetables in a small market town en route to Tabriz. Later Hussein pointed out little sponge cakes filled with mock cream at a roadside stall. The brakes came on in a hurry and hungry punters jostled to buy the decadent morsels. Locally made chocolates, confectionery, dried nuts and local delicacies are famous throughout Iran. Even Hussein didn't observe the last day of Ramadan. He took our teasing in good fun, grinning sheepishly.

As the day was thinking about turning to night, we free-camped forty-five kilometres from Maku south of Dogubayazit. As the cooks prepared dinner, the rest of us enjoyed the waning light and warmth. The air was still and sultry. Temperatures were dipping.

I awoke at 6:30 a.m. feeling grubby. I was sustained by a Beachboys album until my unkemptness was remedied thirty minutes later. I pulled over, stripped off and soaped myself in a stream in the warm early morning sun. A rippling brook fed by snow melt. Bracing! Feeling clean and with fresh clothes on revives me for a couple of hours. I love being close to nature.

The air was perfumed with pine and juniper and bright red mountain flowers. Clumps of wild garlic and spring onions gave off pungent odours. Insects hummed and jumped in the tall grass beside the brook, some with the manic energy of those with short life spans, as the end of summer approached.

At the same time as we were filling up with diesel at Maku, we filled every plastic container we had. Diesel was dirt-cheap here. It could only get more expensive, and probably elusive, in Turkey. We washed the bus down before completing official paperwork and proceeding up the hill to the final customs area at Barzagan behind a long queue of trucks. We can comfortably crossed the country in seven days. The air outside *Lemming* hummed with rumbling, idling engines and when I descended, the smell of diesel was everywhere. Tendrils of heated exhaust fumes rose from the trucks and big multi-wheeled rigs.

Iran. February 1980: Winter

Befa's journey through Iran was a complete contrast to Lemming's. Temperatures steadily dropped from Lahore as we travelled southwest and along the 'Pakistani Highway' to the border.

Although there was no hint of snow crossing into Iran, temperatures were dropping and becoming bleak. Punters started to pull on extra layers. Befa drove via Kerman, Rafsanjan and Yazd on the A2. I looked for 'Camp C', the British Marples-Ridgeway Civil Engineering firm. Their workers made us very welcome, glad to hear English voices, see femininity and catch up on events in the outside world. They offered us shelter and the facilities in their huge hangar-like workshop.

That evening, while the passengers raged in the bar, Iain and I did running repairs: repairing cupboards and fittings jolted loose by the 'Pakistani Highway's' rough roads. We finished by fitting a new stereo, then after hot showers made our presence felt at the bar. Seeing glassy eyes and hearing slurred voices, we forgot about trying to catch up. We had missed a handful of friendly Afghanis wielding machine guns who had made a cameo performance. Jo-Anne had a selfie taken with them banishing their hardware. Everyone was more than a little merry by the time it came to crash.

I was weary and freezing. Fortunately someone offered me the warmth and comfort of her sleeping bag.

Photograph below: John Hutcheson. Outside Isfahan.

Approaching Isfahan, we encountered a light sprinkling of confectionery snow. It continued to get heavier. As it was Valentine's Day, Rita organised a poetry competition. There were a few literati in the group. Iain and I bought carnations in the markets for the ladies. He was doing spadework on Nadine and a carnation would add to his self-image of 'the man about town'. The gesture went down as well as the later poetry recitals. They were all very good but two were memorable. Motorboat's was very creative but crude. As to be expected. Jo-Anne grimaced and gritted her teeth and did the obligatory eye roll. Estelle's was a gem aided by her impeccable delivery and diction.

Estelle took the honours.

Whoops. *I piloted Befa into Isfahan the next morning. Intending to sightsee. I had 'a brain fade', forgetting that Friday was the Muslim holy day and I blundered into the Meidan-i-Shah. This huge open 'square' had tradesmen's shops, including brass, silver and copper work. Prayers had finished. Huge numbers were pouring out of the Masjid-i-Shah mosque. It has a multitude of pale-blue tiles which were in stark contrast to the brown, dry desert. We were definitely in the wrong place at the wrong time!*

A dog's life

Soon we were completely surrounded by people making their way to the exits. Veiled faces with wide curious eyes stared up at us in disbelief. Men looked the bus over in curiosity. But none were angry or threatening. More inquisitive. Youths thrust cardboard cut-out puppets of Jimmy Carter into the cab. Despite the smiles of the crowd, I was concerned that this could turn nasty. We were invading special ground. I inched our way out without incident.

Whilst in Isfahan, driver Iain also 'blotted his copybook'. We seemed to take turns with making blunders so no-one ever had the upper hand, the moral high ground. We located a side-street hardware store off the main square. Long and narrow, inadequate lighting made it dark and gloomy. A musty woody smell predominated. I picked my way past wooden ladders, brooms, rakes, hoes, axe handles and broom handles to the hinge and screw section.

Iain browsed tool-filled aisles. He was then exceedingly stupid! Customers were thankfully talking to and distracting the proprietor. Turning his back to the owner Iain slipped two long tools inside his jacket. I stood there like a stunned mullet. Taking a few seconds to register as everything ground down into slow motion*, I shook my head. Noooo. He grinned, glided deftly around me with all the aplomb of a ballroom dancer, paused to pretend to briefly look at more things, then ambled nonchalantly out of the door.

*Apparently the amygdala area of the brain lays down an extra set of memories in times of stress. I had noticed it before during a motorbike accident in which I was tossed over a car when it abruptly turned in front of me. Fortunately it was a Fiat Bambina. I noticed it much later again when I plunged over a 100' waterfall whilst on a school camp.

"That was insane," I reprimanded him. "Where are we? Iran! A fundamentalistic Islamic State. They chop the hands off thieves!

In public. Not only the perpetrator but accomplices. Me! All over two paltry tools worth not more than a few dollars. What about the store owner? He was barely scraping a living. Probably as poor as a mosque mouse."

The journey from Isfahan to the Barzagan on Befa was a COMPLETE contrast to Lemming's .

In fact, the polar opposite.

Within an hour of leaving Isfahan, the countryside was blanketed in thick snow. Upstairs, passengers prepared well. They huddled together under piles of sleeping bags to keep warm. Couples snuggled together. Jo-Anne hinted that there might have been a little groping going on beneath the warm layers to raise body temperatures!

The Top Deck brochure states "Buses doing Winter Overlands are generally heated".

Yeah, right. Yeah … nah. Although the bus had heaters fitted, these were impractical as they used up huge quantities of camping gas. One gas cylinder every two days. Gas was difficult to come by at times so heater use was curtailed.

Earlier in Jammu, I had chatted with Top Decker Geoff Bowden who had winter tour experience. "Dog … expect the worst—minus thirty and forty-degree temperatures where diesel, oil and even camping gas freezes. Toothpaste freezes and oranges and apples become as solid as cricket balls." At night, Geoff had kept the engine running or he built a small fire under the fuel tank to keep the diesel liquid. Diesel, unlike petrol doesn't explode. "Beware of wind chill," he added, "how fast the wind is blowing. Exposed flesh freezes after about a minute in minus nine degrees centigrade in a 40 kph wind. Keep everything well covered and don't hang around in the elements too long!"

A dog's life

It sounded tough going. As a kid, I read about Ernest Shackleton's 1911 journey to the Antarctic. He advertised in 'The Times'. "Men wanted for hazardous journey. Low wages, bitter cold, long hours ... safe return doubtful. Honour and recognition in event of success." Top Deck could have used that wording for winter overland crew. Safe return = initiative. Still waiting for the honour and recognition.

Iain and I considered driving eight-hour shifts until we reached Goreme. We shared the idea with punters. It was bitterly cold at times. We got the 'green light' to begin.

The countryside was picturesque. Spectacular under deep falls of snow. Snow everywhere. No longer fluffy but iced up. On the ground and drifting through the air. Shrivelled to sharp stinging fragments. Icicles hung from trees. Some of the small towns we passed could have been anywhere but for the mosques with their pencil-thin minarets. The world seemed slow and silent outside the bus. Traffic was light. Occasionally small convoys of vehicles joined us for a short distance and crept along in narrow, snow-rutted lanes in the middle of the road doing twenty-thirty kilometres an hour at the most. Little rooster tails of snow shot up from their back wheels.

Eastern Turkiye

It took Befa three days to traverse Iran, climbing up without incident to 4,000 feet above sea level towards the Central Anatolian plateau.

Parking for the night in nearby snow-shrouded Dogubayazit, 5,000 metre Mount Ararat loomed beside us in the inky darkness. Legend has it that Marco Polo went looking for Noah's Arc "the ship of the world", in 1270. He mentions oil in his diaries. Used to light lamps. So much oil that it could not be loaded onto a thousand camels.

In frontier town Dogubayazit, I found a carpark easily. The place was deserted. It looked like a Hollywood Wild West town except it was under ankle-deep snow. There were other parked vehicles. All were encrusted with hefty layers of snow. Climbing out of the cab I felt punched in the chest by the temperature. It took my breath away. The scene was spectacular. An image I still remember today that I should have caught on film. How many times have you seen a classic shot worth capturing? You don't photograph it and live

to regret that indecision … often long afterwards. It was 'Doctor Zhivago' cinematic quality. Photos fade but not as much as the mind's images.

I walked through crunchy mud. On iced-over puddles. Drifts had iced over on the road curbs and powerlines. I looked past the glassy, slithery road to a two-storied hotel across the street. That could be quite an expedition to get there. Zig-zagging might achieve it. The hotel was lit up like a beacon. The street-level windows were pasted over with snow. I asked after showers but was refused. I exited, peered into other establishments which had their lights on. By the time I wobbled, slipped and slid my way back to the bus, my face was tingling with the cold and going numb. Desensitised. My feet were glacial. My footprints from a few minutes ago were already dusted white. I climbed back in the cab drawing freezing air and a gust of snow with me. Turned on the wipers. They just scraped over the ice. I asked for a mug of hot water and went outside again to pour over the windshield. Inside again, I rubbed the windshield vigorously with my sleeve and huffed and puffed until I had a melted oval hole of clarity.

After scrutinising my Lascelles map, instead of taking the E23 and encountering the icy Tahir Pass, I took a punt and diverted to the military road north through Igdir, Tuzluca, and Kagizman. Snow-laden terrain. The punters were uncomplaining troopers if, on odd occasions, tempers were a little taxed when they were unable to stretch their legs. We were mere kilometres from the Turkish– Armenian frontier. Armenia is on a high rocky plateau at a juncture between Europe and the Middle East. It's said 'it has its head in the west and it's heart in the east'. North of that is Georgia, the birthplace of Josef Stalin.

In the small village of Tuzluca, a highland retreat for asthma patients, I was ripped off when I changed money. I queried the amount the Bank teller had given me but he insisted he was correct. US notes are the same size and colour but have different historical faces to indicate different denominations. The teller got confused. I conceded to his explanation only to realize later … I was right. I am pretty careful with both my own and other's money. Rip-offs rarely happen. Tuzluca was now twenty kilometres behind us. My error. It would have to be deducted from my princely £50.00 a week.

Lonely Planet's "Across Asia on the cheap" describes Eastern Turkiye as the harshest part of the country and as "the area where the opium poppies used to grow and ... the kids, if not egged on by their parents are certainly not restrained and specialise in hurling stones through car windows."

Mooning the Police. *Befa was flagged down several hours inside the Turkish border, en route to Erzurum. Snow was ankle-high. A tall, authoritative police superintendent sauntered up to Iain's cab window, leaned his elbow against the window frame and, other hand out-stretched, palm up, demanded our bus paperwork. He had an intelligent savvy face, hardened by both the summer sun and winter wind. Flicking through our paperwork and apparently finding one item out of date, he curtly summoned Ian and I to the police station, a Spartan wooden building to the side of the road. Beside it was a huge pile of chopped wood in a corrugated iron lean-to. Inside, the wooden floors were strewn with well-worn Turkish kilims and peasant rugs. Three filing cabinets, a large wooden desk cluttered with disorganised paperwork and two smaller tables for the red deputies completed the furniture. A stern Mustafa Kemal frowned down from a photo above the main desk. Beside a clock hung the superintendent's tertiary qualifications.*

Iain and I downed bitter black cay and gratefully warmed ourselves in the heat emanating from the pot-bellied stove. On it sat a double tea-pot, samovar style. The commandant was less concerned with the legitimacy of our paperwork and more about chatting to foreigners. "Where are you from? Where are you going?" He was keen to boast that he was one of the youngest police chiefs in the country.

"I am not surprised," I thought, "this cold, remote location would hardly be sought after by qualified competition." He was more astute than Barney Fife (the archetypal overzealous, inept deputy from the '60s 'The Andy Griffiths Show') but this was far from a thriving metropolis.

As time ticked on, my attention waned and my vision glazed over until, looking through his window, smudged and smeared by road dust ... I was stupefied to see three female punters possessing generous bare bottoms squatting to pee on the far side of our bus. I hastily rose, stuttered and blustered a few hasty words to distract the chief's attention, thinking we were amazingly culturally insensitive. He DID see the three female butts but didn't mind and, stifling a wry grin, waved away my apologies ...

When questioned later the three flashers (or was that mooners?) apologised profusely saying they were caught short! There was a nearby farmer checking his fences so they had limited choices. They were going to flash someone! I thought the obvious solution would have been to ask to use the police station's facilities.

Fifteen minutes later, youths just outside a small township threw missiles accurately and smashed a back window. They scattered before we could catch them. The 'inflated ego' police chief also arrived, but could not find the culprits!

The tour before, Casper and Rag's had taken the alternative **Tahir Pass**, *2400+ feet above sea level. Demanding. Hence I thought for Befa, the military road at lower altitude would be easier. On Casper, I was roused from my sleeping bag just before midnight. "Everyone out!" Still groggy from slumping into a deep sleep after an extended driving period, I descended into a snow storm. Guaranteed to have you awake in seconds. Icy cold. Stinging snow was sleeting down diagonally to assault my face and hands. Casper was descending a winding gravel incline down a gully. Steep banks on either side.*

Inching along. Sliding. I went cab-side where Loxley shouted "Walk in front of the bus, Ian. Can we grip the road or will we slide into that bank?"

The next fifteen minutes was bitterly cold. I was inadequately dressed. The snow was bright in the glare of the spotlights but beyond that it was all guesswork. My face quickly became deadened and my feet were Arctic. I had to stamp them to get circulation moving. My body heat was leaching away ... rapidly. Shivering uncontrollably, I glanced at Casper and through the headlights I could see the wipers swiping snow away in a metronomic rhythm. Behind them Loxley was squinting, peering, rubbing the condensation away from the inside, endeavouring to see the way forward.

Eventually the gradient straightened and flattened out. The punters clambered back in and we made progress.

The next morning, Casper and Rags were confronted with a Turkish articulated truck blocking the road. Its cab hung precariously over a bank. The driver had experienced similar icy issues the night before. Other drivers looked subdued. They puffed on cigarettes and conversed. Stamping up and down on the berm's mud to see if it could take a heavy weight, I stood with Trevor, both silently taking the situation in and weighing up our options. It was the first time I'd seen Trevor go so long without uttering a word. His mind was working overtime. I pointed out a possible way to get our buses around the truck. Trevor pondered.

The passing manoeuvre was successful with Casper but Rags, quickly descended further into the soil to tilt alarmingly. Steve in the cab seemed remarkably calm. Unfazed. I later learned Lodekkas could lean over to an angle of twenty-eight degrees before toppling. A Turkish lorry came to our rescue. Trevor asked if he had a strong cable which he then wrapped around the two towing lugs attached to Rag's chassis.

By reversing, Rags was successfully hauled out of the quagmire.

Lemming found the road to Erzurum corrugated. Like my Scottish grandmother's wooden washboard. Stones popped under our tyres. Lemming alternated between swaying, shuddering or skidding in the thick coarse gravel.

Sitting on the top deck it feels like slow motion, lurching along as if riding a camel. In the cab you experience more of a sensation of 'speed'.

A dog's life

If you can call 60-70 kilometres speeding. Morris, Trish and Jeff all squeezed into the cab at different times to keep Camel or me company. We reached Erzurum by dusk and while dinner was being prepared, some passengers discovered the local liquor shops. Time to 'wet the whistle' and have a drink or two after 'dry' Iran. If nothing else was available, I was prepared to knock back a raki or two. Cheap and potent.

Erzurum is the capital city of Erzurum province, 1,700 metres above sea level. It has a 'wild east' frontier feel. A University city renowned for its impressive Seljuk (1030-1190) architecture and monuments. A NATO Air Force base during the Cold War. The US got upset by nuclear missiles in Cuba in October 1962. 1820 kilometres from Havana to Washington DC. Did this air force base have nuclear warheads? Moscow is only 1800 kilometres away. Tit-for-Tat.

Later we drove to the outskirts, parking overnight only to be hassled by youths wanting to ogle the girls. The girls had to go in pairs to the extremely grotty starting-blocks toilet during the night. One went inside while the other took up sentry outside. I was slumbering downstairs behind the cab and whenever any girls went to the loo, I peered through the curtains to keep an eye on them. Restful sleep?

No! Hygienic conditions? Decidedly not.

The eastern route wound through verdant hills and valleys and alongside clear, fast-flowing streams still fed by snow melt. Civilisation seemed a long way away as did the woes of the world. I liked that concept. Even more so in later years when I became a principal. When the going gets tough, get out into the country. Unwind. Get back to nature. Stress is a temporary, false world.

The scenery was rustic: farmers in the wheat fields were rhythmically slicing their crops with scythes, donkeys hauled carts laden with hay, threshers ground the wheat, old men wore tweed-like vests and flat caps and puffed pipes, women were hunched over in the fields. Hayfields were stubby after being baled. Life as it used to be. Life as it should be.

Away from Sivas by 6.00 a.m., I soon spied another inviting stream where Camel and I, forgoing all inhibitions, stripped off completely and plunged in. This was rather rash as we quickly realised that the stream, fed by snowmelt, was frigid. Thankfully, it was too early for female punters to witness the rapid shrinking of our 'family jewels'.

I have seen a few Top Deck photos over the years of buses taking advantage of unexpected but very welcome opportunities to get clean and feel fresh in mountain streams.

The landscape changed from lush to dry in **Cappadocia**. Urgup's camping ground was crowded. The height of the summer season as compared with my March and November visits. Stretching out before us were panoramas of olive trees, vineyards, layered dry-stone walls and serrated bluish hills in the distance peppered with windows and doors. Troglodyte-style cave dwellings. Surreal.

With punters I spring-cleaned the bus then took my leave to stroll into **Urgup** to arrange a national meal. Urgup's a favourite. Idiosyncratic and quirky. Steep decline. Houses sculpted from honey-coloured, russet-brown and even pink rock and stone. Some house facades contained Greek columns. Others had Seljuk or Ottoman influences. The house exteriors depicted a range of past empires. Did the owners know that?

Some were new. Hewn out of the soft rock of the hill behind Urgup. There was plenty of greenery with family parks scattered about. The region grows a variety of vegetables and fruit here and made quality wine in the mineral-enriched volcanic soil.

Purely by chance, I came across Assiz, carrying a stack of cardboard grocery boxes containing vegetables, his head just visible over the top. "Merhaba, Assiz. Is that you?" He grinned recognising me. 5'8". Black hair. Lean. Thick moustache. Genuine personality. One of the delights of being a tour leader is meeting up with locals on successive tours.

If travelling west to London, I usually arranged our first Turkish National meal in Urgup. If travelling east to Kathmandu, we would go to the Galata Tower. A study in contrasts.

I had taken Befa's group to a restaurant and got chatting to Humdi, a Turkish secondary school teacher who was seated at a table behind me. We got into an animated discussion about education. As you do. A worthwhile topic to get passionate about. Later Humdi heard me propose a toast to "Turkey my favourite country." Accepting that as a compliment, he slipped away to fetch Assiz who played the Saz, a balalaika-type instrument with a long narrow neck and a distinctive sound. Word of mouth quickly got around and other musicians miraculously materialized. The songs they played on the saz were folk songs about unrequited love and sadness or … as we discovered that night—joy, happiness and pleasure.

A rousting, very energetic evening of **Turkish music and dancing** *followed. Memorable. The girls were less inhibited than the guys and hauled the bashful up to dance. We were all flushed, perspiring and breathing deeply by the end. Such generosity and hospitality by locals! I offered to buy the musicians a beer or raki. They refused. Their pleasure!*

As our group weaved their less than sober way up to the campsite, there was a very satisfied vibe. "Dog! An exceptional night. Well done."

For some reason my world was spinning. Ahh… the Raki!

That earned you a few brownie points … err, a bone or two, Dog.

Piddle had been driving with us in tandem. In Zahedan they were still waiting for punters to return from exploring a local mountain when we left. We expected them to catch up within a day.

They didn't.

One of their punters fell from the mountain and was killed. Piddle diverted to Tehran to make funeral arrangements. Arriving in Urgup late that afternoon, they were badly in need of alcoholic frivolity and a chance to grieve. Just the tonic!

An empty bunk space was a constant reminder of that tragedy.

A dog's life

This was the second death of a punter I'd encountered on an overland tour. The other death was that of a fellow punter on Capricorn P33H. Overlands are not to be taken lightly.

Assiz now owned the Cimenli Restaurant, which he proudly ushered me around. It was only fitting to book his restaurant for Lemming's punters. A 'win-win'. I bet he would call on his musicians again. I negotiated a price for: meze (starters) and vine leaves stuffed with rice, herbs and nuts. Fried eggplant. Deep-fried cigar-shaped pastries. Then Adana kebabs and Iskenderun kebabs. The Efes beer and raki would be at punters' expense!

During the meal, Assiz snuck off to gather his maestros. Another rousting night of terrific Turkish food with intoxicating alcohol, music and dancing ensued. I tried to master the Turkish 'line dancing'. On the surface similar to Greek sirtaki dancing. I thought I was doing a reasonable job of getting it even if I wasn't up to Alexis Zorba's standards. But then again, I'd had a couple of Efes followed by a raki chaser.

Cappadocia was created 30 million years ago when volcanoes covered the region in ash with solidified into easily erodible 'tuff' overlain in places by harder volcanic rock. Over time the 'tuff' eroded further leaving towers of 'fairy chimneys', either cone-shaped, mushroom-shaped or phallic like.

Punters explored the rock formations, some of the girls staring long, hard and admiringly at the 'erections', blushing, giggling discreetly behind their hands or laughing raucously out loud. Others scrambled up steep stony banks or climbed slanting, angled slopes or spindly fragile ladders to explore the caves. Some caves had faded damaged frescoes of a bygone Byzantine era. Brilliant colours now faded and scratched out by vandals. There were living areas, tables and benches carved out of the stone, drains and circular depressions where grapes had been trampled for their juices. Wow! Sophisticated.

After school, Humdi drove me to see a hermit who had a dwelling hollowed out of the sandstone cliffs. We passed veiled women riding donkeys home from the fields and men wearing flat caps and tweed-like jackets on carts loaded with produce driven by mules. The house had an expansive view over olive and vine groves. It had been shaped

A dog's life

around an earlier Christian abode and had a long spacious porch. Inside were shelves hewn out of sandstone rock on which were precariously perched books, a television set and a cassette player. All out of context with the natural rock surroundings. Another surreal moment. We had cay on the porch. At times I had to force myself to concentrate on the engaging conversation as I was mesmerised by the view. Wow. Simple but almost inconceivable. I was privileged to be experiencing this.

By now, I had driven excessively and pushed myself hard. I was tired and grouchy. Grumpy and curmudgeon-like. Sleep deprivation. Totally my fault. I should have let Camel drive more. He was a gem to work with and his mechanical skills kept *Lemming* humming along without a noticeable hitch. His spadework (courting) had been successful and he and Jan were an item. Although opposites! Therein lay the attraction. He was more than happy to let me drive anytime I wanted.

Somewhere in the Goreme valley I got into an animated discussion with effervescent Cress and said something inappropriate. As guys are wont to do. Cress burst into tears. Dramatically. Theatrically. Loudly.

I almost had a panic attack. My normal reaction to my making women cry. The incident attracted everyone's attention. Instantly. All female frowns and scowls swivelled my way, like a bank of Gatling machine guns. I could hear the ammunition being chambered. I was not a popular chappie.

Haven't been that way since Khetri House, Jaipur!

Dog! Time out! Into the doghouse.

I needed sleep. Uninterrupted. Recharge the batteries. I was attempting that the next morning when two punters, with impeccable timing, knocked and asked …then pleaded … to shower. Graciously I said yes but this generosity backfired. Playtime! We became juvenile again. A water-fight and much flicking of towels towards derrières followed. Towels and clothes were hidden by the two not having a shower and much flesh was displayed. The tour leader did *not* achieve a sleep-in. But he did have fun.

One came back late that evening to apologise for the earlier interruption, admonished me for trying to do two jobs and acting like a grizzly with a sore head. I agreed. She suggested I de-stress and recommended that I needed to sleep, meditate and have a soothing massage! Perhaps all three.

Maybe she could help …

On two of my tours, I took groups to the underground cities—either at Kaymaki or Derinkuyu. They are linked by kilometres of tunnels. Each city is least eight stories deep, built to protect people from their prosecutors of the day. You have to stoop low, walk down steps, through corridors and past labyrinthine rooms, churches and mills. Wine-making areas have holes in the ceiling above where grapes were dropped to be trampled. The juice flow off via channels to the next part of the wine-making process. 'Conference' rooms had sculpted long tables with bench seats either side all sculpted out of rock. At times, round sculptured stones, Indiana Jones style, could be rumbled into place separating one area from another. The temperature is fresh and cool but even.

A dog's life

A side trip to Ankara and Istanbul

Lemming journeyed to Ankara to secure those essential but elusive Syrian visas. Ankara has been the capital of Turkey since 1923. There was a Hittite settlement there 4,000 years ago. Often one settlement builds on the remains of a past settlement, chosen originally for its strategic location, its height compared to the surrounding hinterland and its water and food supplies. We negotiated our way through a maze of narrow busy streets to the Cankaya diplomatic enclave to drop off the visa applications. "Come back in two days."

We inspected the Ataturk memorial. Stark and Soviet-like, all concrete pillars and columns and sharp-edged angles. Deciding that two days would be better spent in Istanbul than Ankara, we headed north-west. Crossing the 1974 Bosporus suspension bridge into Europe, the punters had fantastic views on both sides. I activated the sound system and pointed out "The Sea of Marmara and ultimately the Aegean is that side and on the other side, the Bosphorus flows into the Black Sea. Hence Istanbul's strategic trading position." Upstairs they jostled each other for the best camera angles as we laboriously lumbered over.

A significant number of Istanbul's highlights are in the Sultan Ahmet area. I escorted the punters around St Sophia, the Blue Mosque, the hippodrome, the underground cisterns and the Topkapi Palace. Some bought leather and suede jackets at the Grand Bazaar. I telexed London to cancel Julia's Beerfest trip (as we could be detouring there) and learned that the Syrian border post was now issuing visas again. Our long detour was unnecessary!

On most tours, I acquired visas quickly and smoothly. It was rare for me to get the runaround. I did have a visa incident on a Tracks Russia/Scandinavian in Moscow which could have turned out badly. Driver

Jack and I went to the Polish Embassy. Jack was enterprising and entrepreneurial, a competent driver with a very good sense of direction but wasn't offered a job as tour leader because, his mentor argued, "He was overconfident and too cocksure of himself."

After eventually edging our way to the front of the queue, we leaned against the counter awaiting our turn. Without warning, Jack offered the official a bribe for immediate service. "What?" growled the official rising abruptly and tipping his chair over. "Do you think we're a third world country? Get out of here." Jack immediately exited stage left. Like the Hanna-Barbera 1960s cartoon character Snagglepuss. Heavens to Murgatroyd, what a blunder.

The official returned to his desk to return to his work. He sharply rounded on me. "Are you with him?" I have a range of responses to the unexpected. Now was the time for the 'innocent, gormless look.' It worked a treat. He took my bundle of passports and surprisingly said "Come back in two hours." I was expecting two days. I found the nearby café where Jack was having a coffee and eating humble pie. I ordered an expresso and a caviar and salmon open sandwich and joined him. "Well, *that* strategy worked a treat didn't it?" I chuckled as I sat down.

A dog's life

I booked a meal at the **Galata Tower**. It dates from the 1200s and has previously been a prison, an observatory and a fire-lookout tower before becoming a night club in the late 1960s.

On London-bound tours, I managed the food kitty so that we could afford a meal at the Galata. Not to be missed. We had already eaten delicious Turkish restaurant food in Urgup but the Galata with its night-club feel, floor show and spectacular night vistas over Istanbul was a marked contrast. Camel agreed to drive us back to the campsite so I could have a raki or two. Camel liked his beer and was looking forward to the Oktoberfest. A sensible trade-off.

Raki is anise and twice-distilled grapes. 45% alcohol by volume. Served with chilled water and ice cubes it gives a milky affect. 'Lion's milk'. The mark of a man.

The show was entertaining. Exotic. Skilled. The belly dancers had supreme control over their body's individual muscles. Each part seemed to be the focus for mere nanoseconds in time with the music—the arms above the head, wrists entwined and palms outwards, hands then slinking out snake-like, the shimmering of the hips either slowly swaying or in rapid motion, the twitching of the shoulders up and down, the bouncing of the boobs in time to the music, the belly muscles sucking in and out.

The first belly dancer was well-endowed and knew how to tremble and shimmy. The next had a plunging neckline and her blouse was only just restraining its two occupants which displayed considerable buoyancy in their efforts to shake free. Up and down. And ... side to side. She elicited a chorus of male catcalls and appreciation.

Yet another spectacular sight was seen from the balcony looking at Istanbul by night. Expansive views. A myriad of twinkling white and yellow lights lit up the shadowy mounds of the surrounding hills. The mosques on the hills over the Bosphorus glowed vividly under their spotlights. Sparkling bright stars. Salty sea breeze. I inhaled deeply. Invigorating. I reflected on the stark contrast. Sophistication in Istanbul. A few days ago, home-grown music and dancing in Urgup.

Returning to Ankara, I collected the passports and visas and we were off but not before Jeff grated the bus under a low bridge and Camel drove up a blind one-way alley.

Lemming's radiator boiled over crossing the Pontic Mountains. Later I sat on the bonnet to pour water over it. Don't know what effect that would have but I did as I was told. We were rescued by a young village girl with a jug of water. Floral cotton dress. Dirty bare feet. Urchin haircut. Engaging smile. Like a female cast member from 'Oliver'. Waiting for the engine to cool we stretched our legs. I breathed in the sharp crisp smell of the pine trees and sweet-smelling wildflowers. Intoxicating. Like inhaling weed but not mind-befuddling. Back to nature.

We pulled over for breakfast in a small mountain village where I cajoled several strips of fatty steak from a local farmer-come-butcher-come-opportunist entrepreneur. Our evening meal.

When I returned in June 2019, I was hoping to repeat the mountain village experience. Seclusion. Isolation. An idyllic forest location. Flowers. Pine trees. Ahhh … the smells. Villagers untainted by the modern world. A motorway now cuts travelling times in half between the interior and the coast. Those unique villages have been bypassed. At times we saw stalls from mountain villages alongside the motorway. They had trekked kilometres to sell their goods. Progress? Yes. Retaining and looking after the rural folk? No.

Syria: Peace be upon you

The Turkish/Syrian border was jam-packed and congested. Lined with dusty, heavy-duty vehicles, dirty juggernauts, articulated multi-wheeled lorries loaded with merchandise. The rumbling and burbling of engines reverberated. The stench of diesel. I liked that smell, and as with the smell of jet fuel, associated it with travelling, adventure and particularly overlands. Drivers clutching well-thumbed, dog-eared papers shouldered, shoved and squeezed their way through scrums to get to customs and immigration counters. We weathered our way through the Syrian border in just over three hours. Par for the course.

At one point, a Syrian officer, chatted to me. He wily softened me up with small talk for five minutes then threw in the innocuous remark, "Enjoy the West Bank." I was half-expecting something devious like this so he received my innocent look. "We're not going there. Just to Jordan —Amman, Petra and Aqaba." As soon as I could, I hustled back to the bus to recount the incident to the punters downstairs. "*Don't* be fooled by him. We are *not* going to Disneyland (our code for Israel). Pass the word on to those upstairs." I took the paperwork from one station to another. Once through, I found a bunk and let Camel take over.

Lemming parked overnight in a parched area inside the border, flanked by a high barbed-wire fence. The middle of nowhere. Barren, dirty, dusty, rubbish-strewn. The countryside was dark red and brown. The majority of fields looked rich and fertile and well-tended while those further afield were dry and desiccated. The landscape was dotted with villages of flat-roofed, one-roomed mud huts enclosed by high walls to form a small private compound. The beehive-shaped houses were used for cooking. More than two thirds of Syria's people work the soil, producing fruit, tobacco (widely consumed), sugar, wheat, cotton and barley.

1980's Syria was a socialist state of eight million people headed by the autocratic Hafez al-Hassad. From the minority Alawite sect. He ruled by force. A 'strongman'. Every time I was there, a rebellion was occurring in Hama, Homs or Aleppo. *In February whilst on Befa, government forces were crushing a rebellion. Armed soldiers were on the roads, lorries with tanks on the back, half trucks with swivel machine guns, tanks and artillery were everywhere.*

On Befa a few punters were taking snapshots of the military activity. When an officer boarded with me a few minutes later, all cameras had disappeared. When the officer commanded. "No taking of photographs", there was a innocent chorus of "Of course not!" from a bevy of upstanding-looking punters. Motorboat was one. He had hastily stowed his camera into the locker of the seat he was sitting on.

24th August 1980. Ahhhh ... a day 'Dog' will remember!

In the 'dog house' that day.

Doing my morning driving stint, I steered towards Damascus. Punters were slumbering. I passed several dusty desolate villages. In one, armed youths stood idly chatting around a table alongside the road. I was intending to drive past with a cursory wave but a machine-gun toting youth strutted out in front of me and held up his arm, palm out. Stop!

Do I ignore and drive past or be cautious and humour him? I climbed down to answer questions and show him my passport and bus carnet. Another macho youth, scarcely past the angry red pimple stage, was particularly cocky. He strode with unmistakable arrogance and demanded an inspection of the bus. I showed him around downstairs and his interest was aroused when he saw drowsy female punters with their pale shoulders exposed in their sleeping bags. Maybe something else was aroused too. He stipulated we go upstairs.

Against my better judgment, I escorted three to the Top Deck. Punters started to stare back in curiosity. The elder of the three militiamen was satisfied but when I touched Mr. Macho on the elbow (as he prodded at a half-obscured black object under Morris' pillow) and tried to steer him outside, he reacted, jabbering to his mate in a bellicose manner.

A dog's life

He ordered me outside. His colleagues raised their Kalashnikovs and ordered me to raise my hands. "Really guys???!!!" By now punters on the top deck were staring down at me with eyes wide and mouths in an O shape.

I called out to Jeff, appointed as a trainee driver, to go upstairs with them as a 'representative' of Top Deck. (Camel was probably still out to it. A deep sleeper that boy! Or … preoccupied.) This manoeuvre was instantly discouraged when one of the militiamen unholstered a stubby black pistol and stuck it into Jeff's midriff. Jeff's enthusiasm at being employed by Top Deck disappeared immediately, his face draining of colour and expression.

Upstairs the militiamen were persuaded by the older, wiser one that the suspected black gun under the pillow was actually Morris' 8 mm movie camera (with a handle) and nothing was untoward. They descended the stairs cackling and guffawing. Macho man signalled his mates to lower their guns. He clapped me on the shoulder and said I could go.

It's interesting how you react in situations like this. I wasn't frightened. I wasn't in danger. Nor were the punters. These dickheads wouldn't want to create an international incident by harming budget tourists. I was just angry! Pumped up and egotistical youths! Grrrrrr!

As *Lemming* motored away there was a distinctive buzz amongst the punters, a palpable sense of animation and exhilaration. It's not every day you see machine-gun toting militiamen arresting the tour leader on his own bus.

Pip, being a Pom, asked me if I would like a cup of tea. That brew, that 'English cuppa', seems to solve everything.

Someone else (an Aussie?) asked me if I wanted something stronger!

Yes! A double bourbon.

Photo: Jeff in happier times before his midriff was introduced to the muzzle of a gun.

Jeff was the centre of attention after initially sitting in a stupefied silence with a blank, unseeing 'thousand yard' stare. I chuckled as I drove for I could swear his voice was a few octaves higher than normal. He would probably dine out on that story a few times in the decades to come. Like the proverbial 'fish catch' story, I wondered if the retelling would get better with each rendition...

I told Morris he had failed 'Filmmaking 101.' All that drama and his 8mm camera was still snug under his pillow. He didn't shoot a frame.

Mark Stephen Bannerman later wrote on the Top Deck website that he had an almost identical scenario in October '81 on *Crunch*. "... but driver Bill Woodhouse *didn't* stop. 100 metres down the road a second checkpoint sprayed the road with a Kalashnikov and a couple of rounds went into the roof above the engine bay. Never known a decker to stop so quick. No one injured thankfully and International incident avoided."

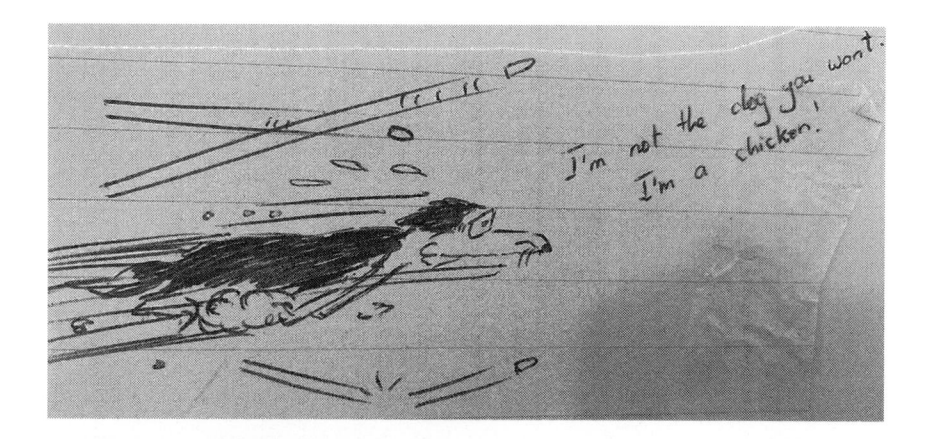

I'm not the dog J, I'm a chicken. won't.

In **Hama** we observed the giant 2,000 year old waterwheels which were 20 metres in diameter. The Norias or "wheel of pots". You could hear the creaking and groaning of the giant water wheels before you caught sight of them.

They were originally designed to distribute water to farms nearby. Now they are more for show. A history lesson.

There were uniformed soldiers with Kalashnikovs stationed on every corner. Trouble was brewing. Yet another protest against the central government.

'**Damascus Camping**', very Spartan, was the venue for *Lemming's* punters to freshen up after sleeping rough. The corpulent campsite owner, belly straining against his shirt buttons, had greasy, greying, receding hair slicked back around his ears, one of which harboured a cigarette, the other a stubby red pencil. He acted as if *he* was doing *us* a big favour by allowing us here. He took his time 'serving' me. There was no one else in the reception area. His voice had the gravelly tinge of many a cigarette. Charging us each seven Syrian £ he added 5 Syrian £ per head for using 'his' swimming pool. Fellow campers told us that they didn't have to pay for the swimming pool. (Approximately 4 Syrian £ to the US $).

Telling him we had fifteen punters, I handed him fifteen passports. By the time he swaggered over to count numbers, punters were everywhere – showers, toilets, the pool, the cooking facilities… Ha, ha. Two can play your game, Buddy. At campsites, I would understate the number of punters. Gave me pleasure with this guy. He was not smart enough to ask for a typed pax list with the passports. Leave that to Munich and the Thalkirchen campsite.

Damascus' history dates back 5,000 years—Abraham, the Assyrians, Alexander, Pompey, Herod, the Umayyads, the Abbasids, the Seljuks, Saladin, the Ottomans, T.E. Lawrence, the Australian 2nd Light Horse Brigade…

Damascus is the oldest, continuously inhabited city in the world. Dominated by its large central square with gardens and water fountains, a myriad of streets and alleys branch off. Also dominant are portraits of President Hafez-al-Assad plastered to building walls. Damascus was crowded and bustling. We bought fresh fruit which was in abundance, oranges hanging enticingly in string baskets over shop entrance ways. Freshly squeezed fruit made delicious thirst-quenching drinks. The local speciality, a banana yoghurt lassi, was a stand out. Ice cubes (of doubtful water quality), keep it chilled.

Delectable mouth-watering kebabs are sold in open-fronted shops where you can see the chef preparing them. It's difficult to resist lamb shish-kebabs sizzling away. It's also hard not to be fascinated by the chicken or lamb döner kebabs cooked on a vertical rotisserie. The meat is seasoned and packed as an inverted cone around a steel rod. This turns slowly on the vertical rotisserie next to the cooking element. The outer layer is sliced into thin shavings with a sharp, wicked-looking, sabre-like knife. After it cooks, it is wrapped in flat bread to which various sauces are added ... ahhhh ... delicious!

Other entrepreneurs, without shops, sell kebabs sitting on the curb side. Rectangular metal trays are beside them, filled with hot coals over which sits a hot plate or grill on which a dozen kebabs sizzle. The smoke waffling up as you made your way past and the smell ... Sooooo enticing! They probably only expected to sell to locals but an ever-hungry kiwi tour leader with a cast-iron stomach ...

Punters bargained for goodies in Straight Street which stretches 1500 metres. It dates back to Roman times. Referred to in 'Acts' in the bible, as a street where the Apostle Paul stayed, several shops are built into the original Roman wall.

It includes the covered **Al-Hamidiyah souk**. The souk is a riot of hustle and bustle, vivid colours, food smells and entrancing perfumes and fragrances. You can find every spice imaginable, leather jackets, shoes and bags, intricate jewellery.

Towards the end of the souk, branch off to visit the imposing **Umayyad Mosque,** one of the oldest Islamic sites of continuous prayer in the world and said to contain the head of John the Baptist and the mausoleum of Saladin, the Sunni Kurd who fought the crusaders in the twelfth century. We quietly and respectfully observed masses of the faithful at prayer, men in one area and women in another. I was impressed by the numbers and their devotion. If it meets their needs …

In Islamic countries, I find the call to prayer by the muezzin five times a day calming and soothing. At dawn, the call to prayer usually makes me smile. It's like a clock's alarm to get up.

On the last tour, I collected punters from Befa and Piddle to go to the 'Hamman Nureddin' between Straight Street and the Ummayad Mosque. The major Turkish bath in Damascus. There are separate entrances and facilities for men and women. You strip off in a small cubicle and wrap yourself in a large fluffy white towel and sip cay until called.

Wearing the thin disposable underwear provided, as well as flip flops, you enter the sauna to be tenderised, to build up a sweat for 15 minutes. After that you proceed into a larger communal section, often an ornately marble room with high ceilings and skylights for natural lighting, where you wait for an attendant.

Now for the exfoliation treatment!

The attendant lathers you up with soap to rub and scrub you down vigorously with a coarse mitten and an exfoliant paste. Then more washing and rinsing in cold water. The extremes of boiling and then freezing temperatures are exhilarating. Layers of dead skin peel off you. The first time I had this treatment was in Istanbul's 'Cagaloglu Baths'. A few days beforehand, I had a game of squash and had been hit in the left nipple by the squash ball. I was in agony when the attendant brushed the bristly mitten repeatedly over my chest. Not only that but the dead skin removal leaves you pink and raw like a cooked crayfish.

A massage followed. To be recommended at least once but these are <u>not</u> relaxing! I thought I was being torn apart limb by limb. I wondered how my arms could get into such unnatural contortions without snapping. After the first punter had the massage, he was asked "Did you lose any weight?"

"Yes—about sixteen stone once he got off my back!"

I had to smile as we lounged back on cushions in our fluffy white towels sipping cay like distinguished gentlemen. Thirty minutes before we were tossing water at each other and flicking towels at our bare butts like secondary school boys. Brett squirmed a little as he sat and reflected rather uncomfortably that he must have "the cleanest a*rsehole in Damascus". He'd also had a free prostate examination.

Jordan

South into **Jordan**. In 1980, Jordan had a population of two million spread over 95,000 square kilometres. Most of it dusty, desolate desert. Uninhabitable. The economy is predominantly agricultural with none of Iraq's oil wealth. Like Syria, it was drawn up with a ruler under the Sykes-Picot agreement during the disintegration of the Ottoman Empire. Tribal and ethnic affiliations were not considered. The Hashemite Kingdom of Jordan was dismembered by the Israelis after the 1967 six day war. It is one of the friendlier Arab countries to westerners. King Hussein had been on the throne since 1953 and was a moderate Arab leader compared to Syria's Hafez al-Hassad.

Jerash is 50 kilometres from Amman, the name deriving from the Greek for elderly. Alexander the Great despatched his loyal, ageing, war-hardened generals to establish a city, later becoming part of the Roman province of Syria under Pompey in 63 BC. Its prosperity was based on mining, agriculture and the caravan trade.

We arrived two hours before full darkness. No problem. A full moon beamed through wispy feathery clouds high above. Perfect timing. 'Fast food shops' opened onto some streets, identifiable by circular holes in the stone where cooks placed bowls to heat food.

Lemmings' punters wandered a colonnaded street 600 metres long and over paving stones burnished and buffed by feet, hooves and chariots. We visited three theatres and two public baths. There were brothels with suggestive etchings carved in stone above entrance ways. Punters walked the ruins of the Temple of Zeus and the hippodrome.

Atmospheric. I suggested we collect our sleeping bags and sleep in the huge oval forum. Most thought that a brilliant idea. I didn't fetch my sleeping bag as a grinning punter, her eyebrows doing the Tom Selleck as Magnum twitch, offered to share hers. Parts of the ruins were shrouded in darkness. Some of the columns caught the moonlight, casting long shadows. Our shadows were elongated as though we were walking on stilts. Silence. Ghostly.

What a treat to sleep in a Roman forum and wake up at dawn.

The capital **Amman**, the Old Testament's 'Rabbath Ammon', I find dusty, dry and unattractive. Little greenery to break the monopoly of white flat-roofed houses. Despite Roman ruins, including a 6,000 seat amphitheatre, it is a place for administrative work before heading elsewhere.

Parking in the 'third circle', the punters went shopping in Mercedes taxis. I descended on the Intercontinental to request tour funds, requisition bus parts, cancel Julia's Beerfest tour as we were probably heading there anyway or arrange further tours for punters.

```
TCC JO
007509 AUG 27 1130 PTS
0518955339+
8955339TOPD G

21.

ATTEN: BRIAN.

    CANCEL JULIA RALSTON'S B.F. TRIP. BILL JAMES HAS AUTHORISED
JEFF SPANN AS TRAINEE. RECEIVED 1000 POUNDS. MANY THANKS. WITH
SAVING AND 4 WEEKS TO GO HAVE 700 POUNDS IN FOOD KITTY TO PAY OUT
ALONE. EXPLORING POSSIBILITIES OF SAIL POWER. PRAYING FOR STRONG
TAIL WINDS TO JOIN YOU AT B.F.

CHEERS. DOG AND CAMEL.
21267 JORHTL JO

8955339TOPD G

058H.))000. 5 MINS
```

One unexpected experience *happened on Casper when the two buses were invited to the Royal Amman Racecourse. We stood out in the bar in our western attire. Arabs wore the white flowing 'dish-dasha' robes with either black and white checked or red and white checked 'shemaghs' or 'keffiyehs' on their heads. They looked sophisticated. Imperious. The event turned out a quaint, very 'country' affair. The horses in the first race failed to take the first bend. With glass of alcohol in hand, mine a chilled rum and coke, friends around you and in the comfort of a well-appointed bar, this could be a day at the races in Ellerslie or Flemington. But No! Those smug regal animals with the prolonged snout and long effeminate eyelashes ambling up to the start line were camels.*

Once started, the camels seem to amble for three quarters of the course then broke into a canter when in sight of the finish line.

A nearby Jordanian said, "Camels are lazy. They only really get a move on if they want to mate."

This did not appear to be the mating season.

Petra, means 'rock' or 'stone' and was on the Silk Road trading route. Inhabited by nomadic Arabic tribes, the Nabateanens, they initially raided the spice and silk caravans before earning better money by imposing taxes. More lucrative, less dangerous. Becoming a client state of Rome in the 1St Century, the Romans built cobbled colonnaded streets and an amphitheatre.

Its inhabitants moved on when alternative 'silk roads' became more viable. For centuries it was probably only known by the Bedouin, then in 1812 it was rediscovered by a young Swiss, a convert to Islam.

A dog's life

Accessible through the narrow gorge (siq) the walls tower 150 metres on either side. In parts they are less than two metres apart blocking out the sun's rays and heat. It is quiet and still, the solitude broken only by the crunching of the stones under our boots. It is a fitting approach to the fabled site rediscovered in 1812.

The first structure glimpsed is the 40-foot-high treasury, Al Khazneh, dating back to 56BC. Motorboat's photo above is of Jo-Anne outside the Treasury. The amphitheatre is close by and the colonnaded street further down and en route to the monastery.

Photo below: Capricorn P33H punters settling for the night opposite Petra's amphitheatre.

On two out of my three tours as tour leader, I encouraged punters to sleep in the caves directly opposite the Roman amphitheatre. The best time to see Petra is at dusk as the sun goes down. The sunlight bounces off the rocks in hues of yellow, orange and brown. Before the sun disappears for the night it turns the desert orange and then a fiery red. The colour changes are in reverse at dawn when the sun rises. The ever-changing plays of light from the desert create a photographer's nirvana.

My first sleepover was on Capricorn's P33H. Under a full moon, Liz and I walked the cobblestones of the Roman road, flanked by Roman columns on either side. I can still see that scene. Feel the roughness of the cobblestones. See the deep grooves between them. See the ruts made by the chariots. Feel the breeze. Smell the desert. See the quality of the light. We were chatting and reminiscing. Dark shadows thrown by the columns made them look like sentries at attention. Watching over us. Dramatic. Romantic. Cinematic quality.

Arctic temperatures and a dusting of light snow discouraged us from sleeping in the caves in February. Any other time, we swept our torches thoroughly around the red dust on the floors of the mop caves—snakes and scorpions anywhere? Wolves could be heard howling, far away in the distance.

I 'got a kick' out of waking up opposite an amphitheatre. Like Epidaurus in Greece, this was built into the side of a hill in the Hellenistic style. It was used for 'the arts' not blood sports. How many people get to do that? This one is partially carved out of rock and has three tiers seating 8,000 people. I like to just sit down in a back row and let the scene wash over me, letting my subconscious wander.

I roused everyone at dawn to climb up 1500 metres to view the monastery (next photo), where Trish, Morris and Jeff, all with a head for heights, would later clamber over. Some punters purchased a cup of black chai, slightly bitter, at a local Bedouin stall. I had sought out the owner the evening before to warn him of our wake-up time. He was keen on earning a little money. Every dina supported his family of five. His smiling, barefooted, eight-year-old, raggamuffin daughter assisted him. She was at that cute age when she was losing her front milk teeth. When she grinned, it was a winsome smile displaying gaps in her top teeth. She confidently carried a silver tray on which were balanced several small glasses of chay on silver saucers. Plus spoons and sugar cubes.

On Capricorn P33H, Bedouins still dwelled in the caves. They drew water from a well. Swept their caves clean with long brooms that witches would have envied. Cooked on primus stoves. Tethered the donkey in a nearby cave. They were friendly and welcoming and, laying down newspaper as a table cloth, they invited punters Cliff and Caroline to share their breakfast of fruit and yoghurt. Although, according to the Trip Book, Caroline didn't realise the newspaper was the tablecloth and walked all over it. On that tour, a Swiss Miss had a Bedouin partner. Her father was about to gift them a much prized goat. A goat = Milk. Cheese. On another tour, a Kiwi girl was married to a Bedouin cave dweller. Those inhabitants were later moved to a village two kilometres away and Petra became a UNESCO World heritage site. How the area has changed in 2023.

Climbing at 30+ degree angles, we eventually discovered Al Dier monastery, 40 metres high. A spectacular structure with extensive views. Breathtaking.

The air is still and silent.

Sitting atop the urn above the monastery you could see the Jordan valley and the Dead Sea through the haze. Towering rocks and peaks, sheer drops in dark shadow to deep valleys. No apparent life.

I wandered away from the chatter to marvel at the construction techniques that created the Monastery and Treasury. And the views.

I let my mind wander. It often does gymnastics, one association triggering another. My reflection was interrupted by elfin punter, Sabrina, who, by opening her lips instantly declared herself an airhead, albeit a cute one. "Is *this* ALL we came ALL this way for Ian?"

Duh? Grrrrrr! Remind yourself, Ian. She's just like your imaginary irritating little sister Ian. Patience!

At the cafe at the Siq's entrance, we relaxed over coffees. I savoured a small Turkish coffee in a minute ornate glass. One by one, the girls slipped away to the restroom to strip down and have a thorough wash.

Some used the hand basins to try and have an overall wash because ... the next apparition in front of me was a big bear of a man, slightly scruffy and unkempt, grubby-aproned and crimson-faced whose burly meaty hands were wielding a mop and a bucket as though they were weapons. He grumbled that *his* restroom was awash with water! I closed my eyes for a second ... or two or three ... inhaled deeply, identified the likely miscreants, shook my head gently, did the obligatory eye roll and muttered "Really girls? Ever heard of discretion? Or subtlety?"

From **Petra** it was a short run down Highway 35 to find **Wadi Rum**. South of El Quweira. East of Aqaba. At one stage we saw an expanded section of the highway which the Jordanian Air Force had constructed. It was used by jets to refuel before venturing forth to support Egypt in the Sinai during the 1967 six-day war.

Wadi Rum. The launching pad for T.E. Lawrence's raids on Turkish railways to disrupt war munition delivery in WW1. Wadi Rum means 'the valley of light airborne sand'. It is carved out of sandstone and granite rock. Massive red and grey towering cliffs with single or multiple domes dominate rippled desert sands. Some have natural bridge-like arches.

As *Lemming* turned off the highway and bumped along the narrow side road, I slipped Maurice Jarre's Oscar-winning 'Lawrence of Arabia' film soundtrack into the sound system. It captures the majestic feeling of vast sand dunes and the wide open desert. The music complements the action. There is also incidental music that accompanies the Arab tribes. Poms Pip and Heather were obviously indoctrinated by the film on UK TV every Christmas. They grinned, nodding in recognition.

Lemming pulled to a stop and we descended. The place is still. Silent. Dwarfed by towering cliffs. Two long black Bedouin tents were clustered together. Three people were inside the nearest tent, a mother and two toddlers ... A ten-year-old girl gave me a shy hesitant wave. Childhood innocence. She stood on a small mound tending a handful of black goats idly chewing on a clump of tussock. Not much of a feed there. A makeshift animal shelter of bleached white poles covered with numerous hides was nearby. Several children give us a wave and come running over. They jammed on their brakes and proceeded more cautiously the closer they got to us.

I saw David Lean's film when I was eleven. Little did I realise I would visit the area several times. Appreciated the film more as an adult. Intelligent screenplay. Compelling performance by Peter O'Toole. Omar Sharif as Sherif Ali was deservedly nominated for best supporting actor. A screen-eating performance by Anthony Quinn as Arab chieftain Aida Abu Tayi. It won Academy Awards for Best Film, Best Direction, Best Editing, Best Sound and Best Cinematography.

T.E. Lawrence was duped by his superiors—firstly British officers, colonels and generals and then further up the pay scales by politicians. He fused an assortment of independent rival feuding Arab tribes together to fight the Turks, believing the tribes would be granted independence after the war. Unbeknownst to him, in 1916, Sykes and Picot had already divided up the area for Britain and France at war's end with pencil and ruler.

Lawrence proposed a state of Greater Syria taking into account tribal and religious—Sunni/Shiite—affiliations, alliances and territories, a smaller Lebanon and a small Palestinian state. Autonomous regions for Kurds and Armenians. Forward thinking for 1917.

I was impressed by the site when I first saw it on Capricorn's P33H. Rugged. Feral. The scattered Bedouin tents. The same as in Lawrence's time? 2,000 years before that? A bony Bedouin woman invited us in for a cay. Very lean, sun-scorched leathery skin. Yellow uneven teeth, some jagged. A smile in her eyes. We were invited to sit on mats.

Several raggedy scallywags ventured in to inspect us. The matriarch carefully made the cay in a black kettle over a small driftwood fire. One side of the tent was folded, rolled back and fastened as an awning. There was plenty of shade. The tent was surprisingly cool. It was sited so that the prevailing breeze came through.

Nearby was a make-shift shelter that doubled as a goat shelter and a kids' den. It was made out of driftwood and clothing rags. It also received a favourable wind.

Bedouins are nomads and their lives centre around searching for food sources for their animals. Goats and sheep mean milk which means food. Bedouins follow regular migration patterns determined by the seasons and availability of pasture and water. During the spring and winter they wander further into the desert when rains bring desert blooms. Nomads set up their tents in places like Wadi Rum and stay as long as there is food for their animals. No rains = no grazing land.

Months after that first November visit, they asked for baksheesh after serving us chai. I initially resisted. 'Taking advantage' of tourists. Then I twiggled ... and was ashamed. Look at what they have. This is living at its most basic. They are dirt poor.

You are meant to be man's best friend Dog.

On Casper, we camped overnight. After dinner, as the sun settled lower in the sky and turned the desert from orange to a subtle pinkish-rose colour, campers gathered up hefty stones to make a circle which they filled with dry combustible driftwood. It fuelled a robust fire. Alcohol was found, sleeping bags were pulled out and an impromptu gathering ensued. The night was dark and still. A desert stillness unlike that in urban areas. A small black scorpion was disturbed and scuttled for refuge, moving rapidly past surprised, squealing punters until shelter was found ... in a sleeping bag. The human occupant jumped up with a whelp and more punters' screams and shrieks followed until the scorpion abandoned that abode too. Off into the shadows to find peace and solace.

I was impressed. First time I'd seen a scorpion. Jet black. Distinctive crab-like pinchers up front. Segmented tail with the distinctive forward curve over the back ending in its stinger. Only a little fella but he could sure scamper on those eight little legs.

After exploring the Wadi Rum 'Beau Geste' fort, and chatting to the Desert Police who watched over the area, it was a smooth run to **Aqaba**, on the Red Sea opposite the Israeli port of Eilat. The scene of TE Lawrence's attack with Howeitat tribesmen upon the Turks in 1917. A surprise attack. The Turks thought the Nefud desert would be a natural barrier against enemies. Impassable. All their heavy artillery was facing seaward.

David Lean's movie told the scene in less than twenty shots. The Arabs on camels and horse come out of the desert culminating in a magnificent panning shot, enhanced by Maurice Jarre's rousing theme, as the tribesmen sweep through the township of white flat-topped buildings to the azure waters of the Red Sea.

Lemming's cooks purchased succulent fresh fish, fruit and vegetables in Aqaba's abundant markets. We drove the beach road until finding a camping spot with a breezeblock toilet and cold water shower. The bus was turned side on so that the salty sea breeze could waft through and lower the temperature. Except in winter, my tours luxuriated here for two days swimming, snorkeling amongst the coral, admiring the small multi-coloured fish and ignoring annoying Aussie comments that this wasn't as good as the Great Barrier.

You had to avoid the spiky little black sea urchins lurking between the rocks ready to pierce the unsuspecting soles of pale feet.

We soaked up the sun, some punters rolling down the sand into the waves in inflated inner tubes. Our fish barbecues were appetising and delicious. A Trevally-like fish smeared with butter and sprinkled with pepper and salt and a few herbs wrapped in tin foil was a treat! Many slept out under the stars.

On some tours we ventured into a local bar, restaurant or nightclub and although we always had a good time, the prices charged were as steep as Wadi Rum's cliffs.

On one tour, I was awake early. Nothing unusual there. Dawn light was emerging. My girlfriend's hormones must have been working overtime as she made it crystal clear she was aroused. Unusually for me, I almost said I had a 'headache'. Reluctantly I decided to 'go with the flow' and accompany her down the sandy beach to a copse of bamboo and palm trees. Just sitting down, we were surprised by a group of youths. We scrambled up turning away from them in the bus' direction. With them behind us, I bulldozed her in front of me to protect her. The adolescents pushed, prodded and bad-mouthed me. We were soon out of the bamboo stand. Onto the open beach. In plain sight.

As we neared the bus, I reflected on their actions. My friend, diminutive in stature and with short, tight curly hair and a less than voluptuous bust presently enveloped in a baggy sweater—looked very boyish! Maybe they thought we were two guys having a rendezvous. Not unusual in these parts. The day before I had seen soldiers walking in Aqaba hand-in-hand. Perhaps I was the object of their desires! I shuddered. I had recently successfully avoided a prostate examination by a masseuse in a Turkish bath in Damascus. That was hair-raising enough. Nothing much was said between us but her ardour was definitely dampened and when I suggested 'a hot cuppa', she smiled wanly and settled for that.

On the Befa tour, and after two-back-to-back tours, I was getting over meals made of dehydrated components bolstered up with fried corned beef and rice. Unfortunately for me the cooks on Befa and Piddle decided that they would exchange punters for that evening's meal. The meal on Piddle was going to be ... fried spam. When Piddle's tour leader Ray Clarke and I retired to a

A dog's life

local Chinese restaurant, my name on Piddle was mud! Ray had had better people-skills than I, because, despite missing Befa's meal, his popularity was intact.

In Aqaba on Befa, I had an amusing incident with driver Iain. Iain was affable, despite being equally frustrating at the same time. He suggested that, whilst punters had free time in Aqaba, us the humble crew, we 'mere males', could cook dinner that evening. To thank punters for their creative meals. Punters would return to pleasant background music to find tables set with tablecloths, knives, forks, wine glasses, wine, beer ...

A good idea so we planned the menu diligently ... went shopping ...

and then ...

the OTHER Iain disappeared. Vanished. Poof!

Apparently he couldn't resist a local's impromptu fishing invitation. And a beer or two. I prepared the meal, seething at his absence and as agitated as a rooster is when marking his territory to scare off competitors. Rita saw my agitated state and tried to sooth my ruffled feathers. The punters clambered aboard, excited with their shopping expeditions. They were delighted by the 'crew's' efforts and enthusiastically tucked in. Iain rolled in midway through the meal, sans poisson, VERY intoxicated. He slid sheepishly into a seat beside girlfriend Janine just as someone proposed a toast to the considerate cooks! Judiciously ignoring my scowls, he raised his glass of wine and crowed "Yyyessss. VVVeryy swell done, hic, Mr. Tour Leader Ian. Cheers!"

Revenge. Iain had told the punters it never rains in Aqaba. As it had drizzled recently, the girls laughingly ganged up on him, dragging him into the tide. I toasted that initiative.

An Aussie jailbird

From Aqaba, *Lemming* headed north to Amman.

Back in winter on Befa, I'd had a dramatic incident as we headed north through snow-covered terrain into Amman. Towards the 'third circle'. Amman has nine roundabouts. Number one is city centre. The higher the circle's number, the further you are from city centre.

Driving through melting ice before starting to climb, stones thrown by youths shattered a back window. Iain jammed on the anchors, the bus squealed, swerved and skidded to an abrupt halt. I spilled out the back door to chase the culprits across an empty building site. I tackled a lanky teenager. By the time I hauled him to his feet other punters reached us.

Locals strode over to resolve the commotion. I turned to talk to the locals then went to confront the youth again.

But he was no longer in front of me.

Glancing down at my feet, he was lying there with a bloodied nose.

Iain had decked him!

One second the youth was standing, the next he dropped like a puppet with its strings severed. Iain was like a coiled spring, ready for another go. "Oh no you don't!" I stepped in front of him pushing him back with the heel of my left hand.

The locals were indignance personified. They ranted and shook their fists. Their faces were puce. Wide-eyed. Streams of Arabic hurtled our way. Accompanied by generous amounts of spittle. You didn't have to speak Arabic to get their drift. We beat a hasty retreat – without the youth. Iain is impulsive and fiery! Not the smartest thing to do.

So it proved.

We drove to the third circle. I went off to the Intercontinental to send a telex for bus parts and funds. Returning to the bus, Iain was missing. Anxious punters informed me he was in jail! The locals at the altercation scene had complained to the police who had wasted no time in tracking down and arresting Iain.

The nearest police station harboured its only Australian guest. His cell was about five feet wide and ten feet long with a wooden bunk bed against one wall and a metallic toilet and hand basin at the far end. The cell smelt strongly of disinfectant. Nadine and I bought him blankets and kebabs. He whiled away the time by composing poetry on the cell walls. They were probably dirty ditties and limericks.

Filing an official complaint on Top Deck letterhead regarding the stone-throwing youths, I requested an interview with the police superintendent. He kept me marinating for over an hour in his Spartan wood-panelled reception area. I had spruced myself up and was wearing a pale blue safari suit. Ex-Hong Kong. I wanted to look respectable and credible as a tour leader. Not touristy in shorts, T-shirt and flip-flops. My opposite number would be in uniform.

I was ushered into his office. Tall and lean with gaunt features, he had a thick moustache, wore a black beret above a stony expression. He sat behind a large wooden desk. In front of him was my letter and a legal pad with a hand-written notes in Arabic. He didn't invite me to sit. He was the alpha male. Neither did he reply when I said that Iain was provoked after the youth had cracked one of our windows. I put forward my case. He advised me that Iain had a court date and dismissed me with a cursory flourish of his hand.

Iain had a Jordanian friend, Mohammed, who said he had 'connections' with the Royal Family and could 'maybe' help us out. A result there wasn't guaranteed so I sought out the Australian Embassy, a thirty-minute walk away. My discussions with senior officials bore results. Career diplomats, grey-suited and well-fed, they talked officious bullish language. Assuring me they were in a position to assist, I departed heartened.

I didn't ring Top Deck. Management's reply would probably be "We pay you excellent money Ian. You don't need us to tell you what to do." That was a nod to Director John Huston telling Michael Caine on the set of 1975's The Man who would be King'— "You are getting paid a lot of money to do this Michael ... you should be able to get it right on your own—you don't need me to tell you what to do."

The next morning, despite Iain goading the guard who escorted him to court, Iain was heard, found guilty and released. We paid a fine. Justice, as seen by locals, had been done. The youth who broke our windows was absent and got off scot-free. Ten minutes later, Iain was warmly received at the bus with a hero's welcome (Grrrrrr). Already packed up, Befa, with me at the helm, made its way from the third circle, out of Amman and slowly down the steep winding road to the Dead Sea.

I had a chuckle at Iain's expense. On the bus, punters handed him mail from the Poste Restante, one post-dated Lahore. Hotel letterhead declared that he had left an item of 'intimate nature' in his room. It was being sent on to the London office. He climbed into the cab, a quizzical look on his face, to share it with me. I had to fight to stop myself laughing. It was a punters' prank. They were chuffed that he was concerned.

The Dead Sea, 392 meters below sea level, was two-and-a-half hours away. The Dead Sea Scrolls, written by a Jewish sect between 150 BC and 68 AD, were found in 1947. *Lemming* pulled into the gravel carpark beside the flat-roofed concrete ablution block containing showers and toilets. Punters dived into the water and 'floated.' The salt density in the Dead Sea means you cannot sink, you always float. The water's salt concentration is around thirty% compared to four% for 'normal' sea water.

At those facilities, there were two changing rooms. On the Befa tour, I accidentally stumbled in on Canadian Cathy in a cubicle. She of the 'coffee made with water from the hot water bottle notoriety'. She was in her underwear, a not uncommon sight on a Lodekka. A torrent of colourful language rushed my way. She over-reacted. So did I. It had been a long day. I simmered and when she reappeared, I took her aside. If I could be tolerant of 20 punters' idiosyncrasies for umpteen weeks, she could overlook an innocent indiscretion on my behalf. Ten minutes after stalking away, I received a bottle of 'Brut' from Cathy as a peace offering. I didn't often snap at punters. I thought I had been particularly patient with her. She was the weak link in the chain of punters. I took to briefing, guiding and monitoring her. The crew/punter distinction breaks down after a few weeks of living check-by-jowl in a double-decker.

The next morning, I was briefing everyone on Israeli customs when we were deafened by Israeli planes flying low overhead. You could hear them rumbling a few kilometres off. We felt we were in the middle of a thunderstorm. That, plus seeing fully-armed soldiers made you realise they were always on a 'war footing'.

The next day we clambered into a taxi at the border to head towards Jerusalem. Cathy was firing off non-stop questions at me. Ric rounded on her and uttered "For God's sake Cathy. Give him a break, won't you? Stop annoying him with your damn-fool questions. You're wearing him down. And us too." I grinned. That was what I'd wanted to say, but was too polite.

The Holy Lands and then... Mesopotamia

Off to Israel. Leaving *Lemming* in a car park, punters caught an Israeli yellow coach over the Jordan River. Somewhere along the length of the Jordan 2,000 years ago, John the Baptist and Jesus Christ had preached. We crossed the Allenby Bridge. General Allenby had worked with T.E. Lawrence to defeat the Ottoman Turks during WW1. When Lawrence realised that Allenby was not going to allow Arab independence, he returned to England.

A soldier and a guide accompanied us. Our carry-ons went onto a conveyer belt to be X-rayed. White entry cards were distributed and later stamped and included in your passport. A body search and the once-over with a metal detector completed the comprehensive 'vetting'. I could see the need for close scrutiny. Israel is bordered by Syria and Egypt who don't recognise her existence and want to destroy her.

After more than two hours, we climbed into dusty cream Mercedes taxis and sped through barren, white chalky hills to Jerusalem. I reflected on the wars and strife that had been fought over this barren wilderness.

Jerusalem. Checking the punters into the Faisal Hotel, the receptionist greeted me with "Shalom". We were on a budget. Our two rooms were large dormitories each with a dozen single beds immaculately made, white sheets and pillow slips and grey blankets. I smiled. Just like the orphanage I spent time in. Allowing time for showers and settling in, I led a walking tour of the Christian, Armenian, Muslim and Jewish quarters. It's reasonably compact and easy to negotiate. We wandered down narrow cobblestoned streets humming with activity. Sellers of postcards and replicated religious icons were numerous. We threaded our way through a market, part of which was devoted to meat including offal and sheep's heads, to the Damascus Gate, which was recreated in Rome for the 1959 epic 'Ben Hur'. Providing punters with local maps,

I pointed out things to do when they had free time. Several punters would ring home from the *Poste Restante*.

We walked to the crucifixion site. A slow, horrific way to die. Iron nails piercing palms and feet. The way the body must have sagged and fallen being secured only by the hands putting weight on the body's internal organs and naked feet.

I believe there was an historical Jesus who preached love, understanding and tolerance to a devoted audience. An audience whose country was occupied by a foreign power. His teachings threatened the Jewish 'establishment'. There was much written about him after his death but it took the first Council of Nicaea in 335AD for Christian bishops to debate the numerous views and interpretations. They reached the consensus that he was not a normal man but the son of God. Any writings and gospels that said otherwise were destroyed. I doubt whether he would have approved of all the blood spilled over the centuries in his name.

A dog's life

The Via Dolorosa, or 'way of sorrows', marks Jesus' journey from trial to crucifixion. The Stations of the Cross run east to west through the narrow streets of the Muslim quarter. Chapels, crosses, plaques and Roman columns indicate the stations. The official site is the Church of the Holy Sepulchre, the original church having been destroyed in 1099 and later rebuilt by the crusaders. It is a huge musty cavern that reeks of incense.

Christ was crucified on Golgotha, a hill that looks like a skull. There is a hill that looks like a skull just outside the walls. The dark gloomy cumulus rain clouds gathering above were an appropriate sombre visual.

From there we took in the Dome of the Rock and the Wailing Wall. The Dome of the Rock, is sacred to Jews and Christians. Walled with eight gates, only two are accessible to non-muslims. Known to Muslims as the Mosque of Omar, it was built between 687 and 691 AD where the prophet Mohammed is said to have ascended to heaven.

The Mount is sacred to Jews and was built on the rock where patriarch Abraham was prepared to sacrifice his son Isaac. Judaism's grand temple was located here. On Temple Mount is the Wailing Wall, so named because Jews come here to mourn their second temple's destruction by the Romans in 70 AD. It replaced the first temple built by King Solomon but was destroyed by the Babylonians in 578 BC.

The Romans erected their temple, dedicated to Jupiter. Byzantine Emperor Constantine had it demolished when he converted to Christianity. Temple Mount fell to Muslim warriors in 638 AD, was captured by Christian Crusaders in 1099 AD then recaptured by Saladin in 1187. Today, sovereignty of the site is claimed by both Israelis and Palestinians.

Orthodox Jews, resplendent in dark flowing robes, fur hats, long braided hair and luxurious beards were in deep reflection and prayers. They were oblivious to everyone else. On this tour we had encountered the major world religions—Hinduism, Sikhism, Islam and now Judaism. Yet another example of intense, focused devotion. Fascinating to observe. We walked to the garden of Gethsemane, among the olive trees, for our own private meditation and reflection. What a gift to be here. Again.

Visiting significant sites of three mainstream religions did not escape us. Several punters were practising Christians. We were visiting the place where Jesus lived, breathed and died. Just to be able to walk in the footsteps of past icons was a huge privilege.

Israel is 26,000 square kilometres. You can visit the main sites in a day. A fleet of cream Mercedes taxis took punters to Galilee and Tiberius and as far north as Nazareth. Galilee was overcast and hazy. It is fertile agricultural land, not as arid as Judea in the south. Jesus recruited his disciples from the fishermen around Galilee and based himself at Capernaum in the northeast to preach.

Visiting a kibbutz. *On Capricorn's P33H, Liz and Caroline got up early to take bus 961 to the Golan Heights. Caroline, had once been a volunteer there at the Quriat Shemona farming kibbutz.*

The two-hour, 250-kilometre bus trip alone was a treat with the driver channelling his inner Steve McQueen by driving fast and careening around tight corners. At one stage he deposited an elderly lady and her groceries in the aisle. He took a corner sharply. She was seated in front of me. She just slid off the slick vinyl seat onto the floor with a plop. A slapstick comedy couldn't have choreographed it better. I helped her up and desperately chased her groceries back and forth across the swaying floor as the bus lurched on. That was a sideshow in itself. But only for me. Other passengers continued gossiping.

An olive-skinned, beret-wearing, female Israeli soldier in camouflage kit was standing beside my seat chatting non-stop, unaware that the snout of her stubby Uzi kept attempting to remove my ear wax. I thought I was

A dog's life

practised at non-verbal communication but my glares were obviously just too subtle.

Caroline's kibbutznik friends Tsolo and Edith, were elderly and welcoming, their dwelling modest but comfortable. They were generous to guests and after showing us around the kibbutz, including the bomb shelters, they made us a lunch of fresh bread, hummus, tomatoes, olives, cheese and fruit. After lunch Tsolo challenged me to backgammon while the girls went for an extended tour.

Their house had an ample supply of books, impressionist prints, TV, a stereo and records. These possessions are all owned by the kibbutz and held in a communal 'treasury'. They receive them when 'their turn' comes around. Tsolo was a founding member of the kibbutz in 1936. His son was killed in the 1973 Yom Kippur war. He harbours no lingering bitter feelings. He wants to live in peace with his neighbours.

One evening on the Befa tour, David, the manager of the Faisal Hotel, invited me to a buffet-style dinner. A chance for me to mix and mingle with locals. Thirty Arabs in long flowing white dishdasha and red and white checked shemagh were digging into the rice with their hands, rolling the long grained rice and slow-boiled mutton into balls and dipping them into a spicy sauce. A lot of flavours came through—saffron, coriander, cumin, cardamom, turmeric. An assortment of nuts! Yum. Right hand only. The left is used for ablutions.

Most of the group were taxi drivers. David dominated conversations getting animated and agitated about the price I paid for the taxis from the border yesterday. Obviously hinting for me to use his services hence my invitation to the 'business dinner'.

A disagreement*. Arabs can be a passionate, volatile lot. On arrival at the hotel, I immediately asked the desk clerk to contact the taxi company that I had used previously to book taxis. He said he would. He never confirmed. Over two days I awaited verification.*

None.

A different clerk was on duty the evening before the tour. No news. In desperation, I had that clerk book another company.

The next morning dawned. I bundled punters into Mercedes taxis for a tour of Israel. They had just departed when another fleet of taxis arrived. The original company! A very aggrieved lead taxi driver started abusing me. He was absolutely frustrated. His face was a striking puce colour and he was trembling. Apoplectic with rage. Reacting rapidly, he reached into the back seat of his taxi. His fingers grasped a beer bottle to smash it against the curb. He attacked me. His more level-headed colleagues restrained him.

The police arrived, listened to their brethren and accused me of not being loyal to the original taxi company. The ruckus was my fault. I tried to explain my attempts at making contact. No reply. I presume it was a cultural misunderstanding. His word (from last time) was his bond. I understood those values. But as a westerner I needed confirmation. Or else my passengers would be swinging 'in the wind'.

In February, despite the bitter cold from a dusting of snow everywhere, I escorted Befa's punters to Bethlehem on the Left Bank. The area had an 'Arab', feel, accentuated when the muezzin called the faithful to prayer from a nearby mosque. The 'Church of the Nativity' was bigger than I expected. The original was built over the cave where Jesus was born. Another was built in the 4th Century when Constantine embraced Christianity and rebuilt again in 575 AD. Later the crusaders fought for possession of the site.

Visa and border hassles. From Amman, *Lemming* trundled north. A tyre was punctured at Jerash. We replaced that and went through Jordanian customs only to find on the Syrian side, we were refused entry. We didn't have the multiple entry visas I thought we had. "Return to the Syrian Embassy in Amman and start again." I was informed. Grrrr! A dark storm cloud started to form over my head. Syrian customs and bureaucracy were guaranteed to bring out the worst in me!

Before we departed for Amman, Jordanian officials apologized for their neighbours. "We are sorry. They are arrogant. We feel for you!" The difference between Syria and Jordan in welcoming and treating travellers is stark. At Jerash, while the passengers washed and cleaned up, our guide Sultan also commiserated showing anger and frustration at the Syrians.

The following day, a peeved and still simmering tour leader stood in the scorching sun for two hours outside the Syrian embassy. This was adding insult to injury. In a long line of malodorous locals, I was one away from being attended to when ... we were told the officials' day was done and everyone had to come back tomorrow. Just my luck.

While punters shopped, I visited the Hotel Continental to send and receive telexes. An hour's time difference with London. I bought a Turkish coffee, read the latest 'New York Times' and 'Washington Post' and relaxed in a deep leather chair in the foyer while awaiting replies.

The third circle car park was *not* the most salubrious. Dusty. Paper litter. Cigarette butts. Curious, leering locals. The smell of urine. I passed the monotony of waiting for the visas by playing backgammon. Camel, Jeff and Morris passed the time by teaching some local ragamuffins a few words of English. However they were not the politest of phrases. In fact blue. *Very* blue. Someone might eventually cuff the waifs around the ear and reprimand them for being obscene!

We had bought firecrackers in Varanasi. One morning I tossed a cracker at a youth who was having a leak near our bus. The cracker exploded in a fountain of dust and pine needles! Boy did he move with a yelp! Jeff soon outdid me. Jordanian youths came into the car park to ogle the girls. Despite being asked, both politely and impolitely, to skedaddle, they didn't. Jeff decided to hurl a cracker at a row of them squatting over by a far wall. He lit it and delayed throwing it so that the wick could burn down. As luck would have it, the cracker bounced a few times like a 'Barnes Wallis bouncing bomb' and ended up at the youths' feet ... before exploding! I thought someone had been dealt a serious injury and started up towards them. I resisted the urge to hum the 'Dambusters' theme' as I walked over to apologize. One thought we had thrown a real bomb. He was amazed to learn it was a cracker.

Befa's punter Estelle dryly called Amman, 'the arsehole of the world'. Interesting. *Lemming's* punters didn't describe it in those terms. They

Overland with Top Deck

were remarkably patient. The tedium of free-camping in the Third Circle carpark was broken a little when I caught up with Waleed, a part-American/Irish guy I had met on the last tour. He was outspoken, verbose and chauvinistic and I thought he would repulse the girls but he took us to a disco one night. On another we had drinks and played pool at his place to while away the hours.

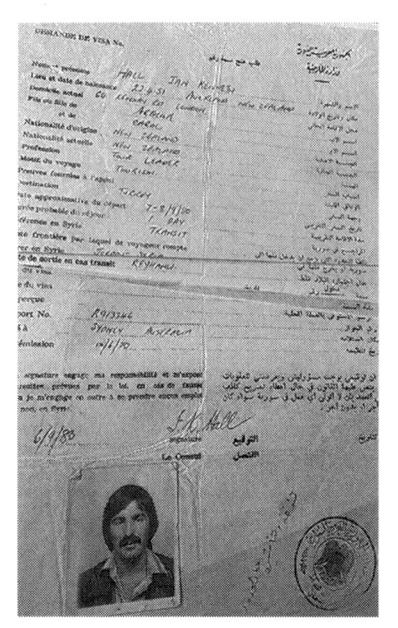

Lemming made her way north to the Syrian/Turkish border. Someone once remarked—the more primitive the country, the more bureaucratic red tape they demand. This certainly seemed to be true. Punters' names were rewritten in Arabic from the English. Several copies of virtually everything was required. I was directed to the bank, to the insurance office, to another two offices to get the Trytique and then backwards and forwards many times courtesy of the whims of the officials. Simple systems were obviously missing and blatant corruption in the form of baksheesh to hurry up the process was rife.

On every tour, my driver—with the bus' paperwork, insurance and carnets—and me with passports and passenger lists were shunted from one office to another—often to one office several times. There was *always* a hold up. Like Groundhog Day. Our paperwork was *always* deemed incorrect in some way. If we didn't have the necessary stamp from the last border, we either had to pay a heavy Syrian fine or go back to Darra to complete the formalities. As we were often behind schedule, paying the fine to happily leave Syria was tempting.

I have met pleasant Syrians. Shop owners and craftsmen in Aleppo were an example. Of course they were pleasant as they wanted a sale. But … Embassy staff, custom officers and campsite owners—people who had power—were made from a different mould.

— 316 —

A dog's life

One border crossing could have been a skit from a Monty Pythonesque comedy. Rain poured down on the custom building's roof and cascaded down the gutterings as Casper's driver and I signed off the paperwork inside. An electrical storm cut off power. We moved around in the shadows. The bulk of our business and paper signing was therefore done in the dark with Loxley leaning over me to shine the torch's beam on the paperwork at the appropriate moment for me to sign. Somehow he kept a straight face.

On Befa, Iain and I were shunted from office to office over a three-hour period. A so-called 'Interpol' officer interviewed us both together and individually. When talking to us, he stood too close, in our 'personal space'. I wondered – which 'team' was he batting for? The atmosphere was awkward and edgy. As Iain and I finally walked back to Befa, he remarked quietly, "Ever get the feeling we were going to be raped?"

My buttocks clenched involuntarily.

En route, I would meet crew from Capricorn/Sundowners. There was mutual respect. Favours were exchanged. I was chatting to a Capricorn tour leader when his driver joined us—Carl Capstick, one of three P33H drivers. I had last encountered him a few months before shopping at Acton's Alliance Store before heading away on *Casper*. We had time to catch up. Later the same tour I caught up with Merv Lapwood, our third P33H driver, at another border.

From Damascus, the road goes north to the Syrian/Turkish border at Kirikan, or you can turn off east to Iraq. Top Deck stopped going through Iraq in 1978.

I visited Iraq and Mesopotamia just once with Capricorn P33H in March 1979. Like Afghanistan, it was soon to close its doors because of internal politics and the Iraq/Iranian war (September 1980 to 1988). I was looking forward to Iraq, the home of the Garden of Eden and Mesopotamia, the land between the Tigris and Euphrates rivers, the 'Cradle of Civilisation'.

I wasn't impressed.

Overland with Top Deck

Iraq was barren and desolate. The 900-kilometre, twenty-four-hour drive from Jordan through to Baghdad was over the most corrugated 'road' I had ever encountered. Tens of thousands of softball-sized chunks of rock. Little chance of sleep during the night drive. An endurance test.

In Baghdad, our 'home' was the 'Hanging Gardens' Hotel. Picturesque name. Drab rooms. Grubby, stained and shabby. Ill-kept. We had to request fresh sheets as the last used ones had just been shaken then pulled tight and straightened up. Two Iraqi dinar a night per person. Exchange rate: 20 fils to the US$.

Baghdad was a dry, dirty, dusty city. Narrow crowded pavements and sidewalks. Litter was abundant often clogging the gutters. Stern-faced men in white dishdasha robes with thick dark moustaches and two-day chin stubble pushed and elbowed past us. Life looked a serious business. It probably was. Saddam Hussein's secret police, the Mukhabarat, were invisible, omnipresent and feared. There were few smiles.

Ninety percent of the inhabitants we encountered had testicles. The women weren't with their men chatting, drinking cay, twirling worry beads and playing chess and backgammon. At home doing the real work, bringing up kids, cooking and cleaning. All shop assistants were male. At Sharjah Bazaar, men haggled, squabbled and negotiated over prices. Conversations were loud and expressive. Arabic sounds guttural. From the throat. The clearing of throats with random spitting onto the ground was also common. When you overheard a hoick coming up nearby, you looked around quickly hoping to avoid it!

Many mosques had intricate, turquoise tiled domes and tall ornate minarets. Beautiful. Red, English double-decker buses were widespread. We visited the Ali Baba fountain, a scene from 'Ali Baba and the forty thieves'. Little dust whirlwinds redistributed paper rubbish from one side of the road to the other. Iraq was expensive compared with the Indian sub-continent but on a par with Syria and Jordan. Two and a half dina for two small fish and a salad. Accompanied by thick, black syrupy coffee. My favourite was the lassi made with banana and yoghurt. Churned up in a blender, it was delicious, cold and filling.

Saddam Hussein and his Ba'ath Party were campaigning. Walls were plastered with election posters showing his smiling menacing portrait. Determined face, eyes fixed on a vision in the distance, thick moustache, traditional homburg hat on head, rifle held high by its wooden stock. Iraq was the second largest oil exporting nation in 1979 and the world's fifth largest producer. It was an unholy alliance between the US and UK and Iraq. Each side using the other. Hussein had minority Sunni Moslems in positions of power where the vast majority of the population were Shi'a. A significant number of the population in the northeast mountains and valleys were Kurds. The average person probably didn't gain much under his rule. Hussein ruled by fear. Would the political tide turn and the opposing sides clash? Time would tell.

We drove from Baghdad to ancient Babylon. The largest city in the world in 1,700 BC. The terrain was flat dusty countryside with the occasional muddy stream, flanked by field after field of date palms. The entrance to Babylon was once through huge ornate towers. Only the foundations exist of the hanging gardens. Built by Nebuchadnezzar, they were a remarkable feat of engineering. One of the seven wonders of the ancient world consisting of an ascending series of tiered gardens with a wide variety of trees, shrubs, and vines, resembling a green mountain.

Babylon and Nineveh, on the other side of the Tigris River, had been neglected. I still felt privileged to be here in the 'cradle of civilisation'. There were fifteen gates to Nineveh and some were being restored with the original building materials. A good move but my overall impression was of rubble, overgrown grass and weeds. Some of the restored stones were engraved with 'Restored by Saddam Hussein'. Trying to get into the history books. He would eventually but not for his good deeds. Infamous not famous.

On the way from Baghdad to Mosul, we stopped to climb the spiralling Samara 'snail shell' tower. Part of the Samara Mosque, built by an early Caliph in 836 AD to announce the presence of Islam in the region and probably to announce to far-off travellers that they were nearing civilisation and a place to rest that night. It can be seen for miles around and at 180 feet is higher than the leaning tower of Pisa. Like the leaning tower, its walkways have worn smooth over time and there are no handrails. I found it scary to say the least.

Having travelled past Tikrit, birthplace of Saddam Hussein, we visited the ancient city of Hatra, once a fortified caravan city on the Silk Roads, now being reconstructed. Hatra was Assyrian. I recalled the Lord Byron poem which I had savoured getting my tongue around when I was a boy. "The Assyrians came down like a wolf on the fold and their cohorts were gleaming in silver and gold. And the sheen of their spears were like stars on the sea, When the blue wave rolls nightly on deep Galilee."

Onwards to Mosul. *400 kilometres. The 'Atlas Hotel'. One Iraqi dinar a night each. A few notches higher than past establishments judging by the following comments in the 'Trip Book' —*

"Happiness is: Bug-less beds. Clean sheets. Black sugarless coffee. Showering without being spied on by a male Arab voyeur. NOT having diarrhoea. Spotless loos. A toilet that flushes. Hot water.

Banana milkshakes. A washing machine. Not living out of a suitcase for two days."

However the last comment summed up many punters' viewpoints—

"Happiness is … saying goodbye to Iraq."

Mosul, Iraq's second city, was cleaner. Less expensive than Baghdad. Fruit and fresh vegetables were abundant. Shops were narrow and shallow with half the produce overflowing onto the path outside. Cay shops were meeting places for men who played backgammon, checkers, or chess whilst twiddling worry beads continually through their fingers and discussing the issues, big and small, of their world. Shoe-shine 'boys' seemed to do a brisk trade. Many a story seemed to pass between client and worker. Social networking.

The food was tastier than in Baghdad. However the hygiene standards were suspect as the following comments in the Trip Book testify—

"Jules crook. J9 crook. BG crook. Brian crook. Neil crook. Tony crook. Barry almost crook! Dog crook".

On our last day in Iraq, the coach pulled over for a picnic lunch beside the River Zan. This was a semi-autonomous Kurdish region. The surrounding countryside was lush and green and dotted with mud brick villages. Sheep and goats were observed by vigilant, weathered, keffiyeh-wearing shepherds.

As we scrubbed the coach beside the river, Kurds came over, unique in their baggy trousers and large hats. Curious, inquisitive and genial. They invited us to their tents. Over numerous cups of cay, they communicated via sign language, smiles, giggles and laughter. We were offered bananas, apples, meat and bread. Humbling hospitality. I didn't eat much. My stomach was issuing noises that it wasn't happy.

Settling back into my coach seat as we set off for the border, I realised my diarrhoea was going to be a problem. Most of that day's journey was tense. My intestines moaned and groaned, tumbled and rumbled, threatening to chance a 'great escape'. A sheen of sweat broke out on my forehead. I wondered if I had control. Yes I did. No I didn't. Yes I did. I fretted. My buttocks had quite a workout. Almost continually clenched. On either side of the coach was fertile flat farmland. No cover to shelter behind...

Just as I could stand it no longer, and gripped the seat in front to rise and plead Merv to stop, there was a sharp loud POP from a tyre causing the coach to come to a shuddering, juddering halt ... beside a thigh-high dry stone wall. What impeccable timing and positioning. Someone was looking after me. Clutching my toilet roll under an arm and still clenching my butt checks, I descended cautiously and waddled awkwardly off.

On Capricorn P33H, we crossed the Iraqi-Turkish border and arrived in Mardin *for the night. A dusty Turkish village, renowned for its historic Arab and Seljuk architecture, perched precipitously and precariously on a dusty limestone hilltop. Unique. Atmospheric. The stone houses seem to cling to each other on the terraces up the steep incline. Mardin overlooks fertile, dark-brown farmland along the Tigris River. Mesopotamia, 'the land between the rivers'! First introduced to me at primary school. Now, years later, here I was. Could never have imagined that.*

A song for Neil. *I shared a room with Neil who was in his early twenties and had been reclusive since beginning P33H. Not many punters were able to get 'close' to him. He stuck near to his parents after unspecified health issues. Possibly mental health. He loosened up to me in the confines of our room. We had shared a room infrequently beginning with day one in Pokhara. His mother genially bustled in to monitor my temperature and make us each a packet soup.*

A dog's life

Two days later, P33H pulled into a coastal layby to have lunch on a beach. Neil went back to the coach to retrieve towels and togs and was bowled over and killed by a truck.

In the Trip Book the day beforehand he had quoted part of Ecclesiastes—"There is a time for everything" which included the line "A time to live and a time to die". You could read a lot into that. Was life too much for him and he'd had enough? Or was it all a coincidence?

Elton John's 'A song for guy' (in memory of a friend who died) was playing on the Capricorn coach the day Neil passed. For me it is forever evocative of Neil. I renamed it in my mind 'A song for Neil' and on future tours I played it along that coast in his memory. Piano solo, bass guitar, occasional shaker. Haunting. Sombre yet uplifting at the same time.

That night P33H stayed in Gaziantep at the more salubrious Mardin hotel (129 lira a night). We were still shocked and grieving for Neil and his parents. I was sharing a room with Cliff and Brian and getting over my diarrhoea. Around 2.30 a.m., I felt the call of nature and rather than use the en-suite and wake the others up with tortuous sounds and the accompanying smells, I went off, dressed only in boxer shorts, to the communal toilets on that floor. Returning to the room, I found it had clicked shut behind me. Locked out! Not wanting to wake up the others, I considered my options. One was to remove the plush curtains at the end of the corridor to wrap myself in to keep warm. Fortunately Cliff was a relatively light sleeper and came to my rescue after ten minutes.

Turkiye: The Turquoise Coast

The Turks call their own country Turkiye. I prefer that to being reminded of poultry. *Lemming* wound her way around the rugged, scenic Mediterranean coast occasionally losing sight of the sea. Periodically we were on tight, looping, tortuous convoluted roads. On the inland side there were towering cliffs or thick pine and cedar forests. On the opposing side—sheer drops to dramatic waves surging, curling, crashing and splintering on glistening black rocks. The distinctive sharp tang of pine and conifer plus the sea's aroma was refreshing. I inhaled deeply. Concentration was the priority though with all the roller coaster climbs and dips and drops. Plus the streaky dappled light filtering through the trees and reflecting off windows and walls played mayhem with my vision.

We passed crusader castles built in the late 1100s. Supply bases for the First Crusade en route to Jerusalem. The 'Maiden's Castle', Kiz Kulesi, was Armenian and was now off the coast near Silifke. According to legend, a king was warned by a fortune-teller that his daughter would be killed by a snake. He built her the castle so that she was isolated from the mainland. The king sent a basket of fruit to his daughter. There was a snake in amongst the fruit. It struck and killed her. Now, surrounded by water, you could swim to the castle.

I dog-paddled.

Aspendos has one of my favourite amphitheatres. Built in AD 162, the amphitheatre seats 12,000 and is part Greek style being built into an existing hill and part Roman with vaulted arches. It has forty rows of marble seats divided into sections by staircases. The stage has dressing rooms. Nearby is a well-engineered aqueduct which carried water from nineteen kilometres, at times carrying the water uphill.

A dog's life

Local women were enterprising. Some made delicious tantalising pancakes with mince, onion, garlic and cheese. Drizzled with olive oil and garnished with parsley. Like Pide, they are cheap and very tasty comfort food.

A coup d'état

12th September 1980. The army overthrew Turkiye's democratically elected government. Suleyman Demirel and Bulent Ecevit had alternated as PM for most of the 1970s but were now in prison.

This, the third coup d'état since 1923, was led by General Kenan Evren. Turkiye had been unstable economically during the 1970s resulting in social unrest and strikes. The general assembly had been unable to elect a president in the previous six months. The coup ultimately had a positive effect on an economy with three digit inflation (great for travellers' spending power but not good for locals), a huge foreign trade deficit and large-scale unemployment. Demirel and Ecevit were imprisoned and banned from politics. Demirel made a come-back and became president, 1993-2000.

Foot soldiers, army vehicles and half-trucks patrolled the streets. We were stopped on occasions, particularly after the curfew began at 10.00 p.m. The last time I'd had to observe a curfew was in Kabul, March 1979.

Past Alanya at the foot of the Tarsus Mountains, we turned inland at Antalya and drove to Pammukkale. Fertile, cultivated farming country. An hour out of Pammukkale, we were pulled over at checkpoint. It was 11.30 p.m. The curfew was 10.00 p.m.! My completely innocent "I didn't know of the curfew" look came into full force. After checking my passport, appropriate stamps and the bus' carnet, the soldier waved me on. We only had a short distance to travel. I was in a Beatles mood again—their early period—so mellowed out with 'Eleanor Rigby', 'Yesterday', 'Michelle' and 'Something'.

Pammukkale

Once *Lemming* arrived at Pammukkale, I crashed, sharing the double bed immediately behind the cab. Someone grunted and wormed over in her sleeping bag. When punters arose at eight, they were delighted to find the bus parked beside Roman ruins and next to a meandering, waist-deep ditch of thermal water. After breakfast we enjoyed standing in the thermal waters as we washed our clothes.

We spent more than a day at Pammukkale during which time we explored the calcium terraces and the Hierapolis amphitheatre behind the bus. During the bus springclean, Morris and Trish came across a hoard of Bachelors' steak and kidney tins. As they would be on cooking duty in Europe, I could hear Trish's grey cells turning over as she wondered how to reproduce these in a variety of ways.

We came across a fruit bat among the provisions. The second bat after 'Bruce' in Australia. Small, scared, fragile and delicate. "Aww isn't he cute?" I nicknamed it 'Bulent the Bat' after the recently deposed Prime Minister and after a photoshoot, we released it into nearby scrub.

Pammukkale means "cotton castle" and refers to the surface of the shimmering, snow-white limestone, shaped thousands of years by calcite-rich springs. Mineral-rich waters drip down the terraces and collect in pools below. The faded colours of my 1979 photo do not give it justice.

Becoming a Greek thermal spa and medical centre in the Second Century BC, it also started minting bronze coins. I warned punters not to purchase 'ancient coins' by enterprising locals. A sister city to nearby Laodicea, one of the renowned seven early Christian churches, Pammukkale was also a Roman healing centre where patients came to "take the waters". The name Hierapolis means 'holy city' because of the many temples built there.

I felt a connection with Pammukkale. Living in Rotorua as a boy, I trudged to school seeing steam arising from gutters, drainpipes and thin fissures in the earth. I loved the distinctive pungent smell of sulphur, soaked in thermal water in Kuirau Park. I had visited the yawning crater of Mt Tarawera, the volcano which in June 1886 erupted, destroying Aotearoa's 'pink and white terraces', the equivalent of Pammukkale's travertines.

On Capricorn P33H, punters stayed in a '60s era motel, since demolished as they drained the thermal waters into their swimming pools causing damage to the terraces. The water supply to the hotels is now restricted in an effort to preserve the overall area and to encourage the calcium deposits to regenerate.

A dog's life

The motel rooms' sliding glass doors opened out onto a decking from which you could descend into your own thermal pool. Making your way to the far side of the pool you could gaze over the travertines and the Pammukkale-Denizli valley.

After having a shower, I slid into the pool first. Thermal waters. Ahhh... Soothing. I was soaking up the vista when Liz joined me. She is blonde and attractive. Statuesque. All the right curves in the right places. Genetics has been kind. Beautiful in looks and in personality. Wearing a smile, brief pink briefs and carrying two glasses of chilled white wine, she asked innocently, "Isn't the view spectacular?"

I nodded muttering, "Which ones?" I feigned nonchalance. We spent the next two hours gazing over the stunning valley. At first the terraces were dazzlingly white and bright but the late afternoon/ early evening sun bounces muted red, gold and purple colours off the terraces. Spectacular. Romantic. Dusk arrived fading leisurely into night.

As much as the travertines, I love the 15,000 seat Hierapolis amphitheatre equally. It was March and a smidgen chilly. We were well rugged-up. Thick fluffy cumulus clouds resembling candy floss scudded across a grey ominous sky. A breeze was blowing. We sat entranced in a back row of the amphitheatre, looking down at the stage. What kind of artistic performances were presented here? Over the amphitheatre's ruins were the travertines and fertile valleys.

Nearby is 'Cleopatra's pool', a public pool. On my visits you could sit on collapsed Roman columns and stare down at ornate and intricate Roman mosaics below you. If you had goggles on (the water stings) you could swim down for a closer inspection. Well-preserved Roman mosaics. Roman columns. With my Top Deck groups I paid for entry for the punters so that they could while away an hour or two and have access to hot, fresh-water showers.

I returned to Pammukkale in 2019.

Disappointment quadrupled! Water flow was nil in parts. In other areas, it had been artificially redirected and channelled. Gone were the startling colours—the blindingly bright whites of the terraces and the vividly contrasting blues and aquamarines of the thermal waters in the basins. The contrast in colours once made it such a magnificent spectacle.

2019's Pammukkale looked as if it had reached its death throes. It was now beginning a slow recovery stage, a transition stage to *hopefully* what it once was. Only part of Cleopatra's Pool was open to the public. Waist-deep murky water. Hundreds of Russian tourists wearing scrimpy, inappropriate clothes.

Pamukkale June 2019.

Carpe Diem. Seize the day. As a tour leader, I was opportunistic and often seized sight-seeing possibilities that were not on the itinerary. Three of them were in Denizli.

Denizli is twenty kilometres down the hill from Pammukkale. 'Dennis Lillee' to Aussies. November 1979. Balmy weather. Late afternoon. Casper was parked on the town's fringes. The cooks went shopping for fresh meat and vegetables. On their way back to Casper I called them over to watch a Turkish woman weaving a carpet. She was totally focused, her forearms, wrists and fingers strong and agile as she moved them across the vertical loom. Her husband beckoned us into his shop where several items of her work were displayed. The punters were fascinated but no sales were made.

Where would we store them? Under the bunks? Most of Casper's punters were on strict budgets.

Back at the bus the cooks concocted dinner. What goes with this? What could we be adding to that? Dinner Creativity 101. Chocolate mousse was being whipped up, fresh fruit was being diced up. Punters were spread about reading, adding to their diaries, playing backgammon and cards, chatting and laughing together. Chilling out after the day's sightseeing.

Loxley and I were slumped in white plastic chairs against the bus, each polishing off our first chilled Efes. Condensation clung to their sides. More to come. We were approached by two Turks who had been observing us. The *alpha male was dressed in smart dark jeans and an open-necked shirt. The buttons of the shirt around his waistline were beginning to strain. His face was slightly chubby with the inevitable moustache. He had longish slicked-back hair around his ears. I formed an immediate impression of him from his gait and bearing. It wasn't altogether favourable.*

Introducing himself as Hasim and his sidekick as Ali, he enquired if we had clothes to sell. He was initially interested in the pants of the light-blue safari suit I was wearing. We chatted and he invited us over to his place after dinner indicating to Loxley he had weed to sell.

My brain cells were precious to me and I wasn't interested in killing off the remaining working ones. I was interested in how a rural Turk lived. Hasim was pleasant enough but was glib. A 'wide boy'. The Turkish version of Arthur Dailey from TV's 'Minder' and later Del Boy Trotter. Buying and on-selling to make a few lira. Plotting. Scheming. Being hospitable to Loxley and I could benefit him in the long run if we returned his way. Quid pro quo.

His house, off an uneven, dusty gravel side-road on the edge of extensive cotton fields, was plaster over brick, a white rectangle with limited windows, uneven mud floors and a tiled roof. It had two rooms—a room with a bed where Hasim slept and another room with mattresses where he entertained us and where his wife Fatima and three kids slept.

We had a pleasant evening. He hauled a few Turkish carpets out to entice us but we politely declined. I didn't know enough about carpets to make an intelligent choice. Late in the evening, Loxley and Hasim went outside for a joint. Fatima laid a checked plastic tablecloth on the floor. I helped her spread out a supper of flat bread, an olive-oil dip, eggplant, olives, yoghurt, nuts and melon. What little they had they were sharing. Hospitality. A hallmark of Islam.

When Fatima said she was a cotton picker, I pricked up my ears. Cotton planting is from March to May. Harvesting is August to September. It was now late October and late in the season. Cotton picking, gathering and sorting is very much 'hands on' work and creates significant employment in rural regions.

Fatima invited me to visit the cotton fields the next day. Several female punters accompanied me to find up to a dozen young women hunched over picking cotton. The crop was bountiful but beneath our sandals the soil was baked and parched with long deep cracks criss-crossing each other. The fields had not had water for some time. A lone male supervisor wandered up and down the rows. Using sign language and basic English, the punters communicated with the workers. To my delight, the workers quickly lost their initial shyness and hesitancy and both sides bonded. We were soon smiling and laughing. "Well, this is a hit," I thought!

It was hot, back-breaking work stooping, tweaking and plucking. A killer on the lower back. The workers had bronzed faces and arms and wore light cotton clothes which caught the prevailing breeze. Their arms and backs of their neck were protected from the sun by long sleeves and scarves. Looped around their waists were white aprons gathered into folds into which they dropped cotton buds. Large bulging grey sacks were nearby. The recipient of the cotton buds. A red rusty dusty tractor sat idle in the next field.

A dog's life

Upon learning that I was a teacher, Hasim invited me to visit the local primary school, a well-worn wooden building with paint flaking off windows and walls. Located down a dusty lane, it was set well back on the section with a towering cedar tree beside it. One class of about twenty-five students, boys and girls around ten years, seated in pairs at dual wooden desks with a wooden bench seat attached. Students were dressed in dark-blue, sailor-type uniforms. Boys had 'number two haircuts' with their hair cropped close to their heads. They all stood up in unison at the teacher's command to greet us.

The room was not lit well. Rather gloomy. There was a row of windows along one side of the classroom but they were high up. Only adults could see out. The room was dominated by the blackboard in the front, above which was a photo of Kemal Ataturk overseeing them solemnly, a large map of Turkiye and the teacher's qualifications and certificates.

I smiled. Like going back 100 years. Rural school. Rote learning and chanting. The teacher the font of all knowledge. No children's work on any of the walls. No desks or tables in collections for group work. These kids were probably lucky to have access to an education. They were clothed and well-fed and engaged.

I glanced up at the photo of Mustafa Kemal. 'Kemal Atatürk', the 'father of the Turks'. Then back at the students. These kids owed their education to him. Plus it was a co-ed class, not single sex. He was instrumental in pushing Turkiye into the modern world and had much to do with reforming education and giving opportunities to women. I gave him a silent nod of gratitude and credit.

Atatürk's reforms made education more accessible to the masses. Between taking power in 1923 and his death in 1938, the number of students attending primary schools increased by 200%, those attending middle schools increased twelve times and those attending high schools increased sixteen times.

Atatürk was a strong supporter of co-education and girls' education. Centuries of sex segregation under Ottoman rule had denied girls equal education. Atatürk thus opposed segregated education as a point of difference between his vision of modern secular Turkey and the previous Ottoman Empire.

Atatürk changed the written Arabic script into the Latin script to better meet the phonetic requirements of Turkish. A new Latin script was created to better project the actual sounds of spoken Turkish. This was a major reform. Atatürk led by example. For a time he travelled the country with a portable chalkboard, teaching locals how to write and read the script.

As we left, I thanked the teacher, Ahmet and Ali. An interesting visit, well worth the diversion. I hoped the education the kids were receiving, and especially the ability to read and write, were going to be their keys to a positive and productive future.

Ephesus

Ephesus is a fabulous site near to the Aegean Coast and close to the beautiful (but touristy and expensive) port of Kusadasi and the charming traditional village of Seljuk.

The city was famed for its Temple of Artemis (550 BC). Sadly, only one column stands today in the middle of a grassy field. Alexander the Great was welcomed here when he visited Ephesus. As was Mark Anthony in 33 BC with Cleopatra. In 27 BC, Augustus Caesar made Ephesus the capital of western Asia Minor. Thus it began its prosperity as a major commercial centre. The city's wealth and success is reflected in the quality of its buildings.

I dropped punters off at the upper entrance, and then, as I walked them downhill to meet the bus and driver at the lower entrance, we had commanding views of the whole site.

Over successive tours, I became friends with Mustafa Urkmez who ran a clothing stall. One of many stalls at Ephesus' upper entrance. I would bring him duty-free cigarettes and take my punters there. His stall's entrance was always flanked with summer dresses. Punters would see me having a cay and a catch-up with him, and regard him as trustworthy.

He had had a tough life as an orphan. In 1983, just before I returned for a visit, he had spent 10 days in Sağmalcılar Prison, of Billy Hayes and 'Midnight Express' notoriety, for arguing with his Aussie girlfriend Leeann in public. Leann agreed to a marriage of convenience to get him to Adelaide. Unfortunately I lost contact with him after that. He was energetic and enterprising. I hope he has had a successful life full of accomplishments. Inshallah.

From Mustafa's stall at the top entrance, you descend a long, winding, cobblestoned promenade. Ruins included the two-storied, partly-restored Celsus Library, the third largest in the Roman world. 12,000 scrolls.

A dog's life

Which way to try look? It's almost overwhelming.

The 25,000 seat amphitheatre stands out. As well as being used for entertainment, it was the preaching theatre for St. Paul.

I clambered about the amphitheatre. Around 9.00 a.m., the heat sets in and sucks the vitality out of you, I took a myriad of well-framed and composed shots without other tourists blundering into them. Some with archways which have seen the ravages of time through to lush green pastures beyond. From the amphitheatre I looked down on 'harbour street' and imagined trading ships and triemes in port.

The long rows of public latrines were the location of a lot of politicking. Patricians sat on their 'thrones', discussed the state of the nation then, when the deed was done, washed their hands in another channel of warm water at their feet.

The Roman public bath system improved upon the Greek model. Water was heated in nearby furnaces and flowed under the marble floors to the baths, thus heating the floors and the baths. (Photo). Baths were not only for washing but also for reading and like the latrines, for talking about philosophy and politics. Some baths had free admission so the plebs as well as patricians could use the facilities.

Kusadasi

A few kilometres from Ephesus is picturesque Kusadasi. Stunningly scenic but ... touristy. Inflated prices. Cruise ships dock here so passengers can explore Ephesus. Shop owners surmise "If you can afford a cruise you can afford inflated prices!"

Kusadasi caravanserai. 1979 postcard.

Centre stage in Kusadasi is its Caravanserai. A roadside tavern. I was impressed and captivated when I first saw it. In the 17th Century it was extended into its present castle state. Travellers freshened up, ate and rested here and recovered from their day's journey. Caravanserais supported the flow of trade, people and ideas across the Silk Road network.

I loved observing the hustle and bustle of the port. A hive of industry. Multiple trawlers arriving and departing, carrying trays of fresh catches. Maintaining boats. Repairing nets. Shop owners sorting, pricing and displaying fish. Living off the sea's bounty.

My first visit on Capricorn P33H left an indelible memory. Late March. Dark clouds blanketed the sky. A biting wind prevailed. In free time I sought out a Turkish café. I walked into a large empty bistro: checked black and white linoleum floor, rows of tables, plastic table cloths, white plastic chairs.

The two teenagers on duty outnumbered the existing clientele. A black and white TV, high up in one corner so that the whole room could see, was broadcasting a local soccer match.

I ordered a mince Pide and a Turkish coffee and mindlessly watched the football game. Turkish Pide (pizza) are made in specialist brick ovens. The chef forms round balls of pliable dough before kneading them vigorously with strong fingers and the flats of his palms. He then flattens them into long 'Viking boat' shapes and dribbles them generously with an assortment of beef or lamb mince, onions, garlic, parsley, cumin, paprika and cheese. Like a slain Viking chieftain being pushed to out to sea in his burning ship, the Pides are slid into a blazing wood-fired oven on the end of a long wooden spatula with due flourish and panache by the chef. It's like watching an artist at work! The golden Pides emerge from the fire accompanied by a whoosh of heat as the oven opens.

The two guys wandered over. Via a few English words and assisted by sign language, we communicated. One 'topic' led to another. Grinning, they sat down and made themselves comfortable. Initial shyness on all our faces evaporated. The conversation got animated. We connected, engaged, chuckled and chortled. My mince Pide arrived. 22.50 lira. US$= 25 lira.

One went off to quickly return with a dictionary. Turkish/English transactions in the front. English /Turkish in the back. One would rifle through 'their' half of the dictionary to a Turkish word. I would see what he meant in English then refer to 'my' back section to find the English word. We laughed. We bonded. We got adept at finding the right word to express ourselves.

I ordered another Pide—mince and egg— (25.50 lira) and coffees. They paid for the second which we shared. I insisted I pay but they were insistent. I was outnumbered. Humbled.

I was elated. Part of the brotherhood of man. Three people with open minds wanting to learn about the others' culture.

I later met people in life who were well-meaning but biased in their views towards Moslems. Could only connect the faith with 9/11, Al-Qaeda and terrorism.

If only they had travelled when they were young and had receptive minds to experience the generosity of the quintessential Moslem.

Selcuk

Two kilometres from Ephesus, is the unique village of Selcuk.

Why unique? It has white storks nesting majestically on Roman aqueduct stumps. It also has St. John's basilica on Ayasoluk Hill. I visited on each tour to stock up on fresh fruit and vegetables and meat.

Selçuk was named by the Seljuk Turks of the 1300s. It was then known as Ayasoluk under the Ottomans until their fall. Then it reverted to its original name. Situated on top of Ayasoluk is Saint John's Basilica, built in the Sixth Century AD by Emperor Justinian and said to contain the apostle's tomb.

Overland with Top Deck

On my visits to Seljuk, I acquired a snapshot of the Turkish way of life. A well-composed photograph is worth a thousand words. I found Selcuk a charming albeit patriarchal, male-dominated society. During the day, women were invisible in the main streets.

Selcuk's day starts just before dawn with street cleaners sweeping the streets and gutters fastidiously. Streets are largely devoid of rubbish by the time the town's inhabitants make an appearance. Shop owners also sweep their section of pavement and kerb then hose everything down. Produce stalls are set up outside with loaves of bread and fresh fruit and vegetables on display. Cay shops set tables and chairs out on the pavement.

Elderly men gossip in twos and threes. They prop themselves up against the backs of chairs and over the shoulders of mates or lean against their spindly, gnarled canes. Most had moustaches, beards were absent. Two-day-old stubble was more noticeable on manual and farm workers.

Many wore flat newsboy caps. They pushed wooden and plastic worry beads continuously through their calloused fingers. Their hands could tell the story of their life. Half of their number, usually the older generation, wore a well-worn jacket, often dark, even in summer. Their idea of formality.

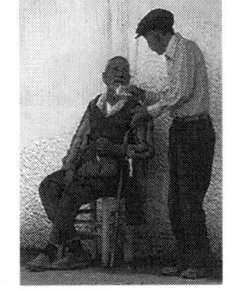

The men's social focus is around tea houses like that at the Efes Hotel, a basic two-star amenity. Serviceable but long past it s halcyon days. Activity was focused in the main lobby downstairs where men sat at tables drinking cay, chatting, playing backgammon or checkers.

A dog's life

The action also spilled outside to the pavement on wooden tables and chairs on the cobblestoned streets. On most of the pavements, shade is provided by well-established, well-tended trees.

Two sets of entrepreneurs, one set being two young boys, had three-wheeled cycles with a large steel container in the front containing ice cream. Cones were in a rectangular box in the front. The owner set up near social gatherings in the afternoon when it was hot. He did a roaring trade. He was protected from the sun by a fold-out umbrella attached to his bike and open above him. The two boys with a similar ice cream cart were more mobile and cycled the streets attracting a younger clientele.

Two owners of a newspaper business had a three-bicycle-wheel cart from which newspapers were sold. They did the rounds with a morning paper and then in the afternoon with the late edition.

Shoe-shine boys also moved around choosing highly visible places to locate. They were rougher-looking. Stubble. Bronzed by the sun. Able to clean, polish and repair shoes.

Horse and carts were often seen. Owners were usually dressed in trousers not jeans, T-shirts and flat caps. Flat newsboy type caps were popular. A guy on a moped zoomed past steering with one hand, clutching his toddler in the other. Casual. No police in sight.

Storks dominate the ruined aqueducts in the village. They have very large, white wings and darker coloured backs. They communicate by rapidly clattering their bills, another almost deafening characteristic of Selcuk at times. Their large nests of sticks are made on top of the remains of a Roman aqueducts, each nest apparently weighing from 60 to 250 kilos.

A dog's life

These high perches on top of broken-down aqueducts afford safety as they are well out of the way of humans as well as ease of take-off. The storks have a wingspan of two metres and need plenty of space to spread their wings and catch the air before take-off or they drop to the ground.

Every year in mid-March the white storks return to Selçuk to mate. Both male and female care for the young, taking turns to fly off and forage for food. The young vigorously fight each other to claim their share—snakes, insects, frogs, toads. rodents, snakes and fish. I chuckled when I saw cats and kittens cotton on and wait expectantly below the nests for cast-offs. When any fish scraps accidentally flew over the top of the nest from a tussle and fall to the ground, there's a scrum of cats who grab what they can and bolt! Head for the hills!

Justinian ordered a basilica built on Ayasoluk hill. One side is slightly more primitive than the other side of town. Less tourists. Less tourist-friendly. White-walled houses. Rows of brown tiles on their roofs.

Broken uneven streets. Deep furrows filled with waste water tossed from dwellings. Women are in evidence here but not in town—baggy Kurdish pants and wearing scarfs, they swept the streets with hand whisks and brooms.

A woman squatted on her haunches on the side of the hill milking a goat and scowling at me suspiciously. I pointed at her and my camera first for approval. She gave me a begrudging nod. Kids, in contrast, grinned gleefully and posed self-consciously and loudly for the photos.

In August 1981, Wendy and I returned to Seljuk to visit Mustafa Urkmez and explore the area. He checked us into Seljuk's 'Efes Oteli' then he and Leann were off to Istanbul to complete the paperwork to get married.

A dog's life

Later, on foot to the beach, a van pulled over to offer us a lift. Two twenty-somethings, Emil and Hussein, operated a newspaper delivery van. Their limited English and our non-existent Turkish wasn't an impediment to attempting to communicate.

They joined us for a swim. For three days we were friends and were impressed by their friendliness, honesty and generosity, traits we had experienced in Islamic countries before.

We mentioned nearby Pammukkale. They had never visited but it was not far from the end of their paper route. They became enthusiastic about going there. Emil pointed to my watch and held up four fingers. We surmised they would pick us up later at 4.00 p.m. That hour came and went and they didn't arrive. We were disappointed. We must have misinterpreted the sign language. The next day perhaps? Wendy and I had dinner and retired for the night.

At four o'clock the next morning, our wooden hotel door vibrated as it was vigorously thumped. The hotel manager Mustafa Baday stood there with Emil and Hussein behind him. Quizzical expressions on all their faces. The Polis were beside them. They had been asked to locate us. They had meant the next *morning's* delivery run! Not the previous afternoon. Scurrying around to get dressed, we were then bundled into their van on top of stacks of newspapers bound together by twine. I loved that fresh newspaper smell. I had been a paper delivery boy for several years. Used to take my Australian terrier with me. Got to know all the local streets well. Earned money for my first stereo and motorbike.

The van's headlights probed the darkness picking up road signs and occasional houses. We pulled over frequently to drop off compact paper bundles. Emil drove. Hussein, Wendy and I counted the newspapers for the next drop. Once stopped, we dragged, hauled and stacked bundles of papers on the pavement outside stores and petrol stations. Hussein checked his clipboard to make sure our numbers stacked up.

Dawn arrived and an orange tinge gradually coloured the sky starting off low and horizontal, rising at its own casual pace. The deliveries completed, we continued onto Pammukkale, stopping first at a Denizli work cafe for a breakfast of soup and piping hot bread from the oven. Fresh bread has a very distinctive aroma as a result of many interactions including sugar and amino acids and sugar caramelisation. The texture was soft and fluffy as we pulled it apart. The soup was made with stock, diced carrots, onions and red lentils and seasoned liberally with salt and pepper, paprika and cumin.

It was Emil and Hussein's first time at Pammukkale. That was humbling. They only lived three hours away. We had done them a favour showing them a scenic historical part of their own country. They were as enthusiastic as schoolboys and, with huge grins splashed about in the brilliantly-blue pools, stretching out and luxuriating as though they were in a hot bath. Most of the basins were shallow, only ankle deep. Emil was the extrovert and wallowed in the warm mud near the basins. He moved his arms and legs up and down and side to side making a 'mud Angel'. There's a boy in every man. And not necessarily hiding.

A dog's life

We tried to enter Cleopatra's pool but entry was only for tourists! No locals allowed! I was appalled. This was *their* country. Wendy and I didn't go in. NOT without our hosts.

Dog: "You'll let tourists into Cleopatra's Pool but not your fellow Turks?! You *cannot* be serious!"

Instead we showed them the Hierapolis amphitheatre. They were impressed.

They insisted on paying for most of our meals including one at a Kusadasi restaurant. When they looked at *that* bill, they couldn't believe the cost and fell about laughing hysterically. Tears welled in their eyes. I insisted we pay but was rebuffed. I berated the restauranteur telling him he was charging his fellow Turks 'tourist prices'. He appeared genuinely affronted. If we came back again, he would throw in a free bottle of wine!

Dropping us back in Selcuk after visiting the Izmir International Fair they thanked us profusely for our friendship, wished us well in the future and then disappeared. Abruptly. I was disappointed. We were having such a good time I wanted the relationship to continue.

I sincerely hope they have had prosperous and successful lives. Inshallah. God willing. A credit to Islam and their country. Forty plus years on, they may not know it, but I remember them fondly. Good deeds are remembered. And cherished.

Back at the Efes Hotel, Wendy and I got acquainted with Mustafa's sons. Eighteen-year old Lulent did a range of jobs for his father. Bulent, at nine-years old, was busy early on hosing down the pavement outside the hotel. He was shy but personable, efficient and focused. He often dressed in pressed trousers with a sharp, well-defined, knife-edge crease, a pressed, short-sleeved white or checked shirt and plastic sandals. He was seen carrying a silver tray on which were balanced several small glasses of cay. Bound for various destinations.

Lulent asked if I could play backgammon. Despite having started when I became a tour leader, I didn't know how proficient I was with locals who play regularly. I pretended I didn't know how. Lulent volunteered to teach me. His teenage mates observed us. We played a few practice games then played a series of five. I won the majority. Boy, did *he* get the raspberry from his mates! They fell about laughing! "You've been playing for ages! You have just taught him and he beat you!"

I felt guilty and to spare his embarrassment confessed that I knew how to play.

THAT brought forth another round of chortles, guffaws and laughter. Tears materialised in his mates' eyes and glistened whilst their fingers pointed at me. I was clapped on the shoulder by several of them and lightly slapped over the back of the head.

You cunning old dog!

A dog's life

Exhaustion

Punters get tired towards the end of a ten-week tour. So too does the crew. Iain and I on Befa were an excellent pairing. I had his back and he had mine. Each was tolerant and patient when the other made a mistake. And we did. But by the tour's last ten days we were fatigued. Available 24/7. Long days. Night drives. In my book, exhaustion exponentially increases the possibility of accidents. Iain and I were physically spent.

Errors came in threes. *We wound our way north of Selcuk, towards Istanbul. I was at the helm around 11.00 p.m. I negotiated my way through a Turkish village. Lights blazed in cay shops. Men were sipping coffees and cay whilst playing checkers, chess and backgammon.*

Following the arrows to the main road, I took a tight left turn. The two left-hand back wheels slid off the cobblestones and lodged securely in soft dirt. Everyone bailed out. Locals assisted, only too happy to oblige. By a combination of sacking in front of the wheels and judicious pushing and levering on the sunken side, we got traction and eventually were on our way.

Error number two. *The next evening. A night drive. Around 11.00 p.m., Iain came to a fork in the roads where the left-hand road, tar-sealed, looked better maintained and the main route. To the right a lesser road, appeared more direct. In the distance, through a thick dark forest were the twinkling lights of the township we were headed for. Iain took the lesser road.*

Five minutes later it dawned on us why the 'road less travelled' was the road less travelled. The tar seal became loose gravel and descended sharply with tight left turns. I walked ahead, concerned by the incline, the road's camber and the precipitous drop into the valley below. I didn't want the bus to tip over. With punters in it. Iain and I exchanged opinions. Punters were roused out of the bus and walked on ahead while Iain gingerly nudged our mobile home forwards. I walked before him on the precarious side and we exchanged views on the road surface, grip of the tyres and the tilt of the bus. Punters piled back within a few minutes when the road flattened and straightened out.

Error number three. *Northern Yugoslavia. Four days later. After midnight Iain took his turn driving. Thinking he may need diesel, I handed him my billfold with two hundred American dollars. Cash.*

Before dawn, a strong grip on my shoulder shook me. Iain wore a worried look. "Wake up! We have a problem!" (Echoing Apollo 13's "Houston we have a problem".) I ushered him downstairs and outside. Whatever it was, I didn't need a 'sticky beak' listening in. We were in a motorway rest area's carpark. Dark except for the light from a lonely lamppost. The light looked ghostly and eerie in the mist.

Iain had pulled in for a rest and a coffee. Climbing into the bus later, Iain realised his pockets were empty. No billfold. Flustered and alarmed, he retraced his steps, checking frantically under tables and chairs and in toilets. At one stage a man had stumbled into him. Iain suspected he might have been pickpocketed.

I took a deep breath. No money? What was Plan B? The car-park was predominantly in shadow. It had been raining recently. Irregular shaped puddles splayed out under our feet. Dawn was due in 15 minutes. The solution was obvious. "Relax, Iain. When it's light enough, we'll do another search." Within 5 minutes I found the billfold, half in a puddle near the carpark's curb. The black billfold was the same colour as the puddle and it merged in.

Troy and Gallipoli

I became interested in Troy when I was eight. A hot summer's school-day. Mr Johnson took us outside to the shade of a large tree. He read an illustrated kids' version of Homer's "The Iliad". Heaps of action engaged the boys and plenty of plotting and scheming by Greek goddesses Athena, Hera and Aphrodite intrigued the girls. Greek gods squabbled amongst themselves to influence the ebb and flow of the Greco-Trojan war.

Dog: "Fight??? Who ME???"

I was intrigued by the Greek armour. The shiny chest plates and full-face plumed helmets. I was impressed by the legendary Achilles but favoured the underdog Hector, brave son of Priam. I had to grin and bear it when he was slain. I was shocked as a ruthless Achilles bound Hector's ankles together and dragged him around the base of Troy behind his chariot.

Two years later, I was 'into' the kid's magazine 'Look and Learn'. In its twenty-four pages were well researched articles. Bold illustrations attracted readers to the text. The historical stories absorbed me the most. One was about Helen—'The face that launched a 1000 ships'. A map showed Troy's strategic location on trade routes between the Mediterranean, the Aegean, the Bosphorus, Istanbul, the Black Sea and the lands beyond. Did trade disputes cause the Trojan War?

March, 1979. My first visit to Troy. To stand at Troy and look over the ruins was a schoolboy's dream come true.

I was disappointed. Just an unruly mass of disorganised bricks. My imagination was working overtime to make sense of it.

Heinrich Schliemann rediscovered Troy in 1876. By not excavating scientifically and methodically, he destroyed much that was valuable. Some say he was more effective than the ancient Greeks in levelling the site. Plundered gold and silver jewellery was taken to Berlin and is now in the Pushkin Museum in Moscow.

Troy is south of the mouth of the Dardanelles. It's located on the Hisarlik hill overlooking flat fertile agricultural land. The sea is now six kilometres away.

I have now come to terms with 'that handful of rocks'. There are nine cities on that site, Homer's Troy being number VI. Scholars think the war occurred around 1200 BC. Homer wrote in 750 BC. There was definitely a large fortified settlement of around 5,000 here, strategically placed for trade, sea-faring and military exploits.

In the 2004 film 'Troy', the reconstruction of the city looked impressive—a walled city close to the sea staggered in terraces up the hillside. Greek armour—like those I had seen as an eight-year old—differed to the Trojan armour which had an Asian/Persian/Armenian look. A wise distinction. Their version of the Trojan horse was presented by the film producers to the town of Cannakkale where it resides along the waterfront today.

Gallipoli is about fifty kilometres from Troy. To visit Gallipoli is an antipodean 'rite of passage'. ANZAC soldiers died at Ypres, Passchendale and the Somme in WW1 but it is Gallipoli that has gripped our collective imaginations. ANZAC ceremonies broadcast from Gallipoli take on an intimate and personal meaning after you have walked the hills, battlefields and beaches. Paid homage. Wept. It's no longer an abstract concept. Instead, it's real images. Spectacularly beautiful forest, beaches and views. Ferns. Bees. Butterflies. Colourful birds. Intoxicating fragrances. Native bush and ferns. Rolling hills. Pebbled beaches. Fastidiously kept graves.

Remember and respect our forebears.

My first visit on Capricorn P33H was a sombre dawn experience made more poignant by the overcast grey skies and cold blustery February winds off the Aegean. We were the only ones there. The Australians and Kiwis had to explain its significance to the Canadian, French and Dutch punters. The English on board did get the significance. Britain had the most casualties of all the allied countries involved.

It's a beautiful site. Approaching it in 1979 along a long windy road, the bus ground and crunched under our tyres and threw up billowing dust clouds. When we descended, we found ourselves on lush grass beside thick verdant pine forests. We inhaled their distinctive scent. The Lone Pine monument was haloed by the rising sun.

"A little spooky" as Dame Edna Everage might say.

I wandered the green bush and fern-laden hills, then the fields, reading the gravestone inscriptions at Lone Pine, Shrapnel Gully and Quinn's Post. Almost 10,000 ANZACs dead. It took mere seconds for tears to well up. 18, 19, 20 year olds ... Only five years younger than the average punter. Boys. Snuffed out. Their first overseas adventure not turning out to be what they expected.

Lemming's punters meandered down the slopes taking in sweeping views of the pine forests and the beaches. We inhaled the fragrance of a multitude of flowers. The rich scent of lavender. Bees buzzing and pollinating. Butterflies swirling about on an invisible breeze, some a relative of NZ's Monarch. This should have been a place to enjoy instead of being the scene of large scale disease, death and destruction.

From the beach, we looked up rugged, steep hills. How exposed the soldiers were. The remains of landing craft still rust in the shallows. All that is left are metal ribs sticking out of the water. Concrete bunkers, worn and weathered over the seasons, stand like mute sentries guarding and remembering those who had died in these shallow waters.

From the topmost ridges and hilltops we looked down from the Turkish point of view. Their homeland was being invaded. Any movement was obvious. Soldiers were isolated. Out in the open. Exposed. A sniper's dream.

I returned in 2019 and the site was just as beautiful … and melancholic. The beaches were calm and tranquil belying their tragic past. The graves were immaculately kept. Respecting the fallen.

Now there is a large Turkish Cemetery. It adds balance to the story. Like the ANZAC side, it is personal, respectful, touching. I watched a young Turk start to leave the site, pause, turn, stand with feet together bowing his head and raising his hands together in prayer closing his eyes to reflect.

In 1979 I knew of Mustafa Kemal's quote and thought it was outstanding. He was a statesman not a mere politician.

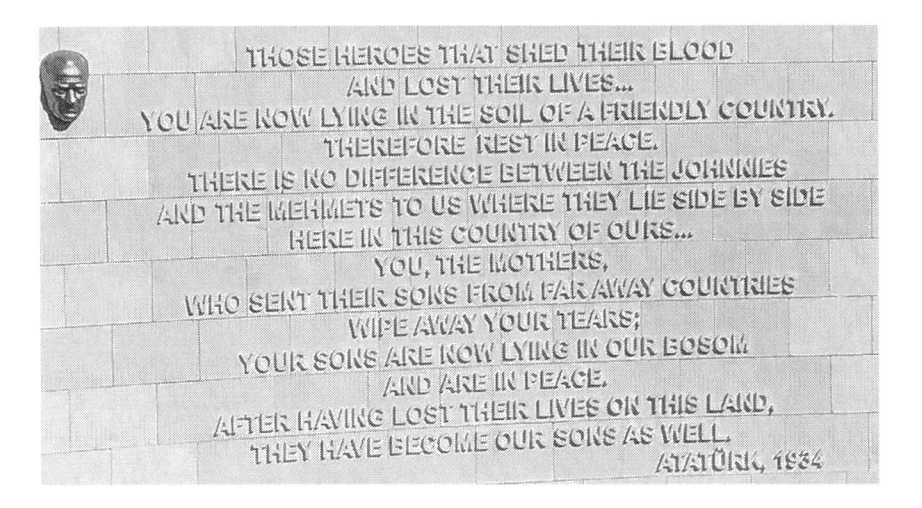

> THOSE HEROES THAT SHED THEIR BLOOD
> AND LOST THEIR LIVES...
> YOU ARE NOW LYING IN THE SOIL OF A FRIENDLY COUNTRY.
> THEREFORE REST IN PEACE.
> THERE IS NO DIFFERENCE BETWEEN THE JOHNNIES
> AND THE MEHMETS TO US WHERE THEY LIE SIDE BY SIDE
> HERE IN THIS COUNTRY OF OURS...
> YOU, THE MOTHERS,
> WHO SENT THEIR SONS FROM FAR AWAY COUNTRIES
> WIPE AWAY YOUR TEARS;
> YOUR SONS ARE NOW LYING IN OUR BOSOM
> AND ARE IN PEACE.
> AFTER HAVING LOST THEIR LIVES ON THIS LAND,
> THEY HAVE BECOME OUR SONS AS WELL.
> ATATÜRK, 1934

I recently saw a TV documentary which followed a NZ Secondary Boys' class touring Gallipoli. In front of Attaturk's words, they did an accomplished Haka to honour the fallen. Feet pounding in rhythm. Angry flushed faces. Eyes wide, staring and challenging. Tongues out. Passion and feeling. Captivating. Hypnotic.

A class of Turkish teenage girls, approximately the same age, stood beside their tour bus, observing quietly. No smiles. Intrigued. When the boys finished, their teacher whispered a few words and the girls, in unison, broke into a Turkish folk song. A complete contrast to the boys' Haka but equally powerful. Soft. Harmonising. Haunting. Deferential. They sang with energy and passion, their hand movements and faces expressing the song's emotions.

A very fitting reposte.

Gallipoli bonds Aussies and kiwis ... and Turks.

In the new millennium, it seems to have become 'the thing to do' to go to Gallipoli for the April 25 commutations. Thousands of people in sleeping bags awaiting the dawn and the beginning of the official programme. Not for me. I feel privileged to have visited several times. Few people. *Whenever you go, it's moving, sobering and poignant.* Should be on everyone's bucket list.

On *Lemming* we wound our way around a spectacular tree-lined coast towards Istanbul. The blacktop was well maintained and made driving a breeze. Well maintained because this is the main route from Istanbul to Gallipoli for tourist traffic. Some hairpin bends are tight and tortuous. On the inland side, the hill climbed steeply. On the seaward side, the bank dropped sharply to the azure waters below. We could smell the sharp turpentine tang of pine trees. The dancing sunlight shafts again played havoc with my vision through the windscreen though! Although a spectacular drive, it was sobering. Istanbul was the launching pad from Asia into Europe. The tour's days were numbered. A little over a week to London.

Istanbul

September 1980. Istanbul bound. On the ferry from Cannakkale to Eceabat, Gallipoli and onto Istanbul.

Istanbul. My favourite city in the world. Its history, location, architecture, and views, the unique atmosphere, the ambience, hospitable people ...

Istanbul was a pivotal point on the overland. Heading east, we were leaving Europe for Asia. The bulk of the tour was in front of us. Heading west, was Europe, 'the hard yards' had been done. The days left could be ticked off on the fingers of two hands.

I had been introduced to local guide, **Sukru** (Sugar) Icimsoy in 1977 and again by Trevor Carroll in October 1979. 'Sugar' was a charming, self-employed tour guide who took tours around Aya Sofia, the Blue Mosque, the Topkapi and the Grand Bazaar. Affable. Energetic. Driven. Resourceful and entrepreneurial. He had an eye for the ladies. It was reciprocated. Turkish men are up there with the French and Italians as being smooth-talking charmers. After completing his compulsory two years military service and assisting in his uncle's Istanbul shop, he was an enterprising tourist guide from 1976 to 1979. After each tourist season, he flew to London in winter to visit tour companies' offices where he promoted himself, collected their brochures, figured out their arrival dates in Istanbul and arranged to conduct tours once they arrived.

He *modestly* billed himself as "the best guide in Europe". He had 'the gift of the gab'. He was highly informative and humorous. I made notes of his talks in case one day he might not be available. That day had come with the *Lemming* tour. He had recently emigrated to South Australia with a Transit punter. He married Lynette and had two children Jonathan and Tamara. He lives in Adelaide today.

Aya Sophia, the Blue Mosque, the Topkapi Palace, the Kapalıçarşi—Covered Bazaar (photo below), the Byzantine cisterns ("From Russia With Love"), the Pudding Shop ("Midnight Express")—are all clustered together in the Sultanahmet area. To really do that justice would take more than just the two days *Lemming* had.

Nearby is the sprawlingly beautiful 16th century Ottoman 'Suleiman Mosque' with panoramic views. From the mosque, wander down narrow, cobblestoned streets packed with people and 'el cheapo' clothes, shoes, caps, sunglasses, jackets, etc. to buy. Goods literally tumble out of shops onto narrow pavements. On a hot day, stop for a freshly-squeezed orange or pomegranate juice. Nearing the bottom of the hill the salty tang of the sea competes with the smell of sizzling kebabs and freshly baked bread. The short sharp blast of ships' horns tell you that the port is close.

At the bottom of the hill is Eminonu, a transport hub. With Casper's punters, I had spent a leisurely afternoon on a ferry travelling up the Bosphorus stopping numerous times along the way on both the European and Asian sides. A huge warship reminded us that the Black Sea, the Ukraine, the Crimea and the USSR were not far away. It was a pleasant day: warm sun, refreshing sea breeze, seagulls circling, gliding and squawking noisily overhead, mixing with locals, playing backgammon, drinking cay, seeing exquisite 19th Century Ottoman palaces and the 1974 suspension bridge connecting Europe and Asia.

Cats seemed to be everywhere in the Aya Sofia, Eminonu and Karakoy areas. Well-fed and looked after. Regarded as clean and healthy. The prophet Mohammed was fond of cats.

The Pudding Shop (2018 photo below) was opposite where the tabby was stretched out. It was a well-known haunt 'back in the day' not only for Turkish sweets and pastries but for meeting travellers and leaving notes for others on their notice board.

A dog's life

Following my walking tour, I issued maps and made suggestions. Some places were walking distance. The cheap metropolitan tram system is a viable option. Mix with the locals. Work out how and where to get a tram ticket and where to get off. There's always a congenial local who will look at where you're pointing on your map and assist.

Once punters scattered, I sought out a barbers in a side street. A place where the locals frequent. A haircut and shave is a "must do" in Turkey. I refrain from shaving for a few days to get the full benefit.

With black hair and a moustache, I could pass as a local. A look of astonishment appeared on the hairdresser's face when he offered me a chair and I replied in English. He offered me a cay. I indicated my requirements via sign language. Hot white hand towels were wrapped around my face. Soothing. Steam opened up the pores letting out sweat, dirt, excess oil and bacteria. The hairdresser poured hot water into a small metal bowl, and used that water and some gel to work up a lather. The water was warm and the lather soon became thick and creamy. He applied it liberally to my cheeks and chin with a short stubby badger brush, like I'd seen my Scottish grandfather use. He honed the cut-throat razor vigorously on a leather strop and meticulously set to work slicing through the shaving cream. The steel hissed through my five o'clock shadow. He massaged a scented cream into my cheeks and put a small hot towel over the shaved area. Eyebrows were trimmed and shaped and any nose hair trimmed. He used a long flaming taper to tap lightly at my ears to singe off any ear hair. I was intrigued by that. Painless but theatrical.

He completed the shaving ritual with two pieces of cotton stretched between one hand and the other. These were used in a quick, deft, scissoring/threading motion to remove 'down' on my upper cheeks. The cotton thread trapped the hair in a mini lasso, and pulls it up and out of the hair follicle.

The hairdresser swapped the razor for scissors and started in on my hair. Ten minutes later he was finished. The craftsman took one step back to admire his handiwork. His client admired his new image. He was indeed an artisan. I wondered if he was following the family tradition.

The haircut and shave cost one NZ dollar. I tipped the hairdresser and his little son who assisted him by sweeping up my fallen locks.

I walked away that first time thinking I *must* make that a habit.

I walked to Cagalolu Hamami, in Yerebatan Street, for a Turkish bath. Cagaloglu Hamami dates from 1741 and has hosted Florence Nightingale and Omar Sharif. If it's good enough for them … Hammans were originally developed as a public service because of city-wide water shortages but now appear a blend of the Koran's emphasis upon bodily cleanliness and a little luxurious indulgence. I was pummelled to the brink of dismemberment on my first massage. Subsequently I opted for 'self-service'. I relaxed in my own time and had the alternate hot dry sauna and cold water experience. That was followed by a cay whilst wrapped in a large towel lounging on soft pillows in the wind-down area.

A dog's life

In Istanbul, a priority is to wander down to the Galata Bridge. Beautiful views of the harbour and the mosques on the surrounding hills. Fishermen, and the occasional fisherwoman wearing a habib or chador, spend hours standing here, not seeming to catch much, just chatting and soaking up the views, the breeze and the salty tang of the sea. Some have small wooden v-shaped blocks balanced on the bridge's railing to support their rods. Some have stools. Most have a small bucket for their catches. I find it relaxing, almost hypnotic. I kept an eye on the small fishing boats tied up at the quay. Who has the freshest looking buns? Who has fresh fish sizzling? Who produces the best looking fish in a bun? Devouring a succulent 'fresh fish in a bun' became a regular ritual for me whenever I was in Istanbul. I always asked for the fish coming straight off the coals. Not those beginning to dry out.

Photo: Mid-October 1979. The anonymous guy in the skiff between the fresh buns and frying fish didn't know it, but he hooked me on 'fish in a bun' for life. Tessekkurler.

Close by is the **Egyptian Spice market.** Originally built in the early 17th century by taxes and duties on Egyptian imports, it is always packed with people. I get swept along in the throngs of people like a piece of debris in a flood-swollen river. Stopping to look at something requires skill. Almost an art form. You make a conscious and deliberate effort to step to one side and stop like a boat docking itself out of the pull of the current. The market is a kaleidoscope of sounds, sights and smells. Mounds of colourful spices and herbs. Nuts and seeds. Honey. Dried beef. Turkish delight.

Egypt

Capricorn P33H Group photo. Indian guide Mr Das extreme left. Carl Capstick driver, back row extreme right, at the Taj Mahal.

Top Deck didn't have Egypt on the itinerary in 1979 or 1980. That did come later—in the '90s. Capricorn did. It was a worthwhile and highlight-filled few days. Our P33H punters checked in early at a bustling Athens Airport and by 6.30 a.m., TWA flight 840 was winging its way to Cairo. I sank back in my seat and enjoyed the flight whilst recalling 1956's 'The Ten Commandments'. I visualised Yul Brynner as Ramses II driving a light, two-horse war chariot.

Egypt experienced early developments in farming, writing, urbanisation and organised religion. Hunter-gatherers settled along the Nile and developed successful irrigation methods. They dug canals and used the crane-like shaduf, which had a lever mechanism, for lifting water up in in buckets from the Nile to tip into irrigation canals. Cattle, sheep and goats were domesticated.

Corn was harvested. Crops were counted and recorded. Memphis and Thebes grew from small settlements into cities.

We were driven through fertile farmland of date palms. Field after field of vegetables were being worked by men and women. Oxen laboured in rutted, never-ending circles as they extracted water from wells. Donkeys and camels carried loads of grass and vegetables. There was no modern machinery. Artisans in the fields were using the same methods that their ancestors used thousands of years ago.

The pyramids of Giza were the tombs of the pharaohs Cheops, Chephren and Mykerinos. They were 2,000 years old when Alexander the Great marched by in 332 BC. Cheops was the highest at 146 metres high. Chephren was 136 metres. Cheops contains two million blocks weighing over two tons each. Time, the elements and thieves have removed the outermost layer of smooth limestone. Quite a feat of engineering and labour. Tens of thousands of slaves worked twenty years to construct one.

To go inside the pyramids we had to stoop low, instantly inhaling a moist musty smell. Like going through the underground tunnels at Kaymakli.

A dog's life

Crouching low, we hunched and hunkered our way along narrow, steep corridors. Outside, Barb, Jules, Jan, Jude and Rosemary considered camel rides. One Egyptian £ per pyramid circuit. I took in the atmosphere. Closed my eyes. Imagined five thousand years ago. The wind whipped up the sand under grey, sultry late afternoon skies.

April 22. My 28th birthday. At breakfast that day, our group received the "brush-off" from an irate waiter. He was aggrieved and indignant at Rose-Marie from the evening before. The likeable but very frustrating 'frenchies'—Rose-Marie and Jackie—had an unparalleled gift for rubbing someone up the wrong way. High maintenance. Very demanding. French. Rose-Marie had ordered a special meal instead of the Egyptian one ... then had not turned up! Not unusual.

I took the waiter aside and attempted to sweet-talk him. A 'mission impossible' until ... I surreptitiously slid a packet of cigarettes into his shirt pocket. Nudge, nudge, wink, wink. The service perked up spectacularly. He was particularly attentive to my table and plied us with fresh buns, butter, jam and numerous cups of tea and coffee.

He purposely snubbed Rose-Marie's table. Just desserts?

The day's sight-seeing included a visit to the Cairo Museum of Egyptian Antiquities. Jam-packed with 120,000 exhibits and displays, a couple of hours soon flies by. I did find the 3,000 year-old 'mummies' just a tad wizened and creepy.

Preparing for dinner, there seemed an endless succession of delays getting to the meal. I was ravenous and was getting increasingly agitated with the procrastination, the reasons why being relayed to me by Liz who couldn't help but sense my frustration.

On entering the dining room, I became aware of the reason for the delays. The tables were arranged in a U shape and were covered with starched white tablecloths. Silver service. Everyone else was seated. And grinning broadly. A chorus of "Happy Birthday" rang out.

Resplendent in the middle of the table? A birthday cake.

I was ushered to the head of the table. Liz sat on my right. Rob Hall, always an accomplished speaker, stood with a smile and with due pomp and ceremony, tapped his fork against his wine glass and called for everyone's attention. He twirled his Hercule Poirot moustache with a theatrical flourish. Not unlike Jack Lemmon's Professor Fate in 1965's 'The Great Race', but without the maniacal laugh. I chuckled. With a gleam in his eye, he read from a large red book. "Dog ... this is your life!"

I settled back and, over the next hour, listened to the 'voices' from my 'doggy' past—Mr Sludge the dog show judge, Mr Henry Snatcher the dog catcher and ... various bitches. Tineke later added in the Trip Book 'Congratulations to those responsible for the brilliant script'.

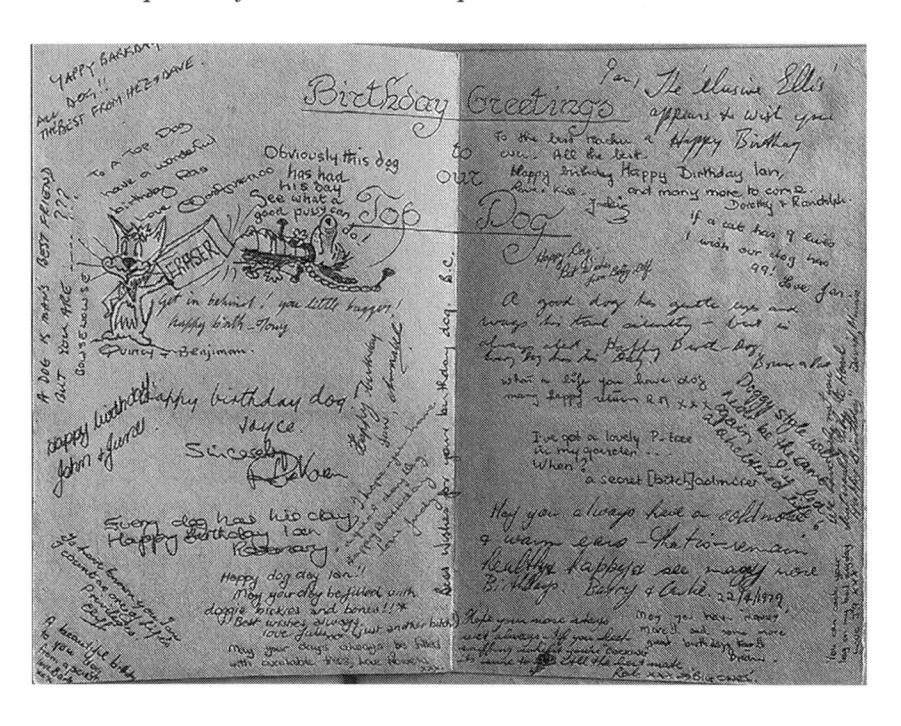

Rob ended the sketches with the line—"Well, I'll make no bones about it. Everyone here wishes you the happiest of birthdays. Dog, this is your life!"

A dog's life

A lot can happen in ten weeks. On Day One of the tour, I hadn't started drawing 'dog'. Now, Day 74, I was the subject of a 'This is your life' send-up!

As Maxwell Smart would have said "And ... loving it!"

I was presented with a massive bone. Via a new collar and chain lead, I was led to blow out the candles on the cake. Following that, eating, drinking and singing followed. A grand night.

The night train to Luxor was Victorian-era. Long, narrow wood-panelled corridors down one side of the train from which you squeezed into 'compact' apartments. The quantity and quality of sleep was minimal. The train bumped, rattled and ground its way through the night — clackedy-clack, clackedy-clack, clackedy-clack. A perfect setting for a 1930s era, Agatha Christie murder mystery!

Fortunately no-one was dispatched during the night. Even 'the Frenchies' survived. (It could have been like the plot of 'Murder on the Orient Express', where everyone on the train, individually, stabs the victim.) We reached Luxor by 7.30 am and were shuttled post-haste to the Hatshepsut hotel by horse and buggy. An hour later we were visiting the Karnak and Luxor temples.

Luxor village housed around 300,000 people and was a kaleidoscopic feast for the senses: dry and dusty with mud and dung houses, broken uneven roads, the smell of urine in open drains, workmen with heavy baskets of bricks on their heads, donkeys laden with huge bundles of grass, flocks of goats and sheep herded by women shrouded in black, bedraggled children running parallel with our carriages with bony arms outstretched crying out for baksheesh. The Nile was flanked by date palms and lush scenery and the paddle steamers, surrounded by smaller Egyptian skiffs and falukas, seemed like extras out of the 1978 Agatha Christie/Hercule Poirot movie 'Death on the Nile'.

'Photo: Jules Skinner and 'Dog' dwarfed by the Karnak columns.

The Hypostyle Hall was built of 134 huge sandstone columns in 16 lines and even now, many of the designs and pictures are clear. A few had been chiselled away. Karnak is usually a highlight of any remake of Agatha Christie's 'Death on the Nile'. The columns are huge and they cast enormous diagonal shadows. Some are sixty-nine feet high. We were dwarfed. Linking hands, it took eight of us to circle one column. Apparently the top of one can accommodate about forty people standing close together. At that height, I wasn't going to try it!

Queen Hatshepsut only produced daughters. The concubine's son was to be king but Hatshepsut imprisoned him for twenty-two years for insulting her. Tough love. When he was finally released, he removed every image of her that he could find. Can't blame him!

Later, we went to see the Temple of Luxor/Thebes. Its glory days were 1540 to 1640 BC. There are huge statues of Ramesses II and an impressive avenue of sphinxes, columns, obelisks, gateways and statues. We were almost in history, information and stunning ruin overload before heading back to the hotel for lunch.

Arising early the next morning to avoid the full heat of the day, we caught a ferry to the other side of the Nile. A well-worn mini-bus carried us to the Valley of the Kings, lying in a nondescript, sun-scorched desert valley surrounded by steep, dry, dusty hills. About fifty tombs have been discovered so far. Not all of them were pharoahs.

As the sun rises in the east, ancient Egyptians built their homes on the east bank of the Nile. The sunrise represented, to them, birth and life. The sunset, by contrast symbolised the end of life. Hence their tombs.

We visited the tombs of Tutankhamun and Ramses VI. Meant to preserve the pharoah's mummies for ever, each tomb is located deep in the ground and resembles how they saw the underworld. A descending corridor leading to a hall connected to a burial chamber. The engravings and colouring still left on the walls was clear and magnificent.

The tomb of Ramses VI was constructed over the top of Tutankhamun's and made it difficult to find by robbers and explorers alike. As it was originally built for a priest, it had frescoes but no engravings. The mummy still lies there, encased in the second casing. Tutankhamun died at the age of twenty-two from a knife incision into his brain from behind his left ear.

The heat, noise and rattling of the overnight train was again not conductive to a decent night's sleep. From the dining carriage in the morning, we saw scenes of Egyptian life. Like taking a step back in time: the Nile, small dusty villages, women washing and scrubbing and kneading clothes in the Nile, small toddlers swimming and playing and laughing in the nude, camels trudging along, laden down with huge stacks of grass, women hunched over picking crops in the fields, others sitting in the shade of date palms.

Overland with Top Deck

After settling into the Fontana hotel again, Liz and I set off on foot to find Gaz Tours to collect mail for the group. Half an hour later we were lost. We hailed a taxi and asked to be taken to the Cairo Museum. We knew the way back to the hotel from there. Not listening to Liz's (wise) counsel, I was persuaded by the driver to be dropped off at the back door of a huge structure which he claimed was the Museum. After disembarking and paying him, I/we discovered that it was not the museum. Liz burst into tears and a few minutes later I lost her in the crowd ...

The next five minutes seemed endless and were very stressful.

Trying not to panic, I banished thoughts of white slavers kidnapping her! She was young, attractive, had a voluptuous hourglass figure and was blonde. Could be worth a few camels. The crowds were thick around us, shoulder to shoulder, jostling past, going about their everyday chores. Liz must be there somewhere. I called out to her repeatedly. My voice was swallowed by the hubbub and din.

We eventually found each other. Liz sobbed with relief and hugged me tight. I was very relieved and grasping her tightly by the hand, hailed another taxi to get her 'home' safely, both chastened by the experience.

A few beverages in the bar followed! My first beer didn't touch the sides! Liz's double rum and coke didn't either. Nor did her Bailey's Irish Cream chaser.

We had about ten days to go on tour. We were going to miss each other. A lot. We had chemistry but ... we had met each other too early in our travels. She wanted to work in London. Receive her 'Duke of Edinburgh' award at Buckingham Palace. Travel more. I wanted to be a tour leader. Really get to know Europe well, not just 'once over lightly'. Do another overland.

You can't always have your cake and eat it too.

Cliff and Dog at Cairo Airport.
Dog is wearing his birthday collar and leash.

— 386 —

The last stretch to London: Europe

Through the Turkish-Greek border and on via Alexandropoulos, Komotini and Xanthi, *Lemming* motored to eastern Macedonia's principal seaport Kavalla and located Camping Alexandros. Well-appointed. Decent sandy beach. Water so clear you can see the sandy bottom metres out.

Reminding everyone that we would have the end of tour farewell party here, we drove into **Kavalla** to stock up on ice, alcohol, fresh vegetables, alcohol, eggplant, olives, mackerel, alcohol, sardines, anchovies, shrimps, fish and meat for the barbecue. Ohh ... and alcohol.

Punters were impressed by the Byzantine fortress and the bustling harbour but showed signs of sight-seeing overload. The senses were overloaded. Just get us back to the beach Ian. No more sights Ian ... please!

That beach barbecue was a success as was the finishing up party. Yorkshire Pip and I paired up to present awards in the Academy Award format—the 'Pooch Awards'. Similar to the first one I did on P33H. Different punters, different awards, different films alluded to. Several punters dressed up and put on their own sketches and skits.

My Jaipur seductress still wasn't 'officially' talking but looked at me with a weary smile, her face silently speaking a range of emotions and acknowledging the tour had been an eventful experience even though her sex life hadn't quite lived up to expectations.

Photo: *Befa's* farewell party, Kavalla, late March, 1980.

Farewell parties are 'bittersweet'. The bitter part being ... the tour was terminating. Punters would soon separate. Maybe to never see each other again. They had been together ten weeks travelling Kathmandu to London. Twenty weeks if they started in Sydney.

The sweet part was punters had had an absolute ball along the way. They had unforgettable adventures, big and small. You knew it at the time even if you were weary and exhausted by tour's end.

Too much alcohol was apparently consumed by *some* of *Lemming's* punters ... who descended to the beach after the awards to build a fire and have more beverages. Once chunky-sized beach driftwood was hard to find, some bright spark loaded one of the tourist paddle boats onto the embers. The 'guilty' were up early to pay the owners for the damage. I didn't find out then. Morris and Trish told me forty years later.

My tour farewell parties have been different but usually of a high quality. The farewell party for Capricorn P33H (going west) was the best ever. Excellent punters. Well-planned and executed. A model to go by. The following overland farewell party on Casper was the complete opposite. The worst. What not to do. We were travelling east. You hit the 'Delhi belly' countries after you have been on the road for seven weeks. Punters were exhausted, ill and disinterested in a farewell party after travelling through Pakistan and India.

Going west? Fewer suspect foods, germs, bugs and upset stomachs.

Befa's farewell party was another superb model. Punters organised it. They were a scholarly, articulate group and did it all. Skits. Teasing. Driver and tour leader mercifully spared. Poetry. Awards went to: 'Mr. Top Deck', 'Miss Top Deck', the snazziest dresser, the best dancer, the smelliest farter, the sneakiest farter, the best cook, the worst cook, the person who lost the most clothes, the person who was often late, the person who swore the most, the most avid culture vultures, the best ad-libber ...

From Kavalla, another express journey through Yugoslavia to Venice to wind down. *Lemming* stayed two nights at Camping Fusina. A Dog-inspired T-shirt was designed and then reproduced at the campground by 'Goose'.

Venice is unique lying in a marshy Venetian Lagoon and sitting on 110+ small islands separated by canals but linked by bridges, the name deriving from the Veneti people who fled there from the Goths. The original people made their homes on islands by driving wooden stakes into the ground and building platforms onto those and buildings atop the platforms.

By the late 1200s it was prosperous city due to its location/ trading position linking Europe and Asia. A republic with a constitution with checks and balances for the populace. Power was exercised by a small number of aristocratic families through a 'Great Council'. The head of the Great Council was the Doge. (Or was that Doggie?) Venice was the launching pad for several of the crusades. At its peak, Venice dominated European commerce with 36,000 sailors operating 3,300 ships.

A dog's life

Venetian traders Niccolo and Maffeo Polo, Marco's father and uncle, travelled to China and met the Emperor Kublai Khan in 1269. Returning to Venice, they collected teenager Marco, and returned to the east where they remained for 24 years. On his return to Venice around 1299 with many treasures and riches, Marco Polo wrote a detailed account of his adventures and the countries they travelled through. He died a rich man in 1324 and is buried in the San Lorenzo church in Venice.

I have seen San Marco's square in excellent weather but also under flood water (aqua alta/ high tide). I love the ambience of the Cathedral and the square, the pigeons on the lampposts, bands playing to tourists sitting outside cafes in the sun. I saw a different side to the traditional image of the Square in 1979's 'Moon-raker'. Bond in a gondola/ hydrofoil combination doing a circuit of the square, with Roger Moore as Bond with a supercilious smirk on his face. The scene desecrated the place but I couldn't help but (reluctantly) smile.

San Marco Square is dominated at the eastern end by the church of St. Mark and the clock tower. The church's bronze horses are replicas of the horses taken during the crusaders' sack of Constantinople in 1204. I showed punters inside the church—St Mark is buried there—and some took the lift up the 300 foot campanile for the views.

Walking the punters around San Marco piazza, we came to the Bridge of Sighs, a covered-over bridge made of white limestone. It has windows with stone bars. Prisoners walked from the interrogation rooms in the Doge's palace via the bridge to the prison on the other side. That view of Venice was the last sight that prisoners saw before their internment. Hence their sighs.

After exploring the streets around the square including the Rialto Bridge, the oldest spanning the Grand Canal, I started to suggest things to do in their free time. I was halted at number three on my list. We could have been on the bridge of sighs. "Ian! *NO* more sight-seeing! (Sigh). Where can we get a coffee, a snack, pizza or a gelato?" (Sigh). I led them through narrow side streets to a sandwich bar. It was the first Venetian café I'd been to. My punters were at a glass factory. When I looked at the menu … I was spoilt for choice. Expresso? Lungo? Ristresso? I chose Cappuccino which was about the only name I recognised. I've learned a lot since then.

Lemming's punters and I spent that balmy afternoon mellowing out in the late afternoon sun as shadows lengthened.

Returning to Camping Fusina, we collected our T-shirt designs and wore them proudly as we tucked into their traditional pork spare ribs, a culinary delight.

Happy hour was on at the bar. Most punters consumed copious quantities of alcohol. The alcohol dulled the pricks of the multitude of mosquitoes lined up like bomber squadrons in battle formation poised to dive. A very pleasant way to (almost) end the tour.

I couldn't resist a diversion to **Florence**. Not on the itinerary but a firm favourite of mine which shouldn't be missed. The birthplace of the Renaissance (1300s to the 1600s), the transition between the Middle Ages and the modern world. Many changes in intellectual thinking happened in this time. Best known for its developments in art. Michelangelo, Leonardo da Vinci and Botticelli walked these streets.

I like small cities. Compact. Historical. Classical architecture. I knew a small area of Florence well. I led punters on a walking tour via a series of linked piazzas to reach the cathedral. In the Piazza del Duomo, the cathedral towers over the russet-coloured roofs of Florence. Begun in 1296, completed in 1436, it is often just called the "Duomo". Designed by Brunelleschi, it is still the largest dome built in bricks and mortar in the world.

Back to the Piazza della Signoria, with its wide arches, Corinthian columns and sculptures. Cellini's bronze 'Perseus' and the 'Rape of the Sabines' are there as well as numerous copies of Michelangelo's David. The original resides in 'The Academia'.

From the Piazza della Signoria, it was minutes to the Palazzo Vecchio and Ponte Vecchio. Rebuilt in the 14th Century from the Etrusan original it spans the Arno River. In the 16th Century, Ferdinando de 'Medici ordered silver shops to replace the original smelly butcheries.

The bridge is renowned for its silver shops and as the only bridge over the River Arno still standing after the German retreat in 1944. Hitler, an art lover and painter, ordered his Wehrmacht not to demolish it.

I would have liked to have stayed the night in Florence and take the punters to the 'Red Garter'. It has character and 'olde worlde' charm. Tour groups usually have a great evening drinking, dancing and chatting. Crew from a variety of companies catch up with each other.

The alternative to the Red Garter was the 'Space Electronic.' Modern. Less atmosphere. I went there once and only remember it for its bar aquarium. Late in the evening I went for a Jack Daniels top-up. The two bartenders were serving people flat tack, mixing cocktails with a flourish, pouring generous spirit measures over ice, passing out labelled bottles of beer, finding change and passing and re-passing each other in impressive, deft, surefooted moves. The cash drawer slammed in and out non-stop.

Swirling ice in my glass whilst waiting, I glanced into the bar aquarium that I was leaning against. I shook my head in disbelief. Maybe I needed to cut back on those bourbons. The flat fish with the crooked buck-teeth staring blankly back at me reminded me of South American piranha.

They were!

If you dropped any change from your drinks into the tank, it was gone. You were definitely leaving it to the tank cleaners.

We stopped briefly at **Pisa** on the way out of Italy. The tower which is the Cathedral's bell tower was begun in the 1100s but gradually began to settle into its foundations resulting in it being fifteen feet from the perpendicular by the 1900s. It has since been shored up.

A dog's life

Munich is the capital of Bavaria and is renowned for its annual Beerfest running the fifteen days prior to the first Sunday in October. The first Oktoberfest took place in 1810 to celebrate a prince's marriage. Until 1896 the festival included other activities like horse racing but from 1896, the annual event became solely beer-focused.

The grounds of the **Oktoberfest** in Theresienwiese are covered by numerous, cream-coloured, aircraft-hangar like marquees each promoting a particular brand of beer. The marquees are packed with revelling punters, Aussies and Kiwis making up a decent proportion of the total percentage! The waitresses are young, blond and attractive, dressed in traditional short black skirts, frilly, white low-cut tops showing abundant natural cleavage which bounced a lot as they were usually in a hurry. They carry several large, heavy steins in each hand. Don't try to walk off with a stein as a souvenir, the bouncers will come down heavy on you! Each stein holds one litre of beer.

Lemming's punters wandered around the various stalls, sideshows and joyrides. I'm not a great beer drinker but food? Lead me to it. The mouth-watering aroma of roasted beef and lamb and chicken on open spits was tantalising and competed with the smells coming from grilled doner-kebab, spare ribs and many types of sausage such as Bratwurst (spiced sausage), Blutwurst (blood sausage) and Weisswurst (veal sausage). As well as getting through 6 million steins of beer, the crowds at each Octoberfest also get through 630,000 chickens, over 350,000 sausages and 90 oxen! Plus unknown but immense quantities of sauerkraut.

We camped overnight in the beerfest grounds. On some tours we freshened up in the public showers (Volksbad) near the Deutsches Museum. You access a small Spartan but clean cubicle with enough room to move around in and a wooden bench to sit on. You strip off, hang up your clothes and enter the separate shower booth. Unlike some camp showers that are on a time switch, these showers were 25 minutes long. And hot. I usually took my time! Luxury!

As *Lemming's* punters were 'cultured out', (no more sights please), I did not take them to the Deutsches Museum, the world's largest Science and Technology museum. 28,000 exhibits from 50 fields. I particularly liked the WW1 biplane exhibition and in particular Baron von Richthofen's Fokker Triplane. Incredibly small.

The end is nigh...

Despite Venetian, Florentine and Oktoberfest highlights, two random events in that last week stood out.

The first occurred at the Italian/French border. Camel had driven *Lemming* on smooth autostrada all day travelling through numerous superbly engineered tunnels. Night had descended and punters were mellow after drinking duty-free purchases all day. There had been many toilet stops. My turn to drive.

I completed the border formalities as punters used the public facilities. Climbing into the cab, an anonymous voice yelled "Ian, Subby's not here. She's in the toilets. She's p*ssed. You'd better round her up. Go fetch her Dog!"

A chorus of snickers, giggles and chortles followed. Briskly returning to the passport office, I found Sabrina wandering around befuddled. Indeed more than a *little* worse for wear. She looked at me through glazed eyes. Ahh... there you are! The dog gathering up his flock!

I draped my arm lightly around her shoulders and quietly barked "Come on (little sister), 'home' is this way." Several punters saw me shepherding her. Kathy commented that the two of us made a poignant photograph! Awww ...

There were several interpretations. A teacher rounding up his students. Herding cats. Herding dogs. Herding sheep.

A teacher for seven years, I *did* feel paternalistic. It's in our training. In our blood. I was acting *"in locus parentis"*, for those parents and family I farewelled in the St Leonard's Station carpark. Their kids were *my* responsibility. I wanted them to have a tour of a lifetime, to love the overland route as much as I did. ALL had to get to London safely. I had achieved that once more. Three times in a year.

The second 'lightbulb moment' came when Camel remarked how proud he was to have successfully done an overland. I thanked him for his mechanical/DIY skills, nursing *Lemming* along in atrocious conditions, his easy-to-get-along-with personality. Putting up with me when I was tired and grouchy in Cappadocia. A reliable dependable team member.

I mused over Camel's comment. I had never thought of it as an achievement before. Any successful completion of a tour was 'a given'. Like my passing a university paper. I started so I would finish! No 'ifs', 'buts' or 'maybes'. Giving up was never considered. Not an option.

To do an overland *was* an achievement. There are crew who have done far more than I. Richard Hewitt has done eleven. Overlands were potentially hazardous tours. Anything could happen. And did. I had experienced first-hand: war-torn and divided countries often in the midst of a civil war, Soviet troops in Afghanistan, revolutionary fervour in Iran, anti-western riots in Lahore, militia holding me up in Syria, intertribal warfare and government crackdowns in Northern Syria, a military coup in Turkey, an irate bottle-wielding taxi driver in Jerusalem, getting a driver out of a local jail in Amman.

Not to mention bad 'roads', sickness, diarrhoea, visa delays, long border crossings ...

Reaching 'Old Blighty'

Camel took responsibility for *Lemming* in Dover and drove to London. Everyone else took the train to Victoria Station on September 24, 1980. About this time last year, I was being interviewed by Bill James. A *lot* of adventures—three Asian overlands and one Australian —had been packed into a year. It was sentimental saying goodbye when you live check by jowl with others for ten weeks. There were hugs, kisses and tears. Promises to stay in touch. "Can't thank you enough Ian," Morris and others said. I received a begrudging nod and a tepid smile from Curly.

Lemming's punters were an excellent bunch. All realised just how big their adventure had been, how enormous the distances covered. 19,000 km from Kathmandu to London alone. Especially the 20 weeker from Sydney. I am sure they got very good value for their A$2583.00 investment. Each had dined well on their A$198.50 food kitty. Punters' adventures would enthral parents, friends and grandkids in the years to come. You did *what*?

Dropping my accounts and the punters' reports off at Top Deck HQ in Kenway Road, I passed Dillon on the other side of the street. He stared straight ahead ignoring me. Still smarting from our telex interchanges? Plus getting the tour in two days late. Hold it! Didn't the 1979/1980 brochure say they were eleven week tours? I was early. *C'est la vie.* Life's too short to hold grudges. Let's have a beer sometime and recall that fantastic era.

I never returned to collect the remainder of my pay. I had already withdrawn some of it. Top Deck usually had cash-flow issues. Time for a little payback. Besides, I have simple needs. I am grateful for small mercies. Skroo did me a favour by starting up the company then employing me. Bill had looked after me handsomely in Australia, offered me the Aussie overland, flown me to Kathmandu via a Bangkok stopover for

Overland with Top Deck

the express tour, put me up in room 107 of Drivers' Alley at the Blue Star for a month and reunited me with my Aussie punters for the 10 weeker.

I'd had an absolute ball and had savoured the Top Deck experience. I would be a better person and teacher because of my experiences. No longer one of those who goes from high school to teachers' college to teaching with no 'real' world experiences. I was grateful. Blessed.

I was now reading 'The Times Educational Supplement' looking for a permanent teaching job in England.

We had a reunion in a London pub within a month. Already many had jobs, either by drawing upon past skills or being prepared to learn new ones. Cress began work in hotel management and hospitality as intended. 'Flo' got work as a nanny and within a short time she became a nanny to the children of Kiwi operatic diva, Kiri Te Kanawa. She got flights around the world when Kiri went touring with her children! Even one back home to Aotearoa NZ. Jeff Spann returned home instead of working for Top Deck. Pip returned to Huddersfield for her sister's wedding and began work as her dentist father's receptionist. Camel and Jan were an item and rumour had it that they were getting married. Several others used London as a base to explore the British Isles and places further afield.

Trish and Morris Tanner got jobs in "The Old Swan" for £45 each a week. A workmate soon invited them home for a homespun meal. "I was going to cook you NZ leg of lamb. But that's probably old hat to you kiwis. So I cooked you a good old English steak and kidney pie instead!" Trish and Morris had been on cooking duty in the last few days of the tour. Meat was expensive in Europe. We had *several* tins of 'Bachelor's Steak and Kidney pie' in storage under the upstairs bench seats. Trish and Morris had worked diligently to produce steak and kidney in a *multiple* of tasteful ways.

Epilogue

I lived in England from September 1980 to September 1985 securing 'supply' teaching at first then a permanent teaching position in Hertfordshire two months after arriving back. Within two years, I won promotion as a deputy principal. Beginning an M.Ed. at Exeter University in 1981, one I couldn't do in NZ, I graduated in 1984.

Taking students on the tube to London to see art galleries and museums and having lunch whilst feeding the pigeons in Piccadilly Circus was a highlight I never grew tired of. A humble kiwi teacher with his class in the middle of London, 1,000s of kilometres from home. As an ex-Outward Bounder, each year I took students on week-long tours to Wales' Wye Valley to kayak, climb and abseil.

Time eventually caught up. I was enjoying learning to scuba dive along the French Riviera when I had a lightbulb moment. Why was I paying good money for sun, sand and sea when I had a holiday home near the beach 'down under'? Time to return.

Terry Pratchett wrote "Why do you go away? So that you can come back. So that you can see the place you came from with new eyes and extra colors. And the people there see you differently too".

In NZ, I taught again, gained a contract as a media lecturer at Auckland College of Education before going on to become a principal for twenty years at three different schools. Now I am semi-retired and relief teaching. Teaching Year 7/8 one day, new entrants the next and most levels in between. For eight years Victoria University has contracted me as a visiting lecturer. At the end of 2023, I will hand in my chalk … err, whiteboard pens.

Forty-plus years on, I wished I'd been a tour leader for a longer period. But at that time, forty-three weeks on the road in a year was a lengthy period. Fifty-four weeks 'on the road' in the sixteen months I was a tour leader, was considerable. Some tours had been back to back. I had crossed Europe and Asia, the Indian and Australian subcontinents.

I met up with wife Carol over a pizza in Earls Court just before Christmas, 1980. She had arranged a meeting to ask for a divorce. I knew that was inevitable. I had not seen her for two years. Tears glistened in my eyes. I was twenty-three when we married. Almost thirty now. I had got over the turmoil around the demise of my family. Had travelled. Had many adventures. Was now ready to settle down and have a family. I knew I should have had those adventures and sown those 'wild oats' before we married. I couldn't expect her to wait.

She said she had no-one else but I was doubtful. She wouldn't be travelling alone. Someone was out there, probably close. In fact, a mate from teachers' college. In 1981, she and her new partner headed home to Aotearoa with Top Deck on—of all buses, *Lemming*. She conceived along the way. When her daughter Louisa was born, Carol gave her a bib inscribed with "I've been everywhere man."

I met up with a former punter and thought ours could be a long-term relationship. That was not to be. We bought a house together. Over five years my charms faded and she fell pregnant to a Frenchman at her work. When we parted, my £10,000 house share converted to NZ$25,000.00, a decent amount to return home with, after almost seven years.

After that relationship imploded, I caught up with an ex-punter. By now, I felt I *wanted* and *needed* a family. My biological clock appeared to be ticking. I didn't want to be the last Hall. However she already had a strong family unit of parents and sister. She didn't need another. I didn't want to force her to have a family against her better instincts. Nor did I want to deny my feelings.

Looking back, I grew up during my tour leader years and undertook the Top Deck challenges, the dangerous and unpredictable, 'in my stride'. I was quietly confident in my abilities, usually unfazed and didn't panic. Just worked through the problem to find a solution. Improvised. Used my initiative. I was particularly pleased with the way I handled the two 'extremes' of overlands.

My knowledge of history, geography, cultures and religions had grown exponentially and undoubtedly benefited me as a person, a teacher and a principal. I was fascinated by other cultures agreeing with Mark Twain when he wrote "Travel is fatal to prejudice, bigotry, and narrow-mindedness …"

My 1979/1980 years were unique and a 'one-off'. I was 'young and bullet-proof'. Travelling changed my attitudes, values and views of the world. Anita Desai wrote "Wherever you go becomes part of you forever."

"Those were the days my friend,
We'd thought they'd never end,
We'd sing and dance forever and a day,
We'd live the life we choose,
We'd fight and never lose,

Those were the days.
Yes, *Those* were the days".
(Mary Hopkin/ Russian folk song)

In the future friends, family and grandkids might ask …

"How did you travel across Asia?"

"Double-decker bus!"

Indeed … an idiosyncratic, quirky and unforgettable way to travel.

Photo #1: Kathmandu: Bagmati bridge.

Photo #2: In the grounds of the Hotel de Paris, Varanasi.

A dog's life

Photo #3: Hotel de Paris. Varanasi.

Photo #4: Leaving the Jaipur Observatory.

A dog's life

Photo # 5. "Boarding the elephants bound for the Amber Fort, Jaipur.

Photo #6: The Amber Fort. Jaipur.

Photo # 7: Lake Dal, houseboats. Kashmir.

A dog's life

Photo #8: Dawn floating markets, Kashmir.

Photo #9: Houseboats, Kashmir.

Photo #10: Houseboats, Kashmir.

Photo #11: Cappadocia.

A dog's life

Photo #12: Zelve, Cappadocia.

Photo #13: Urgup, Cappadocia.

Photo #14: Urgup, Cappadocia.

Photo #15: Bathing at the Bolan Pass.

A dog's life

Photo # 16: Camel train. Entering Quetta, Baluchistan, Pakistan.

Photo #17: Flax weaving, Quetta.

Photo #18: Takeaways, Quetta.

A dog's life

Photo #19: Wadi Rum, Jordan.

Photo 20: Wadi Rum, Jordan.

Overland with Top Deck

Photo #21: Ephesus.

Photo # 22: Ephesus Amphitheatre. **1979.**

A dog's life

Photo #23: Oct '79. Aya Sophia. Istanbul, Turkiye.

Photo #24: Interior. Aya Sophia. Istanbul, Yurkiye.

Overland with Top Deck

Photo # 25: Ominonu, Istanbul, Turkiye.

Photo # 26: Fish in a bun. Istanbul, Turkiye.

A dog's life

Photo #27: Hierapolis, Pammukkale, Turkiye.